SCALIA v. SCALIA

RHETORIC, LAW, AND THE HUMANITIES

SCALIA v. SCALIA

Opportunistic Textualism *in* Constitutional Interpretation

CATHERINE L. LANGFORD

The University of Alabama Press
Tuscaloosa

The University of Alabama Press
Tuscaloosa, Alabama 35487-0380
uapress.ua.edu

Typeface: Caslon

Cover image: Antonin Scalia, associate justice of the Supreme Court of the United States, March 21, 2013; courtesy of the Collection of the Supreme Court of the United States
Cover design: Michele Myatt Quinn

Library of Congress Cataloging-in-Publication Data

Names: Langford, Catherine L., 1974–, author.
Title: Scalia v. Scalia : opportunistic textualism in constitutional interpretation / Catherine L. Langford.
Description: Tuscaloosa : The University of Alabama Press, 2018. | Series: Rhetoric, law, and the humanities | Includes bibliographical references and index.
Identifiers: LCCN 2017020442| ISBN 9780817319700 (cloth) | ISBN 9780817391607 (e-book)
Subjects: LCSH: Scalia, Antonin. | Constitutional law—United States—Philosophy. | Constitutional law—United States—Interpretation and construction.
Classification: LCC KF8745.S33 L36 2018 | DDC 342.73001—dc23
LC record available at https://lccn.loc.gov/2017020442

To James Arnt Aune

Contents

Acknowledgments ix

Introduction 1

1. Textualism as a Response to the "Living" Constitution 9

2. Textualism in Scalia's Speeches and Extrajudicial Writings 24

3. Interpreting a Clear Clause: The Eighth Amendment's Cruel and Unusual Punishments Clause 51

4. Interpreting Competing Clauses: Mediating Religion between the Establishment and Free Exercise Clauses 72

5. When the Constitution Is Silent: Rejecting the Right to an Abortion 97

Conclusion: Scalia's Opportunistic Textualism 116

Notes 129

Bibliography 145

Index 155

Acknowledgments

The conceptual roots of this project—and my interest in the jurisprudence of Antonin Scalia—began many, many years ago. During that time, several scholars mentored me: James Arnt Aune, Leroy Dorsey, J. Michael Hogan, John Murphy, and Vanessa Beasley. These scholars cut across time and institutions. Jim Aune taught me that I could, and should, study what I loved. Leroy Dorsey taught me that intellectual pursuits could be fun. Mike Hogan taught me to persevere and to improve. John Murphy convinced me to duct-tape myself to my chair. Vanessa Beasley modeled what it looks like to be a woman who is a successful scholar, teacher, mentor, community member, and family person. And when Jim Aune passed away, Miriam Aune stepped in to encourage me to keep going.

I was lucky enough to have been extended a Faculty Development Leave opportunity from Texas Tech University in 2013 to complete a first draft of this manuscript. I am especially grateful to the graduate students who helped me collect data to analyze during that leave, particularly Andrew Potter and Amanda Schwertner. I am also grateful to the numerous graduate students who participated in my Historical Critical Methods seminar, for listening to, and providing me feedback on, my ideas. My graduate students have demonstrated a generosity of time, intellect, and encouragement. Some of my advisees, in particular, have expressed an interest in my work on Scalia, regardless of their place on the political spectrum: Prairie Endres Parnell, Kevin Garner, Jessica Reynolds, Kyle Dennis, Brendan O'Grady, Jared Bressler, David Braz, Kathryn Starkey, Alyssa Fiebrantz, Lauran Schaefer, Kevin Gene Thompson, Jennifer Duckworth, Austin Tyson, JT Seymore, and Nicole Brown. Sarah Crim and Josh Abbott are two former graduate students who are always available to talk about Supreme Court opinions and judicial appointments. My undergraduate students as well have provided me a space within the classroom to float and to test ideas—thank you all.

Within the discipline, I have been lucky enough to develop a group of people that I consider to be my partners in crime: Jeremiah Hickey, Eric Gander, and David Grassmick. These men have provided me with a circle of intellectual thought. From conference to conference they have been willing to hear my analyses of Scalia opinions and to press me to think in different ways. I have enjoyed "taking our show on the road" and look forward to many more years of doing so.

During the heaviest times of my writing, the people who held me accountable and offered me encouragement on a daily basis were my accountability group: Gina Castle Bell, Marjorie Buckner, and Justin Eckstein. My Lubbock family—Melanie Neal, Wendy Humphrey, and Cash Langford—made sure my physical and emotional needs were provided for while I wrote. They also made sure that I took time away from writing to be a human being. Paul Fowler, Bryan Williams, David Fry, and Cathy Fry helped make Lubbock home. My Redeemer Lubbock family made sure my soul was fed. My Empty Nesters walked with me throughout the writing of my manuscript, surrounding me with love, care, and interest in what I was doing. I started attending a new gospel community while I completed revisions. When I learned that my manuscript had been accepted, this group celebrated with me with a joy that increased my own.

My biofamily doesn't always understand what I do, but they support me nonetheless. My mom, Ann Langford, modeled for me unbelievable strength and resilience throughout my life—both qualities that came into play as I drafted and redrafted this manuscript. My brother, David Langford, was always willing to listen, and to give brotherly advice, when I called. Some of my biggest supporters include my extended family: Sug and Big D, Chuck and Susan David, Warren David, Michael David, Daria Hoffine, Debbie and Mike Keneson, and Libby Langford. Certain neighbors have become like family to me: Claudia and Paul Crocombe, Louise and Jeff Nuttall, and Joy and Larry Gadeken.

Others have played a significant role in my life that cannot be easily categorized. They are, in no particular order: Shantel Eilenfield, Courtney Byrd, Bear Wilson, Kim Horton, Kristin King, Justin Hughes, Zoë Hess Carney, Andrea Terry, Lauren Dent, Tina Delahunty, Shelley Christie, Robin Johnson, Kirsten Davis, Holly McIntush-Mobley, Matthew Randazzo, Jeff Harris, Ed Banayat, Steve Bayne, Monica Yancey, David Gore,

David Dewberry, Darby Dickerson, Narissra Punyanunt-Carter, Erik Bucy, Harry Weger, Melanie McNaughton, Lyn Freymiller, Brian Horton, Rob Layne, Justin Keene, Julie and Larry Doss, Holly Haseloff, Megan Graham, Kimberly Copeland, Lauren Douglass, Sara Ratliff, Montené Speight, Joe Barlow, Robert and Kathy Dean, Paul Miller, Judy Poffenbarger, John Poch, Jerry Dwyer, Jaclyn Cañas-Carrell, LeAnne Lagasse, Joy O'Steen, Joshua Barron, Suzanne Tapp, Micah Logan, Richard and Victoria Pineda, David Beam, Patrick Hughes, Rob Stewart, and Lawrence Schovanec. I thank you all for the ways you have, whether you know it or not, touched this work. You are my people.

Lastly, my dream of having this book in publication wouldn't have been realized without the support of Clarke Rountree. Words cannot express my gratitude for Clarke's vision for the Rhetoric, Law, and the Humanities series at the University of Alabama Press. Anonymous reviewers of his editorial board provided me with thoughtful feedback to advance and to improve my work. The entire board is filled with people I respect and admire and whose work I seek to emulate. I am also grateful for Daniel Waterman, editor in chief, for going above and beyond the call of duty in advising me as a new author. *Grazie mille.*

SCALIA v. SCALIA

Introduction

In the mid-1980s, a rumor floated that President Ronald Reagan was considering Robert Bork and Antonin Scalia for a Supreme Court vacancy. One day, as Scalia tried to enter an elevator in a parking garage, a security detail blocked his entrance. "I'm sorry, sir," one of the security team stated, "This elevator is being held for Attorney General Edwin Meese." Scalia pushed his way past the security detail and into the elevator. After punching the button for his floor, he pointed his finger at the security detail and proclaimed, "You tell Ed Meese that Robert Bork waits for no man!" The doors to the elevator closed and Scalia ascended to his destination.

This story tells us a lot about Scalia as a person. In it we observe his willingness to stand up to authority, pushing past any resistance to achieve his goal. We also can see his sense of humor at play. We do not know whether the security detail knew who Scalia was, or who Bork was, or if they relayed Scalia's message to the attorney general. We can imagine, however, Scalia retelling this story, with a wicked gleam in his eyes and a chuckle. Most importantly, however, we witness his willingness to tell a tale that lacks veracity to achieve the end he desires.

Known as an intellectual force for conservatism, an ardent advocate of strict forms of judicial interpretation, and a wordsmith, in his speeches, extrajudicial writings, and legal opinions Scalia crafted a persuasive narrative to reform judicial interpretation. The hero of Scalia's national narrative is the Constitution—perfect in construction and timeless in application—not the justice interpreting it. The villain is the activist justice who seeks to pervert the meaning of the document. Scalia's textual tale tells the story of legal decisions, bound by the confines of the constitutional text, that reflect the original meaning of the founders. This tale allows the Constitution to regulate the operation of government, to protect the majority, and to allow states the right to enact diverse policies.

Appointed to the US Supreme Court by President Reagan to fill the junior justice position left vacant by William Rehnquist's appointment to chief justice, Antonin Scalia was confirmed unanimously by the Senate in 1986. Graduating magna cum laude from Harvard in 1960, Scalia practiced law for a private firm in Cleveland for seven years before resigning to teach law at the University of Virginia in 1967. He then served in various capacities in the Nixon and Ford administrations. After the Republicans lost the White House in 1976, Scalia returned to teaching, this time at the University of Chicago Law School. He remained at Chicago Law until Reagan appointed him to the US Court of Appeals in the District of Columbia in 1982.

Of his years before the Supreme Court, judicial scholar Christopher E. Smith tells us that Scalia "became known as an advocate of deregulation and increased power for the executive branch, two ideas reflecting his criticism of the exercises of authority by the Democrat-controlled Congress."[1] Scalia's criticisms of congressional action were in line with the ideological perspective of then-President Reagan, who sought to appoint strict constitutional constructionists to the bench. In a radio address to the nation on August 9, 1986, Ronald Reagan justified his nomination of William Rehnquist as chief justice and Antonin Scalia as an associate justice. In that address, Reagan remarked: "Too many judges were taking upon themselves the prerogatives of elected officials. Instead of interpreting the law according to the intent of the Constitution and the Congress, they were simply using the courts to strike down laws that displeased them politically or philosophically. I argued the need for judges who would interpret law, not make it. The people, through their elected representatives, make our laws; and the people deserve to have these laws enforced as they were written."[2] President Reagan hoped Scalia would be a justice who would "interpret law, not make it." The president sought justices who would interpret the Constitution in a narrow fashion, limiting judicial intervention into social policies.

Following the judicial appointments of Rehnquist and Scalia, Reagan's efforts were successful; many constitutional scholars have commented upon the "conservative turn" of the modern Court.[3] Political scientist Richard A. Brisbin Jr., however, argues that Scalia's decision-making better reflects a knee-jerk reaction against the Warren and Burger Courts, which furthered New Deal legislative aims, rather than a consistent conservative ideology. Scalia's opinions advocated reversing earlier opinions in cases involving a wide array of fundamental rights, from free speech and freedom of religion to abortion rights, criminal due process, and equal protection of the laws. In Scalia Reagan found an articulate advocate of conservative views and a justice willing to overturn New Deal judicial decisions.

A vocal advocate of textualist interpretation, which limits constitutional meaning to the written text of the Constitution, Scalia was one of the most visible and controversial justices on the Supreme Court. His decisions and opinions led some to caricature his tenure on the bench. Cartoonist Ruben Bolling took to posting sketches about Scalia in his "Tom the Dancing Bug" cartoon on Salon.com, depicting Scalia as "the crusading judge who travels the land doling out tough justice"[4] and as the "justice of action—not activism."[5]

During his thirty years on the court, Scalia altered several judicial customs. First, he increased the divisiveness of oral arguments. The most vocal presence during oral arguments, Scalia was known to interrupt appellate advocates and his colleagues with both hostile and friendly questions, biting commentary, or witty quips. Although most justices interrupt counsel with whom they disagree, Scalia interrupted both sides equally. Second, he increased the fragmentation of the court's judicial opinions. Scalia did not believe in judicial restraint when it came to opinion writing. He wrote opinions—concurring, dissenting, concurring-in-part and dissenting-in-part—whenever he felt the need to let the public know his views in a case. Before Scalia, the members of the court worked hard to present cohesive opinions. His propensity to write encouraged other justices to follow his example.

On February 13, 2016, Scalia died at the age of seventy-nine, while on a hunting trip in West Texas. His sudden and unexpected death, which occurred during a presidential election cycle, set off a flurry of news coverage as commentators discussed his life, his legacy, his judicial philosophy, the circumstances surrounding his death, and the political consequences and legal obligations of replacing his vacated seat.[6] Scalia's death presented an opportunity for advocates and critics of his jurisprudence to reflect upon Scalia's influence, for this controversial justice was not merely an interpreter of the law but an energetic advocate of strict forms of constitutional interpretation in his public speeches, extralegal writings, and judicial opinions.

In response to his passing, his peers praised Scalia's intellectual prowess and acknowledged his legal legacy. Conservative justices characterized Scalia as a larger-than-life figure whose intellect forced the legal community to rethink how we interpret our most sacred document. Justice Clarence Thomas, Scalia's conservative ally for a quarter of a century, described the deceased justice as a man of "towering intellect" and as "a legal giant."[7] Fellow conservative Justice Samuel Alito echoed Thomas's sentiment, declaring that Scalia was "one of the most important figures" in Supreme Court history.[8] The conservatives on the court were not the only ones to recognize Scalia's influence on contemporary jurisprudence. Justice Anthony Kennedy, the court's moderate member who frequently acts as the court's swing vote, noted Scalia's "wisdom, scholarship, and technical brilliance."[9] The liberal delegation of the court remembered Scalia fondly as well. Justice Ruth Bader Ginsburg, well known as one of Scalia's dearest friends, praised him as "a jurist of captivating brilliance and wit."[10] Justice Stephen Breyer, Scalia's most formidable opponent regarding questions of constitutional interpretation, characterized him as "a legal titan."[11] Justice Elena Kagan, a longtime academic before her appointment, described Scalia as "one of the most transformational" justices in US history.[12] Each of Scalia's colleagues remembered him as a person of intellectual depth and ideological commitment whose unfailing advocacy of "originalism" and "textualism" as acceptable methods of constitutional interpretation has resulted in the rest of America being concerned with how laws are interpreted.

Conservative politicians characterized Scalia as more than an important legal mind; they also touted him as a heroic figure in the American political scene. Praised by presidential hopeful Ted Cruz as "an American hero,"[13] by Marco Rubio as "one of the most consequential Americans,"[14] by Donald Trump as a "remarkable person,"[15] by Jeb Bush as "my favorite justice,"[16] and by John Kasich as "an essential, principled force for conservative thought,"[17] Scalia's death left big judicial shoes to fill. A pioneer of the conservative cause for GOP presidential candidates, Scalia's unexpected death during an election cycle led most of these presidential hopefuls to praise the recently departed in one breath and demand that Scalia's seat be left vacant until after the upcoming presidential election in the next. The hope of these candidates was that a Republican would win the top of the ticket and appoint a conservative justice to replace Scalia—a hope fulfilled when Donald Trump became the forty-fifth president of the United States.

Following the mantra of not speaking ill of the dead, politicians on the other side of the aisle also celebrated Scalia's intelligence and influence. President Barack Obama described Scalia as "a brilliant legal mind with an energetic style, incisive wit, and colorful opinions," stating, "He influenced a generation of judges, lawyers, and students, and profoundly shaped the legal landscape. He will no doubt be remembered as one of the most consequential judges and thinkers to serve on the Supreme Court."[18] Hillary Clinton and Bernie Sanders both acknowledged that they adopted different stances regarding public policy issues than did Scalia. Clinton nevertheless recognized Scalia as "a dedicated public servant who brought energy and passion to the bench,"[19] and Sanders called him "brilliant, colorful, and outspoken."[20]

Although most legal scholars did not offer public remarks following the news of Scalia's death, a few constitutional scholars joined the chorus of praise. Harvard law professor Cass Sunstein said Scalia was "not only one of the most important justices in the nation's history; he was also among the greatest."[21] New York law professor Richard Epstein described Scalia as "a most memorable friend" and a "passionate and articulate defender" of his views.[22] Many former clerks recounted the tales of working with Scalia and the lessons they had learned, expressing their admiration for the justice.[23] Legal professionals respected Scalia's jurisprudence and shared stories about his affable personality.

In their news accounts, journalists recognized Scalia's influence and explained his judicial philosophy to the larger public not attuned to the academic debate over judicial interpretation. In the *Guardian*, Godfrey Hodgson recounted how Scalia's judicial philosophy, which appeared "reactionary and eccentric" three decades ago, nevertheless has become "increasingly influential on the bench and especially in the great American law schools."[24] CNN columnist Ilya Shapiro described him as the "highest-profile and most powerful expositor" of textualism and originalism.[25] The *New York Times* correspondent Adam Liptak characterized him as a "champion of originalism."[26] The *Washington Post* columnist George Will described him as "a jurist of colossal consequence."[27] Writing for *Fox News*, Judge Andrew P. Napolitano explained: "This theory of constitutional interpretation has two names—textualism and originalism. Justice Scalia argued that the Constitution means what it says; it says it is the supreme law of the land; and all American judges have taken a solemn oath to be subject to what it says. It is superior to the jurists who interpret it. It is what it says, not as they might wish it say. Thus, all judges are bound by the text. Hence the world 'textualism.' . . . If the text of the Constitution is ambiguous, it then becomes the duty of the jurist to ascertain the original public meaning of the words that form the ambiguity. Hence the word 'originalism.'"[28] Their accounts tell a story of a justice whose passion for the Constitution resulted in his judicial philosophy moving from a marginal perspective to a mainstream ideology.

These accounts of Scalia's passing confirm that Scalia's judicial hermeneutic was such a prevalent aspect of his personal persona that it was discussed when marking his passing. Such widespread recognition of Scalia's judicial philosophy acknowledges Scalia as a judicial revivalist—a justice who took his message of textualism and originalism to the masses and was heard.

Scalia's message was not just heard, however; his advocacy achieved a revolution within constitutional interpretation. Echoing Justice Kagan, Shapiro concludes that Scalia's philosophy of interpretation "has had a transformational effect on the law."[29] As one example, Shapiro recounts how the Constitution was not included in constitutional law textbooks before Scalia's assuming a seat on the High Court. Scalia's advocacy of the constitutional text led to the Constitution being included first as an appendix to textbooks and then as part of the front matter. Scalia's influence did not end with publishers of constitutional law volumes. As law students moved from the classroom to the courtroom, they brought with them the primacy of the text. Appellate attorneys began discussing the textual meaning of the law in their briefs and oral arguments, which they had not done in large measure before Scalia's advocacy of the text. "Substantially as a result of his influence," Shapiro explains, "no advocate today would write a Supreme Court brief about the meaning of a statute that does not focus first on its language."[30] Appellate attorneys now address the plain meaning and the original meaning of the law before the court, and other judges and justices take into consideration the original meaning of a text when deciding what the law means.

Scalia's influence even reached to the nomination process of Supreme Court justices. During the second day of her confirmation hearing, Senator Herb Kohl (D-Wisconsin) asked Elena Kagan what type of justice she would be. He clarified what he meant by comparing Scalia's judicial philosophy with Justice Souter's and then asked her with which philosophy she would better identify. Although Kagan attempted to demur, stating she did not think she needed to fall within either camp, when pressed she went so far as to declare, "We are all originalists" now.[31]

One cannot ignore the fact that Scalia was the justice liberals loved to hate. In an interview with the justice in 2008, *60 Minutes* correspondent Lesley Stahl shared, "I'm surprised at how many people really, really hate you."[32] In its "Democracy in America" blogpost, the *Economist* ran a short piece on Scalia's response to the *Bush v. Gore* (2000) decision, entitled "Why People Hate Antonin Scalia."[33] In 2013 Mark Joseph Stern of *Salon* identified Scalia as a "homophobe."[34] In 2015 Senate Minority Leader Harry Reid described Scalia's line of questioning in the *Fisher* oral arguments as "racist."[35] Also in 2015 Tom Gualtieri identified Scalia as the "Worst Person in America" because he is "melodramatic, illogical, condescending, self-serving, ignorant, hysterical, and a big, fat balding, foot-stomping sore-loser in judicial robes."[36] After his death, liberal citizens and journalists did not follow the adage, "If you cannot say anything nice, do not say anything at all." *US News & World Report* published the eight worst tweets about Scalia. One characterized Scalia as an "evil, soulless, and hateful man"; another wrote, "Obi-Wan confirms Scalia's death: 'I feel a great disturbance in the Force, as if millions of voices suddenly cried out in orgiastic joy'"; and the *Onion* joked, "Justice Scalia Dead Following 30-Year Battle with Social Progress."[37] Tomás Ríos, senior sports editor for *Vocativ*, described Scalia as "a monster."[38] David Ehrlich of *Rolling Stone* asked, "How long do we have to wait till we can openly not be sad about it?"[39] Silvia Killingsworth of the *New Yorker* tweeted, "Wish I could be a fly on the wall for Scalia's chat with the Devil."[40] The *Daily News Bin* described him as "one of the most cartoonishly evil villains in the history of the United States government, having intentionally brought harm to a great many Americans."[41] *Slate* columnist Dahlia Lithwick characterized Scalia as a "cartoon supervillian."[42] Lithwick also opined, "As a liberal you are certainly free to hate Scalia, and sometimes it seemed he worked overtime to earn your hate. He gloried in it. He wrote cruel, demeaning things about whole groups of Americans."[43] A number of people tweeted their intention to find his grave to urinate on it.[44] Anna Merian declared him to be "a titanic, sweeping, one-man disaster for LGBT rights, racial justice, abortion access and general human decency." Rachel Anspach of the *Huffington Post* and Eric Zuesse of *Washington's Blog* both labeled him a "bigot."[45] Liberals believe Scalia to be not only a bad man but also evil, bad for America, and rotting in hell.

When I began studying Scalia many years ago, I was a young, conservative scholar interested in the hermeneutics of constitutional interpretation. No individual offered a richer site of analysis than the outspoken jurist, Justice Antonin Scalia. In Scalia I found a man who articulated his viewpoint in extrajudicial speeches and writings. Although he refused to allow his speeches to be recorded, thanks to the Internet age I was able to obtain several of his speeches on the speaker's circuit that focused on constitutional interpretation. He also wrote about his judicial philosophy in law reviews and books. Intellectually, textualism appealed to me; the Constitution should be read in such a fashion as the language of the law supported it to be read. I decided to take Scalia at his word and analyze how he interpreted the law in his legal opinions. Influenced by close textual analysis, I attempted to give "an account of the rhetorical dynamics implicit" within Scalia's opinions.[46] I operated from the question, How does one interpret the Constitution in different areas of law according to a textualist perspective? Or, more colloquially, What does a textualist interpretation of the law look like in different areas of law?

This book examines Scalia's use of textualism in his speeches, extrajudicial writings, and judicial opinions. Throughout his judicial opinions and extralegal writings, Scalia argues that textualism is the only acceptable form of constitutional interpretation. Yet Scalia does not clearly define his textualism, nor does he always rely upon textualism to the exclusion of other forms of argumentation. Scalia is the standard-bearer for textualism, yet only so far as textualism supports his ideological aims. When textualism fails to support his ideological aims (such as in cases that pertain to states' rights or the separation of powers), Scalia reverts to other forms of argumentation. Textualism relies upon a notion of limited linguistic meanings, yet it does not mandate *how* a strict reading of the Constitution should be focused and applied. My analysis of Scalia's opinions in three areas of law shows that Scalia uses rhetorical strategies beyond those of a textualist approach. My analysis led me to conclude that Scalia was an opportunistic textualist and that textualism is as rhetorical as any other form of judicial interpretation, contrary to Scalia's advocacy of textual interpretation as the form of constitutional interpretation closest to the Constitution's original meaning and least vulnerable to political influence.

I

Textualism as a Response to the "Living" Constitution

The text and intention of the Constitution must be understood to constitute the banks within which constitutional interpretation must flow.

—Attorney General Edwin Meese

As can be observed through accounts following his death, Scalia consistently articulated a particular way to interpret the Constitution. His advocacy helped constitutional interpretation become one of the most important issues facing the United States today. The debate about forms of constitutional interpretation remains important, because it perpetuates the myth that the law can be interpreted in an unbiased and nonpreferential fashion. Debates over how to interpret the Constitution have arisen because the *method* of legal interpretation is a rhetorical maneuver to support judicial legitimacy, for how justices interpret the law creates the *reality* of the law as a social practice. The thinking goes that when the process is fair, the results are fair. Scalia's advocacy of textualism was not new; the proper scope and function of judicial review has been debated for a century.[1] Rather, Scalia's perspective represented a new chapter in an ongoing narrative about constitutional interpretation.

Split courts resulting in a plentitude of opinions, including majority, concurring, dissenting, and concurring-in-part and dissenting-in-part, result from different understandings of how to interpret the Constitution. Some justices support a "strict" interpretation of the Constitution, believing that the text should be understood in as limited a fashion as possible. Other justices support a "loose" interpretation of the Constitution, believing that the text can be interpreted differently at different times to respond to shifting social needs.

In *Constitutional Fate: Theory of the Constitution*, Cornell law professor Philip Bobbitt argues that justices employ six different types of commonplaces while interpreting the Constitution: historical (original intent/meaning), textual (plain meaning), structural (macro perspective), prudential (cost/benefit analysis), doctrinal (precedent), and ethical (telic ends).[2] Justices do not use new forms of argument every time they write an opinion. Rather, they use common forms of argument to which they return in opinion after opinion. Bobbitt presents each type as an independent argument, but justices rarely cleave exclusively to one type in their opinions; they typically embrace several forms of interpretive rationale.

The debate over methods of judicial interpretation communicates to the public that certain forms of judicial interpretation are more legitimate than other forms. Judges such as Scalia who employ textualism claim that their method of interpretation exists within the narrow confines of the constitutional document, which results in their interpretation more closely corresponding to the system of governance that the Constitution created. Their approach is more democratic, in other words, because it separates the political from the legal and leaves the political to the people.

Textualism as a Method of Constitutional Interpretation

Textualism is a response to loose interpretation, such as the notion of a "living" constitution. Textualists, Bobbitt tells us, rely upon the "plain meaning" of the constitutional text. Recent scholarship on textualism has focused on three distinct applications of the term: strict textualism, rigorous textualism, and new textualism. Prominent legal theorists use the term differently, based upon the aspect of the constitutional document to which they grant agency. For strict textualists, independent articles or amendments have the agency to determine how each should be understood; for rigorous textualists, the entire document has agency as a whole; and for new textualists, it is the Constitution interacting with the community that has agency. Although Scalia does not identify himself using this language, his speeches and extrajudicial writings advance ideas found in each of these perspectives.

Strict textual construction limits judicial interpretation to the language of a particular article or amendment. Rather than hold the entire document to have significant meaning, strict textualists emphasize key articles or amendments. For strict textualists, language has limited meaning that does not change quickly. Strict textualism's limited perspective on language use gives stability and continuity to constitutional meaning, yet it cannot respond to changes in the popular understanding of language.

Whereas strict textualism examines distinct elements of the Constitution, rigorous textualism emphasizes the importance of the Constitution in its entirety. "A rigorous textualism," constitutional scholar Mark Tushnet explains, "insists that every constitutional provision—every jot and tittle—contributes meaningfully to the creation of a constitution structured by a set of principles, all of which cohere tightly with each other."[3] Rigorous textualism relies upon the premise that the constitutional text asserts its own abiding purpose, extrinsic of meaning created by a judge's opinion. For rigorous textualists, linguistic meaning remains consistent throughout the document.

In contrast with the first two forms of textualism, both of which assert that the constitutional text has meaning within the boundaries of the text itself, new textualists believe that the Constitution has meaning only within certain linguistic contexts.[4] New textualists place agency within the text only when the text is "clear." When the text is not clear, the new textualist defers to the legislature, granting Congress the agency to interpret the meaning of the text. Meaning derived from context allows the new textualist greater flexibility in interpretation. New textualists recognize that law toggles between constituting community and being constituted by community.

Each type of textualism relies upon the actual text of the Constitution to respond to constitutional questions. Each type favors judicial restraint, prefers that the legislature clarify nonlegal issues, and denies the role of the judge in determining legal outcomes. Each type has a different strength. Strict textualism simplifies constitutional law by holding that a few principles take primacy over other legal considerations. Rigorous textualism's breadth means that most legal questions can be answered by looking to the overall purpose of constitutional provisions. And new textualism, with its emphasis on constitutive meaning constantly recreated by community interaction with the law, has the flexibility to respond to shifts in contemporary understanding of legal principles.

Generally, critics present three challenges to textual interpretation: The language of the Constitution has no "plain meaning"; the supplemental materials used to support textual interpretation are not definitive accounts of original meaning; and limited linguistic meaning forces twenty-first-century America to be governed by the principles of eighteenth-century America. Some critics who claim the Constitution does not have a plain meaning believe that the text is neither self-determining nor self-justifying. Rather, judges, lawyers, administrative agencies, and state and local governments each determine what the text means to them. Following in the line of the early living Constitution debate, agency resides within the judge who does the interpreting; a text does not have agency on its own. Other critics challenge the idea that no other documents are necessary to understand the constitutional text. Legislative history, founders' documents, state ratification debates, and dictionaries are not authoritative statements of original meaning. Which state ratification debate, for example, would determine how to interpret a particular statute? Linguistic meaning is not constant—either across a document or through time.[5] Other critics maintain that basing decisions on the Constitution, as it was understood at the time of its ratification, means that our dead forefathers, who cannot demographically, socially, or morally represent the modern republic, still govern America. According to University of Chicago Law Professor David Strauss, "In the textualist vision, there was a time—a moment—when someone got it right."[6] Yet the Constitution was not perfected at the time of the ratification; judicial interpretation and recent constitutional amendments continue to expand liberty and suffrage. Thus, the twenty-first century should not be bound to the principles of the founders.

Not all scholars are critics of textualism, however.[7] Attempting to resolve the criticism that textualism treats the Constitution as a cadaver, tying the needs of the present people to the will of the past, Yale Law School Professor Jed Rubenfeld maintains that textualism grants authority to the persons who ratified the Constitution and that the Constitution continually is enacted by the people unless (and until) they alter the constitutional text through the amendment process. Other scholars acknowledge textualism's resistance to change as its greatest strength. This view holds that textualism gives the Constitution stability and predictability, both over time and across levels of governance. Theoretically, responding to judicial questions with the belief that language is static would mean that all levels of the judicial branch—from state courts to the Supreme Court—would arrive at similar answers to the same questions.

At issue in the debate over constitutional interpretation is the role of the judge. In more strict forms of interpretation, such as those favored by Scalia, judges act as a nonpartial entity that merely observes and applies the law. In loose forms of interpretation, the judge is viewed as making the law. Although textualists claim that the Constitution should be read in a strict fashion, allowing the plain meaning of the document to be adjudicated, the Constitution cannot be interpreted apart from the individuals who read it. The historical debate about a living Constitution demonstrates how early commentary on judicial interpretation recognized the role of the judge in explaining what the law is. The idea that the text has agency on its own—whether that agency is through its living nature or through the plain meaning of the text—is a recent phenomenon. Thus, the modern conception of a "living" Constitution is a new narrative that does not have roots in the historic uses of the term.

The Living Constitution

Public discourse about a living Constitution dates back more than a century, as politicians, judges, legal scholars, and historians began to consider the organic metaphor. The conversation appears to have been introduced in 1912 by then-progressivist presidential candidate Woodrow Wilson. According to Wilson, government and society both are organic; for the system to work, we need to view the constitutional text as organic as well. Early academic understandings of the concept disagreed as to the nature of the "living" Constitution. Some scholars deferred to Wilson's metaphor, allowing for an awareness of the role of the judge in saying what the law means. Other scholars personified the Constitution, arguing that the document has the power to change itself. Over the years the meaning of the metaphor changed as the public abandoned the role of the judge in the interpretive process, understanding the metaphor rather as the ability of the constitutional text to alter itself. The perceptual shift regarding the relationship of the judge to the text, as well as to the political and the juridical, is important, because debates over constitutional interpretation, constitutional scholar William F. Harris II tells us, "most paradigmatically represents the connection between law and politics—actualized in verbal and governmental practices."[8] Namely, how we talk about the Constitution expands or restricts the role of the judges in our democratic republic, as well as constitutes the rights and liberties of our citizens.

In his 1912 campaign speech entitled "What is Progress?" Wilson presented both the machine metaphor and the body metaphor of constitutionalism, rejecting the former in favor of the latter. Wilson's speech performs the rhetorical work of justifying the Constitution as an organic text and requires his auditors to rethink how they understand the functioning of government. Wilson explained:

> Government is not a machine, but a living thing. It falls, not under the theory of the universe, but under the theory of organic life. It is accountable to Darwin, not to Newton. It is modified by its environment, necessitated by its tasks, shaped to its functions by the sheer pressure of life. No living thing can have its organs offset against each other, as checks, and live. On the contrary, its life is dependent upon their quick cooperation, their ready response to the commands of instinct or intelligence, their amicable community of purpose. Government is not a body of blind forces; it is a body of men, with highly differentiated functions, no doubt, in our modern day, of specialization,

> with common task and purpose. Their cooperation is indispensable, their warfare fatal. There can be no successful government without the intimate, instinctive coordination of the organs of life and action. This is not a theory, but fact, and displays its force as fact, whatever theories may be thrown across its track. Living political constitutions must be Darwinian in structure and in practice. Society is a living organism and must obey the laws of life, not of mechanics; it must develop.[9]

According to Wilson, the Constitution is neither held captive to the thinking of the founders nor governed by the rule of law; thus, it is not a static document difficult to amend. Wilson's claim created a rhetorical space for the Constitution as a changeable document, able to facilitate progressivist ideology and to protect the body politic.

Wilson's idea that the Constitution is organic found its way somewhat into Supreme Court Justice Oliver Wendell Holmes's opinion in *Gompers v. United States* (1914) two years later. In his opinion, Holmes claimed the machine metaphor could not apply in judicial cases; rather, each case must be considered in light of how the area of law has evolved. According to Holmes, "The provisions of the Constitution . . . are organic, living institutions transplanted from English soil. Their significance is vital, not formal; it is to be gathered not simply by taking the words and a dictionary, but by considering their origin and the line of their growth."[10] Holmes's words, however, cannot be understood to justify loose readings of the Constitution, as the text of the Constitution itself is not organic; rather, the *products* of its enumerations live and take shape beyond its textual boundaries.

Other judges quickly followed and extended Holmes's line of thought regarding constitutional interpretation. In his landmark *Olmstead* (1928) judicial dissent, citing *Weems v. United States* (1910), Justice Louis Brandeis opined that the language of the Constitution "should not . . . be necessarily confined" to earlier legal applications.[11] According to Brandeis, the Constitution contains *aspirational principles* that must be given new effect within each generation, according to the needs and experiences of that period. Benjamin Cardozo agreed, writing in *The Nature of the Judicial Process*, "The great generalities of the constitution have a content and significance that vary from age to age."[12] Although these great legal minds concur that the constitutional text needs to be read according to contemporary standards, they do not make the intellectual leap that the Constitution is living per se. Upon the latitude of acceptance regarding constitutional interpretation, these remarks indicate that within the first part of the twentieth century several judges shifted their thinking away from the Constitution having a fixed, static meaning and toward the Constitution being interpreted more expansively than it had been in the past.

The idea that the Constitution contains broad premises that can be applied to a variety of contexts was brought before the public again in President Franklin Delano Roosevelt's 1932 inaugural address. "Our Constitution is so simple and practical that it is possible always to meet extraordinary needs by changes in emphasis and arrangement without loss of essential form," FDR declared.[13] Through his remarks, the public heard the president, who had just taken an oath to uphold and to maintain the Constitution, tell them that the Constitution has the ability to respond to contemporary social needs. Although he did not characterize the Constitution as living, his statement nevertheless allows for the document to adapt to new social conditions. Roosevelt's inaugural indicated that the Constitution could respond to "extraordinary needs." Although the debate over the living Constitution would take place mostly within academic circles, the oppressive economic conditions of the Great Depression created a rhetorical situation in which the discursive construction of the Constitution as living and able to respond to their suffering would have appealed to a large percentage of Americans.

Constitutional scholars swiftly began to discuss Wilson's idea that the Constitution is living; they offered pragmatic justifications for how a document, perceived as unchanging for more than a century, can be applied to new contexts and circumstances. In his 1927 work, *The Living Constitution*, Columbia Law professor Howard Lee McBain considered the rule of law and how even the provisions that the founders implemented (such as the written text, the division of powers, the federal system, and the Bill of Rights) necessitated interpretation.[14] McBain recognized different means through which the constitutional text could be altered, including customs, nullification, legislation, and judicial interpretation. According to McBain, the contemporary Constitution is not the document that was adopted at the time of the founding. McBain's claim is a simple one: Because the document has changed, it is living. He makes no claims about the nature of the document itself or about the acceptable vehicles of change. He merely uses the organic metaphor to *identify* change.

In 1930 James M. Beck, former solicitor general to President Warren G. Harding and congressional representative from the state of Pennsylvania, delivered an address to the *American Philosophical Society* titled "The Changed Conception of the Constitution."[15] In his remarks Beck traces the origin of the shift to the debate between Robert Y. Hayne and Daniel Webster about the Foot Resolution in January 1830. During this debate, Hayne used John C. Calhoun's nullification doctrine to argue that the Constitution was a compact between both the various state governments and the national government and the state governments. Hayne also argues that states could, if they desired, nullify a law that violated the compact. Webster disagreed, determining that the nation must be preserved and cannot be split apart by sectional rivalry. Although Hayne and Webster differed as to the nature of the Constitution, "none of the speakers," Beck tells us, "had any conception of the Constitution as a living organism. All regarded it as a static instrument, whose letter was as unyielding as the stone upon which the Ten Commandments were graven."[16] Nevertheless, Beck identifies different forms of law as the point of tension between the two men's thoughts. Two forms of law exist in constitutional law: written law and unwritten law. Certain laws are expressed (written) and self-determining; other laws are not. He explains that the Due Process Clause means nothing in and of itself; the clause requires knowledge of legal precedent and context. Therefore, full understanding of the written law necessitates knowledge of the unwritten law, or law outside the text. Such unwritten law can include precedent and common law.

Regardless of the Hayne-Webster understanding of Constitution as a static document, Beck himself viewed the Constitution as an organic document consistent with current thinking. Beck's understanding of the Constitution as a living document differs from McBain's or Hayne's and Webster's. Beck personifies the document as its own agent that can adapt and grow. Although he recognizes that earlier thinkers did not understand the Constitution in such a fashion, he nevertheless opined that the Constitution extends beyond its textual boundaries. Beck's opinion invites the contemporary living viewpoint of the Constitution as a document able to realize its own aspirational will.

Other scholars writing during Beck's time temper his call for an organic Constitution, recognizing the role of the judge in saying what the law is. In his 1934 article, "The Elasticity of the Federal Constitution," legal practitioner and scholar Horace H. Hagan promotes a living Constitution, arguing that the only way for the government to respond to new problems is for the Constitution to be interpreted in different ways.[17] Hagan advocates the ability of judges to respond to new political and social issues, abiding by shifting notions of morality and social needs. Hagan refuses to abandon the agency of judges in the interpretation of the constitutional text.

The idea of a living Constitution became increasingly difficult to refute as scholars provided pragmatic justifications for nonoriginalist readings. Constitutional scholar Edward Corwin claims that a malleable constitution is both rational and reasonable. In a 1934 law review essay, he wrote, "The constitution must mean different things at different times if it is to mean what is sensible, applicable, feasible."[18] James Hart presents a bifurcated argument, asserting that observers think the Constitution is either unchanging or adaptable.[19] In 1936 historian Charles A. Beard published an article entitled "The Living Constitution" in which he acknowledges the role of the judge in interpreting the Constitution. The text of the Constitution is vague and must be interpreted for society to know what it means, Beard explains.[20] Beard's conception of the Constitution follows McBain's. He argues that the Constitution cannot be understood on its own accord; a text can be given meaning only when a human being—namely a judge—interprets it.

Apparent in McBain's, Hagan's, and Beard's analyses of the Constitution is an awareness of the judge's role in determining what the law is. The Constitution itself is not living; the judicial *interpretation* of the Constitution changes to respond to contemporary social needs. The Constitution is not self-determining; the judges, through their judicial opinions, alter the meaning of the document. Moreover, judges can expand the contemporary meaning of the Constitution by using unwritten law. During this era, the constitutional document was unchanging but supported by additional forms of law such as statutory law, civil law, and common law, in addition to various legal traditions. The substance of the Constitution largely was immutable, altered only through the amendment process.

In his analysis of the ways judges interpret the law to construe new meaning, rhetorical theorist Kenneth Burke, in his 1945 work, *A Grammar of Motives,* found that Supreme Court justices altered their form of interpretation toward consistency with FDR's political ideology. Burke cites Justice Owen Robert's vote in *West Coast Hotel Company v. Parrish* (1937)—the first time the court upheld New Deal legislation and referred to as the "switch in time that saved nine"—as an example of the High Court allowing contemporary political issues to influence its adjudication of the law and, thus, its use of a loose form of interpretation.[21] The living Constitution, brought into material reality in *West Coast Hotel* (1937), altered the legal landscape by personifying the text that founded the nation. Importantly, however, Burke acknowledges that the *judges* made the decision to interpret the law differently; the law did not constitute *itself* as an organic being.

Contemporary rhetorical constructions of the Constitution as living have abandoned McBain's, Hagan's, and Beard's understanding of the role of the judge in deciding the law, and have thus obfuscated the part judges play in determining social policy. In a practice that began in earnest in the 1950s, the Warren Court's reading of the Constitution expanded individual civil rights and civil liberties in significant ways,[22] with the court becoming more influential in social policy than elected officials were.[23] By perpetuating the idea that the Constitution is living, judges are not held accountable for legal interpretations that violate majority will and historic practices. Judges henceforth could assert that their interpretation of the document remained consistent with the spirit, if not the letter, of the law.

In 1976 William Rehnquist revisited the question of a living Constitution in a speech he delivered at the University of Texas School of Law, which was printed in the school's law review[24] and reprinted in the *Harvard Journal of Law and Public Policy* following his death.[25] In his remarks Rehnquist identifies two meanings of a living Constitution: the Holmes version and what he calls the "brief version." The former is consistent with early uses of the term "living" and the latter is in line with contemporary uses of the phrase. The Holmes version, derived from Justice Holmes's opinion in *Missouri v. Holland* (1920),[26] claims that the framers used general language when writing the Constitution, language that must be enacted in different contexts to be understood. Rehnquist offers the brief version as an example of another form of living Constitution that has become prominent in recent years. Rehnquist tells us the brief version encourages the idea that nonelected judges can address social ills when other branches of government have not resolved the problem.[27] The brief version allows a nondemocratic, counter-majoritarian body to determine public policy when the political process fails to do so. Rehnquist addresses Marshall's defense of judicial review in *Marbury v. Madison* (1803), concluding that Marshall aligned with Holmes's version of a living Constitution.[28] Considering previous and contemporary uses of the living Constitution enables Rehnquist to argue that neither Holmes nor Marshall, with their loose interpretations of the Constitution, empowered the document (or the judiciary) to extend beyond its accepted textual boundaries. To wit, present uses of the living Constitution concept lack historic basis and adopt an unsubstantiated perspective regarding judicial interpretation.

Today the debate over constitutional interpretation revolves around the same questions: Is the Constitution static or elastic? Does an unwritten Constitution exist? What is the role of the judge in constitutional interpretation? Great legal minds differ in their responses to these questions. Former Attorney General Edwin Meese,[29] Justice Antonin Scalia,[30] Judge Robert Bork,[31] and Professor John Ely[32] all agree judicial interpretation should be limited to the constitutional text, a perspective constitutional scholar Thomas Grey terms "interpretive."[33] On the other hand, Justice William Brennan,[34] Justice Stephen Breyer,[35] and constitutional scholars James Boyd White,[36] Thomas Grey,[37] and Jack M. Balkin[38] all are of a mind that judicial interpretation should be allowed to utilize extraconstitutional sources, which Grey calls "non-interpretive." Since the Constitution does not offer guidance as to how it should be read, scholars do not have a definitive answer as to whose opinion is correct.

Pushback against the living Constitution did not begin in earnest until the mid-1980s. The debate regarding constitutional interpretation was brought out of the law schools and into the public sphere when then-Attorney General Ed Meese gave a speech before the American Bar Association (ABA), a speech discussed widely in news commentary.[39] In this speech the attorney general advanced originalism as an ideology that should be given preference over living Constitution approaches.

The Great Debate

When speaking to a meeting of the ABA in July 1985, Attorney General Edwin Meese addressed the issue of constitutional interpretation, advancing a hermeneutic of strict construction.[40] Meese's ABA speech started what the Federalist Society refers to as "The Great Debate,"[41] triggering the public's interest in how judges interpret the law. In a rare occurrence, Meese's speech elicited responses from two sitting Supreme Court justices: William Brennan and John Paul Stevens. Both disagreed with Meese's strict form of judicial interpretation. Meese responded to Brennan's and Stevens's critique, expounding upon his ideas and asserting the importance of a written constitution to upholding the rule of law. Judge Bork also gave an address in which he supported the idea of a strict reading of the law. The Federalist Society concluded the debate with remarks from President Ronald Reagan following the appointment of William Rehnquist as chief justice and Antonin Scalia as associate justice.

In his speech, Meese advocated what scholars today would refer to as an ethic of original intent. His speech considered the role of the judiciary in the governmental system and of judicial interpretation in three areas of law. For Meese, the decisions presented during the previous court term lacked coherency. After examining the court's decisions in three areas of law, Meese concluded that the decisions crafted political policy rather than expounded upon constitutional principles. Such decision-making, Meese explained, has "given us questionable economics, governmental disorder, and racism—all in the guise of constitutional law."[42] According to Meese, many celebrated judicial opinions, in fact, merely overturn judicial mistakes caused by loose interpretation.

Meese argued the United States should not have judge-made law; in other words, the constitutional text should not be altered by the whimsy of whoever resides on the bench. According to Meese, when justices make decisions, they need to attempt to understand the original intent sought by the Founding Fathers. He asserts, "Those who framed the Constitution chose their words carefully; they debated at great length the most minute points. The language they chose meant something. It is incumbent upon the Court to determine what that meaning was."[43] If justices use original intent to determine legal outcome, then our democracy, Meese promised, would be strong and our Constitution would remain intact.

In October 1985 Justice William Brennan, at the Text and Teaching Symposium at Georgetown University, proclaimed the Constitution to be an aspirational document altered by changing morality and social conditions.[44] According to Brennan, the words of the Constitution were "not crystalline": "The phrasing is broad and the limitations of its provisions are not clearly marked. Its majestic generalities and ennobling pronouncements are both luminous and obscure."[45] The vagueness of the Constitution's textual meaning therefore "calls forth interpretation, the interaction of reader and text."[46] Although Brennan did not cite Meese's speech directly, Justice John Paul Stevens, in a speech before the Federal Bar Association a week later, refuted several of the attorney general's ideas regarding the incorporation of the Fourteenth Amendment.[47] In his speech, Stevens claimed that many different ideas were advanced during the founding period and that judges cannot determine which views should be upheld. From Stevens's remarks, determining original intent presents an unachievable goal, as the founders were not monolithic in their values or in their thinking.

The next month Meese expanded upon his earlier speech in remarks to the DC chapter of the Federalist Society.[48] Addressing the issue of constitutional fidelity, Meese declared that specific language should be followed, that consensus about the meaning of the document should be abided, and that when the language is vague, the text should be interpreted in a manner that does not contract the text. For Meese, constitutional interpretation does not rely upon original intent alone; yet bad judicial decisions derive from not following the original intent of the framers.

Judge Bork joined the debate when he spoke about constitutional interpretation at the University of San Diego School of Law in November 1985.[49] Bork began his remarks by arguing that the constitutional text provides parameters through which the law should be interpreted. For Bork, interpretivism (which he also refers to as intentionalism) does not limit a judge to what the language of the text meant at the narrow time frame of the founding. Rather, he claims, "all an intentionalist requires is that the text, structure, and history of the Constitution provide [a judge] not with a conclusion but with a premise."[50] The premises upon which he relies are core values of the nation, including liberty, justice, and equality. Upholding the "historic intentions underlying each clause" has three benefits: judges will neither craft public policy nor implement their own viewpoints, and the US system will remain under the Rule of Law.[51]

In his remarks upon the appointments of Rehnquist and Scalia, Reagan did not engage in a theoretical debate about different forms of constitutional interpretation. Rather, he advocated judicial restraint and reminded the public that our Constitution is a written document and that the Rule of Law governs. He ended his brief speech with a warning from Daniel Webster that implied that if the courts engage in loose interpretation, then the Constitution will fail and anarchy will reign.

Conclusion

The question of how to interpret the US Constitution is not a new one; politicians and legal scholars have disagreed about constitutional interpretation for almost a century. Legal scholars study the issue of judicial interpretation in an attempt to understand what judges themselves think they are doing when they "interpret" the law, for how justices interpret the law has material effects on social reality. Scholars find that judges employ predictable arguments when they write their judicial opinions. Scalia refers to himself as a "textualist" or an "originalist." Within the modern Supreme Court, different judges employ characteristically different commonplaces or different combinations of commonplaces. One form of interpretation can result in vastly different interpretations of the law, depending on how one uses the text of the Constitution. Hugo Black's textualism, for example, led to liberal, New Deal opinions, while Scalia's textualism favors conservative agendas that overturn New Deal decisions. Variance in opinions as a result of different forms of constitutional interpretation, however, creates a space to question the legitimacy of judicial opinions.

Legitimation is not a linear development. When applied to a judicial context, we can know that (1) legitimacy is a contested state and can be increased or decreased and (2) the legitimacy of a method of interpretation, a justice, an opinion, or an institution can be denied. Legitimacy does not need to be determined by the public as a whole; experts can influence how the public thinks. The court's decisions are open to public debate and to criticism, with certain opinions criticized as horrible decisions and as negatively impacting the perceived legitimacy of the court in the public sphere.[52] A well-respected institution (e.g., the Supreme Court), a person (e.g., a particular justice), or our democratic system (e.g., the Constitution) can offset the negative impact of what is perceived as a poor decision.

Following the tradition of consensus legitimacy, our political actors, institutions, and processes have legitimacy because the people of the United

States confer legitimacy upon them. Although not all decisions will have the consent of the people, the institution is empowered to act because it was given the authority to do so. The High Court's legitimacy derives both from the court as an institution and from its decisions. Social scientists ask whether the American people accept the opinions of the court as legitimate policy actions. Present studies are not conclusive. Political scientist David Adamany concludes that two forms of organizational legitimacy exist: content legitimacy and symbolic legitimacy.[53] Content legitimacy exists if the public supports the content of the decision; symbolic legitimacy exists if the public sees the decision as the authoritative position on the issue. Method of interpretation is a means by which to imbue legitimacy upon a decision. If observers perceive a decision of the court to be political, the legitimacy of the court is challenged;[54] similarly, if a method of interpretation is perceived to be political, then the legitimacy of the court is challenged.

The arguments sparked by the Meese/Brennan debate focus upon the use of historical and textual interpretations. Beginning with an emphasis on the original intent of the founders, many textualists now look to the original meaning of the text for direction in interpreting the Constitution. When we compare and contrast the living Constitution debate with the Great Debate, we notice several similarities. Both recognize that the Constitution is an important text within our governmental system. Both agree that where the Constitution is clear, the language of the law should be followed. Trouble begins when the language is not clear or is absent from the document, as observers then disagree as to who has agency to determine the law: Do judges act or do they defer to other branches of government? And if judges act, what do they use as their authorizing agent: the founders, the founding time period, the guiding principles of the nation, history, economic principles, previous case law, their own reasoning, or something else?

Before the Great Debate, the discussions primarily occurred within law schools. Following them, the debate became part of the larger public discourse. The average person now talks about "strict" construction or the "living" Constitution, espousing a stance about how the Constitution is, or should be, read. Most importantly, however, the debate about hermeneutical choices within constitutional interpretation is important because it is the nexus between language and politics. How the justices interpret the law becomes material reality for millions of Americans.

My survey of the early public discourse about the living Constitution and the Great Debate reflects the responses of experts well versed in legal theory. Yet legal language and principles require an expertise that excludes the majority of US citizens from the debate. Judges and legal scholars acknowledge the role of the judge in altering the constitutional text. While the public understands the importance of who is elected president for the selection's impact on future Supreme Court nominees, a disjunction exists between the political appointment to the court and the rights and liberties that individual members of the public experience. Regardless of high school civics classes, most people do not know what the Constitution says or what rights it guarantees. The common person takes up the language of the debate without understanding the legal theory behind the debate. The public largely accepts that the Constitution is an organic agent with the power to evolve. To state that the Constitution is "living" means, to such a public, that the document can be altered through judicial declaration; the textual boundaries do not need to be inflexible. Scalia disagreed.

2

Textualism in Scalia's Speeches and Extrajudicial Writings

In textual interpretation, context is everything, and the context of the Constitution tells us not to expect nit-picking detail, and to give words and phrases an expansive rather than narrow interpretation—though not an interpretation that the language will not bear.

—Justice Antonin Scalia

In every speech he delivered and in every essay or book he wrote, Scalia constructed a narrative in which the Constitution has a limited range of meaning and was not created to respond to shifting public needs. In an earlier time Americans understood the limited meaning of the constitutional text, Scalia tells us, and to alter that meaning the legislature passed a constitutional amendment. In his public speeches Scalia liked to reference the Nineteenth Amendment as an example, declaring it evidences how the Constitution has a limited range of meaning. If we were able to make the Constitution ensure voting rights for all persons at will, then we would not have had to pass the Nineteenth Amendment, granting women the right to vote. Scalia thus contends that the courts should defer to the legislature in the crafting of social policy unless a right or liberty *expressly* is protected in the Constitution.

I begin with an examination of Scalia's public speeches and extrajudicial writings because doing so gives us an idea of what Scalia understood himself to be doing when he interpreted the law. Scalia explains his method of constitutional interpretation to the lay public and legal audiences within these texts. Maintaining his concern with what the founding generation understood the text to mean, rather than with the intent of the founders per se, Scalia advocates limited judicial action and narrow readings of the Constitution. From his speeches and extrajudicial writings we can see that his advocacy of textualism evolved over time and addressed different challenges to strict readings of the Constitution.

Scalia as Orator

As an American orator, Justice Antonin Scalia was strangely present and absent in the public sphere. He frequently spoke to bar associations, foundations, institutions, think tanks, civic organizations, religious groups, school children, law school commencement ceremonies, and the news media, yet because he refused to allow his speeches to be recorded, little evidence exists of what he actually said.[1] Other justices are not so reticent. Since May 2000, the US Supreme Court has hosted a Web page with speeches delivered by the justices. Justices William H. Rehnquist, Stephen Breyer, Ruth Bader Ginsburg, and John Paul Stevens allow their speeches to be posted most frequently.[2] Although Scalia was one of the most prolific speechmakers on the court, none of his speeches were published on the official Court website while he resided on the bench (nor will they be published posthumously).[3] Scalia spoke widely and frequently, but, with a few exceptions, he demanded in advance that the hosting entity not record or publish the speech.[4] Scalia did, however, allow news programs as well as question and answer sessions to be recorded.[5]

One is left to wonder why such an articulate and forceful advocate of textualism would not allow his public speeches to be documented and publicized. One of the reasons might be because he essentially gave the same speech repeatedly. David Savage of the *Los Angeles Times* recounts, "He delivers the same speech over and over. But, as he has told friends, it remains fresh for those who have not seen it."[6] Another reason may be that had Scalia allowed his speeches to be recorded and placed on the Supreme Court's official website, his own thoughts would have been included in the institutional memory of the court and offered as an additional perspective to the institutionalized voice of the judicial opinion. Speeches reflect an individual's personal thought, not a professional's opinion or an institution's position.

Scalia's refusal to allow his public speeches to be recorded rhetorically supports his claim that a justice's personal reflections do not matter. As media theory scholar Marshall McLuhan tells us, "The medium is the message."[7] The channel of communication imparts meaning extraneous to the content of the message itself. How does a speech impart a meaning different than a law review article or a judicial opinion? Do not all of these articulations communicate the reflections of a judge? A majority judicial opinion reflects the judicial branch's institutional position.[8] Dissenting and concurring opinions reflect additional institutional perspectives.[9] A law review article provides the assessments of a professional person with legal training.

A speech offers external projections of an individual's personal thoughts. Speeches such as Scalia's are ethereal—delivered in a moment and gone (unless his will was violated and the speech was archived via digital technology). Consequently, a speech would offer tangible evidence violating his claim that the personal predilections of judges do not matter when interpreting the law.

In this analysis I examine five of Scalia's speeches made available through different websites, typically via the research institute or think tank that hosted the event at which Scalia spoke: his 1989 Sibley Lecture, entitled "Reflections on the Constitution," to the University of Georgia School of Law; his 1996 Catholic University of America speech, entitled "A Theory of Constitution Interpretation"; his 1997 Wriston Lecture to the Manhattan Institute for Policy Research, entitled "On Interpreting the Constitution"; his remarks to the 2002 Pew Forum on Religion and Public Life at the University of Chicago Divinity School, entitled "God's Justice and Ours"; and his 2005 Woodrow Wilson International Center for Scholars, entitled "Constitutional Interpretation the Old Fashioned Way."[10] An examination of Scalia's speeches—the ones that have become a part of the public record regardless of his prohibition against publishing his speeches—shows that Scalia repeated the same themes in every speech he gave. Following the political consultant's creed that consistency of message is important to achieving your aims, Scalia articulated the same message in speeches spanning multiple decades.

The three dominant themes of his speeches were constitutional interpretation, judicial deference, and the democratic process. According to Scalia, the Constitution should be interpreted as a statute. In other words, for Scalia the Constitution's meaning was fixed at the time of its adoption. Moreover, justices should not take the law-making process into their own hands, since in a democracy the government is to be ruled by the people. According to Scalia, the Constitution was meant to be fixed and rigid; it was not intended to respond to the changing needs of society.[11] Such is his thought regardless of what he states. I point this out because in "Constitutional Interpretation the Old Fashioned Way," Scalia maintains that his is a "flexible" Constitution. In his statement, however, Scalia did not use the term "flexible" to mean that the document is elastic. Rather, he contends that the document is not flexible at all—it is static and must be altered through the process of constitutional amendment. Although he claims not to attribute original intent, Scalia nevertheless asserts that the founders intended the laws to be changed only through legislation or constitutional amendment—and until recently the practice of the country supported the founders' intention.

When read in turn, Scalia's speeches unfold temporally as part of a larger national dialogue about constitutional interpretation, judicial deference, and the democratic process. The speeches, delivered across sixteen years, shift the hermeneutic lens from one aspect of the textualism argument to another. In one speech Scalia emphasizes how the Constitution is a special document, in another he promotes a return to strict readings of the Constitution, and in yet another he encourages judicial restraint. Considering each speech separately highlights the ways in which Scalia's textual tale developed and how different appeals were made to particular audiences, even though Scalia discussed the same themes in every speech with little variation. Although my sample is small, these speeches reflect his public voice and correspond with newspaper accounts from his other speeches.

"Reflections on the Constitution": 1989 Sibley Lecture to the University of George School of Law

In his 1989 Sibley Lecture, Scalia emphasizes the symbolism of the Constitution, the founders' purposes in establishing a written constitution, and the difference between the United States' Constitution and the constitution of another nation, the Soviet Union, which he refers to as the Union of Soviet Socialist Republics. He argues that the Constitution should not be altered easily and that it means what it means, even when that meaning is not consistent with the personal predilections of a justice. His claim relies upon *argumentum ad antiquitatem*, which argues that the Constitution should be followed because it has existed for so long.

Scalia's speech begins, as most of his speeches do, with a reflection on the distinctive nature of the Constitution. Difficult to alter, the Constitution is the most celebrated document in the history of the nation and represents the identity of the nation. Scalia asserts, "When statutes are amended you take the old one, throw it out, and insert the new one. . . . Not so with the venerated document that is our United States Constitution. . . . We append all of the amendments at the end. That is how reluctant we are to touch that venerable document, that symbol of our nation."[12] Etched in the national consciousness and our government systems as a sacred text, Scalia tells us, the Constitution's corpus is untouched by physical alteration. Unlike other nations, the United States has preserved the same Constitution for more than two hundred years—much longer than any other nation.

Scalia's argument from tradition implies that the United States' governmental system should continue as it has in the past. The ideals of the founders, Scalia concludes, were captured in the specific enumerations the founders chose to include in the articles and the amendments to the Constitution and were meant to be enduring. Thus, not only have the people been reluctant historically to change the Constitution, because they respect it as a sacrosanct document, but the founders also did not intend for the text to be altered. Scalia cites a speech by Benjamin Franklin, given at the signing of the Constitution, as evidence that the ideals embodied in the Constitution were meant to guide future governmental decisions: "For having lived long I have experienced many instances of being obligated by better information or fuller consideration to change opinions even on important subjects which I once thought right but found to be otherwise."[13] Franklin's statement appears to advocate keeping the language of the text vague, and thus the interpretation of the text broad, so that additional information or changing circumstances could allow readings in line with contemporary issues. One also could understand Franklin to mean the Constitution would be cast aside in favor of a new document. Nevertheless, Scalia asserts that Franklin encouraged his auditors to leave the text of the Constitution alone, allowing future generations to understand the document in a different fashion—a point in direct contradiction to Scalia's underlying message that judges should interpret the text as a static document, its meaning set forth at the time of the founding. Scalia's point is, in fact, a subtle admonition against judicial activism—judges should not alter the constitutional text through Supreme Court opinions. Public opinion will change; the constitutional text represents enduring principles. According to Scalia, the court should rely upon the meaning of the constitutional text as understood by the American people at the time of its adoption.

If his audience accepts Scalia's premises that the Constitution is enduring and that momentary opinion may not be the best guide to the future, they also likely agree that judges should not base judicial decisions on personal predilections. This leads to Scalia's conclusion that viewing the Constitution as a living document degrades and debases the text. Scalia notes that such an approach would bring "compromises of principles" and "misperceptions of liberty" to the bench. Scalia does not elucidate what these possible misperceptions of liberty can be; he merely states they exist. Scalia's critique appears to foreshadow Justice Breyer's speeches and extrajudicial writings, which compare "the liberty of the ancients" against "the liberty of the moderns."[14] Breyer advocates pragmatic judicial interpretation, emphasizing how the theme of "activity liberty" can achieve legal results that are beneficial to the functioning of democratic participation. Activist judges, Scalia contends, misconstrue liberty, which results in readings of the Constitution that lessen the integrity of the text.

Scalia's Sibley Lecture strives to convince his audience that the Constitution is a special document and is to be treated in a revered fashion. We should not deal with our founding document as we would any other governmental text. Specifically, constitutional law was created to be enduring;

it should be less easily altered than laws created by the legislature.[15] In his address to Catholic University, Scalia emphasizes this theme yet shifts his focus to the actual interpretation of the Constitution. If his audience agrees that the Constitution is a unique document, and if we have treated it as such in the past, then we should look to the Congress, rather than the courts, for a response to contemporary public needs.

"A Theory of Constitution Interpretation": 1996 Remarks to Catholic University of America

Scalia's remarks to Catholic University can be viewed as a judicial jeremiad in which Scalia calls back the people from their forgotten practice of constitutional interpretation. According to Scalia, the Constitution is a fixed and static document that is to be understood as it was when it was adopted in the eighteenth century. If the people want to change their governmental system, they need to do so "at the ballot box" rather than seek redress in the courts. The judicial branch and the public need to realize their errors in engaging in loose forms of interpretation and return to the covenant they established when the predecessors founded the country, namely, that the Constitution creates a system of government and protects broad rights and liberties.

The role a Supreme Court justice plays in the maintenance of constitutional covenants is an important one. The justices sit on the bench to interpret the Constitution, although Scalia acknowledges that no consensus exists as to how they should go about doing their job. Scalia himself identifies a preference for textualism, explaining that a textualist seeks to understand the original meaning of the Constitution (what it meant to the American people at the time of the founding) rather than the original intent of the Constitution (what the founders meant for the Constitution to mean). Scalia is not alone in his thinking, as previous Supreme Court justices similarly understood their role in maintaining the covenant. Citing the Nineteenth Amendment as an example, he argues: "As you know, there was a national campaign of 'suffragettes' to get this constitutional amendment adopted, a very big deal to get a constitutional amendment adopted. Why? Why did they go through all the trouble? If people then thought the way people think now, there would have been no need. There was an Equal Protection Clause, right there in the Constitution in 1920. As an abstract matter, what in the world could be a greater denial of equal protection in a democracy than denial of the franchise? And so why didn't these people just come before the court and say, 'This is a denial of equal protection'? Because they didn't think that way."[16] People did call this a denial of equal protection, regardless of Scalia's claim. He asserts that because women who advocated for voting rights did not appeal to the courts for the elective franchise, ipso facto broader interpretations than have been employed in the past are not allowed. (In fact, Susan B. Anthony appealed her denial of voting rights and the matter was heard in *Minor v. Happersett* [1874]).[17] According to Scalia's version of history, his contemporaries should read the Constitution in such a way as to understand how the populace perceived it originally. Since the document's meaning is fixed, the only way to alter its meaning is via the amendment process.

As the extended quote above shows, public perception regarding the role of the judge is important. Rather than seek judicial remedy in the courts, the public should introduce statutory policy to address contemporary problems. Abortion and the death penalty offer two examples of areas of law that should be regulated by the political process rather than adjudicated. According to Scalia, justices should not construe their own version of what the Constitution ought to mean in these areas of law. If Scalia can persuade his audience—and the larger public—that they should not take political issues before the courts, then his peers will have fewer opportunities to engage in judicial activism that bastardizes the Constitution's meaning.

Scalia denies that his version of constitutional interpretation leaves the United States with a rigid system of government. Rather, by leaving the outcome to the people via the political process, the people can achieve results that align closely with their interests. Being one of nine aging justices on the highest court of the land sheltered Scalia from common complaints and vogue trends. "I am so out of touch with the American people," Scalia declares, "I don't even try to be in touch. . . . If you want someone who's in touch with what are the evolving standards of decency that reflect a maturing society, ask the Congress."[18] He asserts that his job is to interpret what the document actually says, not what it *ought* to say. The Constitution is not an "empty vessel," waiting to be filled with whatever legal doctrine du jour the justices wish. He concludes that if America does not heed his warning to return to a limited view of the Constitution, then our democracy will be weakened. When judges intervene and interpret the Constitution beyond its original meaning, they alter the meaning of the sacred document. Scalia continues his jeremiad regarding constitutional interpretation in his Wriston Lecture.

"On Interpreting the Constitution": 1997 Wriston Lecture to The Manhattan Institute for Policy Research

In his Wriston Lecture Scalia continues to emphasize the main points of his earlier speeches. The Constitution is not a living document; judges should not loosely interpret the document; and the proper channels of redress are through the legislatures. In this speech, however, he adds a criticism of the political Right and a warning about the strength of the American political system.

Scalia constructs the audience of his Wriston Lecture as intelligent and consubstantial with the justices. Scalia identifies his audience members as "an assembly of intelligent people from high school age onward," specifically not including persons who are minors or persons who are unintelligent. Using rhetorical questions to pose possible interpretative scenarios within his speech, his erudite audience acts as a confidant, privy to Scalia's ruminations about judicial interpretation. As he addresses what sort of questions the court should consider and how they should read the Constitution, his audience affirms his preferred interpretive reading.

Judicial interpretation, Scalia tells us, is different from policymaking. Advocating originalism, which he again describes both as textualism and as original meaning, Scalia contends the justices cannot consider just any matter that the public brings to them. Rather, the Constitution needs to be read according to the plain meaning of the text, as well as according to how the public understood the document to mean at the time of the founding. Scalia again offers suffrage as the archetype for constitutional amendment, with the right to vote being denied for a plentitude of reasons, including sex, property ownership, and literacy, all of which he finds to be constitutional. If the public wants different laws, they need to pass either statutory laws or constitutional amendments, Scalia argues, not allow judges to make the law into whatever they want.

Treating the Constitution as if it is living, which justices do when they consider matters about which the Constitution is silent, violates the textual integrity of the Constitution and harms the democratic system. The Constitution, Scalia explains, guarantees the legal *process*, not the legal *result*. "Due process of law never meant you've got the right answer. It meant the process was fair," Scalia declares.[19] By trying to create a nation that the judges deem fair, the courts have ignored how a constitution differs from other types of laws. "A constitution is not for flexibility," Scalia opines. "A Constitution is for rigidity."[20] Conservatives and liberals alike are to blame for anthropomorphizing the Constitution. Citing multiple examples of areas of law in which the text is silent (abortion, homosexual conduct, product damages, and how to rear one's children), Scalia concludes that if the Constitution is silent about an issue, then the courts cannot adjudicate the matter. The people must decide matters of public policy at the ballot box.

Concerned with the deterioration of the democratic state, Scalia places the burden of a healthy democracy on the refusal of the Supreme Court to determine the outcome of political issues. Rather than work to achieve popular support of the majority, groups need only to win five votes out of nine to effect social change. The loss of democratic processes "is a great sadness" to Scalia.[21] Judicial legislating is a threefold problem for Scalia. First, making the Constitution mean whatever we want suggests that it does not mean much of anything at all. Second, we have no criteria by which to interpret the Constitution if it can mean whatever we want. Third, judicial legislating exposes the Supreme Court to the political pressures placed upon other political branches. Scalia contends that these three points detract from the court's prestige and make the court vulnerable to political attack.

Scalia's Wriston Lecture concludes the court must refuse to engage in the political battles that frequently come its way in order to prevent political attack. The distinction between belief (what the court thinks should be done) and action (what the court actually does) is one Scalia continues to address in his "God's Justice and Ours" remarks to the Pew Forum. Whereas in earlier speeches Scalia distinguishes between the belief and action of the court as a body, in his Pew Forum speech he distinguishes between belief and action as an individual justice and clarifies how his religious beliefs do not determine his judicial actions.

"God's Justice and Ours": 2002 Pew Forum on Religion and Public Life Remarks

Scalia begins his remarks about constitutional interpretation in his speech to the Pew Forum on Religion and Public Life, given at the University of Chicago Divinity School, by distinguishing between personal belief and professional action. Returning to one of his most common examples, Scalia emphasizes that his actions reflect the constitutionality of capital punishment; his opinions do not abide by his personal religious beliefs against capital punishment. For Scalia the death penalty can be administered because the Constitution says it can. "That statement would not be true if I subscribed to the conventional fallacy that the Constitution is a 'living document'—that is, a text that means from age to age whatever the society (or perhaps the Court) thinks it ought to mean."[22] Justices who reject the constitutionality of capital punishment should resign, Scalia asserts.

Scalia's speech to the Pew Forum is perhaps his most surprising. In his remarks Scalia contends that he has no moral problem with upholding the death penalty, despite his being a Catholic. Although one would hope that a Supreme Court justice would not adjudicate based upon his or her religious beliefs, what is surprising about this speech is Scalia's argument that the state is the "minister of God" in the administration of justice.

Scalia's role in the death penalty—the Supreme Court being the court of last resort for someone sentenced to death—poses no problem for Scalia, because he claims that the state was the minister of justice for God. Quoting the book of Romans, he declares the United States was built upon the concept of God as manifested in the Christian Bible and as reflected in our practices and traditions. Such a belief in God, Scalia tells us, is exhibited in the words "In God We Trust" stamped on our money, the words "under God" stated in our Pledge of Allegiance, and the prayers that open Supreme Court sessions.

Speaking to a group of religious intellectuals, who had gathered to consider the relationship between religion, politics, and public life, Scalia assumed that his audience accepted Christian references as evidentiary support. For this audience, Scripture is a valid text and the Christian viewpoint asserted in Romans is the heritage of the American people. Importantly, Scalia would not have the liberty to argue the state is the "minister of God" in one of his judicial opinions. Such a claim would reflect his religious views rather than his secular legal deductions.

Scalia does not merely consider a religious perspective on capital punishment. As his title suggests ("God's Justice and *Ours*"), he also addresses the constitutionality of capital punishment from a legal standpoint. According to Scalia, whether society has evolved beyond the need to employ capital punishment does not matter; the Constitution allows the state to take a life following due process of the laws. In fact, Scalia argues that society's enlarged capacity for destruction, murder, and death have *increased* the need for the death penalty, as people can harm others in more cruel and destructive ways than the founders ever could have imagined. Therefore, he disagrees that the death penalty was not morally acceptable. For Scalia, the practice of capital punishment is more necessary now than ever before.

Scalia's Pew Forum speech is significant in his oratorical corpus because this speech clarifies how a judge adjudicates the law regardless of his or her personal opinions or beliefs. The text of the Constitution may violate the ideology of a judge; nevertheless, the judge has to uphold the Constitution as he or she swore to do. If the people desire to change the document, the amendment process through which they may do so is available to them. The Constitution may not say what we want it to say; it should always mean, however, what the founding generation understood it to mean. Scalia continues his crusade against expansive readings of the Constitution in his Address to the Woodrow Wilson International Center for Scholars.

"Constitutional Interpretation the Old Fashioned Way": 2005 Address to the Woodrow Wilson International Center for Scholars

In his Woodrow Wilson International Center for Scholars remarks, Scalia presents himself as part of an elite minority of people who interpret the Constitution as it should be interpreted. He refutes the "false virtues" and details the "principle vices" of the living Constitution doctrine, insisting that loose interpretation does not produce progressive results. He argues that nonoriginalist readings can result in the loss of rights just as much as they have the ability to secure new rights.[23] In addition to several of his standard examples (e.g., capital punishment and women's suffrage), Scalia offers a few fear appeals (including sodomy laws, jury trials, and the Confrontation Clause) as well as a decision that angered many conservatives (flag burning) to support his claim that judges should abide by originalism when deciding cases. His discourse engages in a form of apocalyptic rhetoric, presenting the demise of the Constitution as well as alluding to the end of minority rights in the United States.[24]

Scalia depicts himself as a "qualified other" within this speech, distinguishing himself as a minority member of legal intellectuals who favor an unpopular form of constitutional interpretation. A rhetorical construction, otherizing separates in-group members from out-group members. The Other typically occupies a negative status as nonnormative and inferior, as members of the otherized group are essentialized and disenfranchised.[25] Scalia's Other simultaneously perpetuates and challenges the traditional Other. Scalia declares: "I am one of a small number of judges, small number of anybody—judges, professors, lawyers—who are known as originalist. . . . This is such a minority position in modern academia and in modern legal circles that on occasion I'm asked when I've given a talk like this a question from the back of the room—'Justice Scalia, when did you first become an originalist?'—as though it is some kind of weird affliction that seizes some people—'When did you first start eating human flesh?'"[26] Aside from his humorous quip about being a cannibal (or a zombie), Scalia constructs himself not only as outside the interpretive norm of his community of professional elites but also as a skilled minority. Although one of only nine members of the highest Court in the land, Scalia implies that he does not maintain a position of privilege. He is part of "*such* a minority position" that he stands out as an uncommon apparition, an unusual entity worthy of examination. His education and chosen career identify him, however, as a Qualified Other. Judges, professors, and lawyers have intellectual *gravitas*, formed through years of specialized schooling and work. As a judge, Scalia can be identified with other legal professionals; as an originalist, he is an interpretive anomaly. To wit, Scalia is a Qualified Other who occupies an intellectual, social, and professional space within a legal in-group, but on the border of said group.

Unlike himself, who he crafts as an interpretive purist, Scalia portrays justices who support loose interpretation as standardless hucksters who implement their own ideological perspectives and do not believe "the Constitution is a legal text."[27] They are, in his words, "willful" judges who "distort" the law. Although he acknowledges that judges who decide the law based upon their own proclivities have always existed, he claims that they used to at least *pretend* to uphold the Constitution. In the era of the living Constitution, these judges do not attempt to maintain the façade; they read the Constitution in whatever manner produces the result they seek. Scalia claims that if a judge does not use textualism, then that judge does not use any form of interpretation at all. "What is the criterion that governs the Living Constitution judge? What can you possibly use, besides original meaning?" Scalia asks.[28] Scalia establishes an either/or fallacy, concluding that a judge uses either textualism/original meaning or no form of interpretation. "There is none other," Scalia proclaims.[29] For Scalia, any other form of interpretation lacks such credibility as to be nonexistent.

In his Woodrow Wilson remarks, Scalia engages in what I refer to as the "anti-argument." Anti-arguments demonstrate inherent fallacies within reasoning, through advancing an opposing position, developing an argument to its logical extreme, or illustrating logical conflicts. Scalia walks his listener through the progression urged by these loose constructionists toward a Constitution that has no textual meaning. The first step is to claim the Constitution means what it did not mean when the document was adopted. Scalia cites libel law as an example, explaining how *New York Times v. Sullivan* (1964) determined that a public figure could not sue for libel if the libel was not malicious.[30] The second step is to create judicial doctrine with no textual bearing. Scalia offers the example of substantive due process. The Due Process Clause does not protect fundamental liberties; rather, it guarantees procedural due process. In other words, life, liberty, and property can be denied once a person has had his or her day in court. The third step, Scalia asserts, is the elimination of the separation of fundamental liberties from other, lesser liberties. Scalia contends that doing so means "the Court has essentially liberated itself from the text of the Constitution, from the text and even from the traditions of the American people."[31] The end result of such a path, for Scalia, "is that it will destroy the Constitution."[32] Moreover, a living Constitution eradicates minority rights and the American system of government, Scalia contends, creating a "recipe for destruction of what we have had for 200 years."[33] Consequently, other judges end up destroying the integrity of the Constitution, which is the foundation upon which our government is fashioned, if those judges do not read the Constitution via an originalist lens.

Importantly, in this speech we can observe a shift in language from textualism to originalism. Although constitutional scholars such as Bobbitt separate the two forms of interpretation, for Scalia they are one and the same. Scalia understands originalism as the original meaning of the document as understood at the time of the founding. Since the text itself is not necessarily clear in all instances, Scalia allows himself the space to consider what the founding generation understood the text to mean. Therefore, when the text is not clear on its face, Scalia contends that the founding context gives meaning to the text—but regardless of the perspective (the language of the text or the original meaning of the text)—it is the text itself that drives judicial interpretation.

Scalia's Woodrow Wilson speech is a culmination of his thinking on the subject of constitutional interpretation. In earlier speeches he asserts that the Constitution is a special document, that judges need to be called back from the error of their interpretive ways, that the separation of powers gives distinct functions to the judicial and the legislative branches, and that a judge should not allow his own political beliefs to influence his adjudication. In his Woodrow Wilson address he offers a vision of what will happen if the judicial branch creates the law: The Constitution will be destroyed. For Scalia, the meaning of the Constitution was fixed at the time of the founding. He claims to reject the intent of the founders, but to support his view he quotes Benjamin Franklin when espousing the significance of the document. In these speeches, Scalia also contends that justices should not determine what is best for society by altering the Constitution's meaning. Rather, the Supreme Court should allow the legislators, who are responsible to their constituencies in frequently held elections, to respond to the changing needs of the people. Scalia claims the justices should distinguish between their personal beliefs and their professional actions, restraining themselves from deciding political issues. In each of these five speeches, Scalia presents a clear argument, supported by examples the general public could easily understand. Scalia crafted these speeches in a language accessible to the layperson. His extrajudicial writings, however, are crafted for a different audience. Scalia's extrajudicial writings are addressed to persons educated in the law and contain more nuanced arguments about the legal process. As he says, "Men may intend what they will; but it is only the laws that they enact which bind us."[34]

Scalia as Extrajudicial Author

Scalia published a number of works that developed and advanced his preferred method of constitutional interpretation following his ascension to the High Court.[35] Each expounds upon Scalia's theoretical justification for a strict interpretation of the Constitution and is cited widely by persons seeking to understand and to critique Scalia's judicial decision-making.

The themes present in Scalia's extrajudicial writings align with the themes from his public speeches. My analysis of these writings shows that Scalia offered a limited vision of the role the judiciary plays in the governance of the United States, advocated strict interpretations of the Constitution, and believed that expansive readings of the Constitution violently impair the functioning of American democratic practices.

In what follows I consider each of Scalia's writings in turn. I quickly move through the first two essays, because neither presents an in-depth examination of how to interpret the text per se. I offer a more thorough consideration of the third essay, "Common-Law Courts in a Civil-Law System: The Role of United States Federal Courts in Interpreting the Constitution and Laws," delivered as part of the Princeton University's Tanner Lecture on Human Values in 1995 and subsequently published in his book, *A Matter of Interpretation: Federal Courts and the Law (1998)*, because it is Scalia's most developed exposition of the practice of textual interpretation. I also do not engage in extensive analysis of Scalia's and Bryan Garner's 2012 *Reading Law: The Interpretation of Legal Texts,* because it does not offer as detailed an analysis of textualism as Scalia's earlier "Common-Law Courts" essay. An extension of the claims in his earlier writings, *Reading Law* takes up the question of how to analyze law—predominantly statutory law—according to existing legal canons.

"The Rule of Law" and "Originalism"

The first two essays argue that how judges decide the law is important because the integrity of the constitutional text must be maintained. To ensure that the Constitution is preserved, justices should not let their own personal predilections influence judicial decision-making. Stability of the law, Scalia tells us, is enhanced through the predictability of judicial decision-making. Nevertheless, these essays show slippage in Scalia's thinking. In "The Rule of Law as a Law of Rules" (1989), Scalia inadvertently acknowledges the possibility that he does not follow his own interpretive rules, and in "Originalism: The Lesser Evil" (1989), he concedes that narrow forms of interpretation have intellectual challenges as well.

The chiasmus set forth in Scalia's title, "The Rule of Law as a Law of Rules," establishes the idea that judicial decision-making should be formulaic. To be arbiters of justice, judges must rely upon criteria of justice external to their personal predilections for the law. Scalia explains that in a rule of law system "*the law is king*,"[36] drawing upon Thomas Payne's assertion in *Common Sense*. Arguing against the use of personal judicial discretion in decision-making, Scalia asserts, "We judges cannot create [general rules] out of whole cloth, but must find some basis for them in the text that

Congress or the Constitution has provided."[37] Characterizing the Constitution as a fixed document that does not necessitate filling in gaps in legal principles, Scalia suggests the outcome of judicial decision-making should be the same over time. The text does not change (unless amended), so outcomes should be clear and predictable.

The above excerpts show that Scalia's brand of textualism does not begin and end with the text. Rather, the text influences a judge's reading. To take his metaphor of the cloth, textualism could be the material that constitutes the fabric or the dye that colors the cloth. Thus, Scalia recognizes that the text cannot be all that is involved in the interpretive process. We can observe that the process includes the constitutional text, the judge, and something else—although Scalia neglects to state what that something else is. Scalia acknowledges that the extent to which the text plays a part varies in interpretative readings.

Although the text influences his decision-making, even Scalia does not rely solely upon the text. Scalia admits, "It is perhaps easier for me than it is for some judges to develop general rules, because I am more inclined to adhere closely to the plain meaning of a text."[38] Importantly, Scalia notes he is *more* inclined, not that he is *fully* inclined. Moreover, this essay frames textualism as a set of "general rules" that are relatively easy to achieve. As we will see in his "Originalism" essay, however, Scalia's form of textualism requires the judge to engage in intellectual archaeology.

In contrast with his speeches and other writings, in "Originalism: The Lesser Evil," Scalia acknowledges that, in comparison to other ways of reading the Constitution, originalism is a "lesser evil." Since no interpretation is good, originalism merely stands as the *less* evil of the forms. Thus, one can infer that *no* forms of interpretation are good; all are evil. When a judge is forced to interpret the law, therefore, he must select the form of interpretation that will corrupt the system the least. From Scalia's writing, we can infer that the Constitution and statutory laws are good; attempts to say what the law is or to interpret the law incorrectly are evil. Judges do not need to go beyond the original meaning of the Constitution to correct social wrongs or to remain consistent with changing values. "Elections," Scalia maintains, "take care of that quite well."[39] While elections were created to respond to contemporary shifts in values, the Constitution was meant to preserve fundamental values, such as free speech, freedom of the press, and due process of law, that remain constant throughout time. Maintaining the founding values is good; deviating from them is evil.

In "Originalism," Scalia recognizes that originalism is difficult to apply correctly, as it is challenging to know the original meaning of the document, it relies upon questionable historical evidence of original meaning, it requires judges to become experts in the political and intellectual context of the founding time period, and it demands that judges cast aside their own preferences. Such interpretation is, Scalia proposes, possibly "a task sometimes better suited to the historian than the lawyer."[40] For if the judge does not interpret the law correctly—in other words, according to the meaning of the text as it was originally understood—such interpretation would be a form of evil. Originalism, on the other hand, brings predictability and clarity to legal decision-making and prevents judges from imposing their will on the Constitution.

These first two essays, published after he had been on the Supreme Court for fewer than three years, reflect Scalia's early advocacy of textualism. Their underlying ideas—that judges must decide cases not based upon their own ideologies, must adhere to the original meaning of the text, and must seek predictability and clarity in the law—remain arguments Scalia returned to time and time again in his speeches, writings, and judicial opinions. In later speeches and writings, however, Scalia refused to admit flaws of textualism or that textualism, as a form of interpretation, can be evil. He also refused to grant his own agency in determining what the law is, arguing instead that meaning is derived from the plain meaning of the text and from the context within which the text was adopted.

"Common-Law Courts in a Civil-Law System"

In "Common-Law Courts in a Civil-Law System," Scalia set forth his most developed exposition of the practice of textual interpretation. In the essay, Scalia presents arguments against a living Constitution and in favor of "reasonable" textual interpretation. According to Scalia, constitutional interpretation is a "science" that has been "neglected." While he condemns other forms of interpretation, he nevertheless fails to set forth the process of textual interpretation, criticizing more expansive readings of the Constitution without offering guidance for interpreting the text properly.

Projecting a dichotomous relationship between the "science" of law and the "art" of law, reminiscent of Socrates's split between rhetoric as an art and dialectic as a science in Plato's *Gorgias*, Scalia differentiates between different types of law. Scalia begins his essay with a statement of his aim: "The following essay attempts to explain the current neglected state of the science of construing legal texts, and offers a few suggestions for improvements."[41] Scalia's characterization of statutory and constitutional law as a "science" implies constitutional interpretation should be objective, predictable, and replicable. For such interpretation to be objective, the judge has to be a neutral party merely applying pertinent legal principles to the case at hand. Legal interpretation should be fairly predictable, because the end result of a case can be foreseen. A judge does not create new legal principles; rather, he applies already existing principles. Lower courts, moreover, should be able to follow previous decisions and reach similar results in similar cases, thus replicating legal decisions and reasoning. Law that is objective, predictable, and replicable values expertise and procedure and devalues opinion and results. Statutory law and constitutional law are sciences in which the neutral principles of the law determine the necessary legal outcomes.

In opposition to statutory and constitutional law, the common law is an art in which the creative crafting of law is more important than the "right" result. Common law can be objective, predicable, and replicable when scenarios similar to those that have already been considered arise, but common law does not necessitate that judges consider only particular questions. Within the common law, judges can create a legal rule when new questions present themselves. Scalia's discussion of the common law is important rhetorically, because it differentiates the common law from constitutional law. The two forms of law occupy separate legal spaces. Common law is judge-made law; constitutional law should not be judge-made law. In an era in which the people think the Constitution is living, they expect judges to interpret the law in such a fashion as to produce the results they want. In other words, they expect judges to use their lawyerly skills to create new constitutional law. But, as Scalia tells us, constitutional law is written law—established by the people and resistant to change.

Scalia's characterization of law as a science leaves us with a legal system that gives agency to the law rather than to the lawmaker or judge. The law wills what it will, and its will is known by what the document sets forth. Yet Scalia tells us that little attention has been given to questions of how the science of law should be performed. Frequently judges try to use legislative intent to understand what the law is rather than rely upon the language of the text itself. Scalia rejects this practice. "Men may intend what they will," Scalia contends, "but it is only the laws that they enact which bind us."[42] For Scalia, the final legal text is the only thing that can be known—the process of arriving at the text does not matter for several reasons. First, Congress does not make clear its legislative intent. Statutory law can be vague, allowing the details to be worked out through the enactment of laws. Second, few representatives actively participate in the lawmaking process. Since only a small number of legislators write statutes or are involved in the committee process, few members of Congress are on the floor during debate, and rarely do all representatives vote in favor of a bill that is passed, judges cannot use *intent* as a criterion for interpretation. Consequently, judges should let the language of the law and the original meaning of the text guide their adjudication of the law, basing their interpretive decisions on the statutory text itself rather than on assessments of legislative intent. The rule of law and the lack of clear and consistent legislative intent create a space for Scalia's solution to the neglected practice of legal decision-making: the use of textualism to interpret the Constitution.

In this essay, Scalia first attempts to define textualism strictly and then later moves to a broader definition of textualism. "When the text of a statute is clear, that is the end of the matter," he proclaims.[43] Yet Scalia does not characterize himself as a strict constructionist. "A text should not be construed strictly, and it should not be construed leniently; it should be construed reasonably, to contain all that it fairly means," he states—a premise he repeats in his speeches.[44] By pronouncing that textualism should be construed "reasonably," Scalia tries to escape an either/or fallacy and to craft a textualism that can be responsive to shifting societal needs. Interpretation should be neither strict nor loose; it should be "reasonable." But what does "reasonable" mean, and how should "reasonable" be applied? In his "Common-Law Courts" essay, Scalia explains that "reasonable" means that "words have a limited range of meaning, and no interpretation that goes beyond that range is permissible."[45] Although Scalia appears to indicate that words do not have one precise meaning, his explanation works from the premise that words cannot be expanded beyond particular denotative meanings that existed at the time of the founding. Supporting his point with the Due Process Clause, Scalia contends the death penalty is constitutional because the Constitution ensures a *process*, not a *result*. A person can be denied life, yet only after due process. He argues that his peers who believe society has evolved beyond capital punishment have no textual basis for their opinion.

A lawyer's training develops in a judge an understanding of how a text could be reasonably construed differently than a lay individual might construe it. A lawyer's training begins the first year of law school, with learning legal concepts and how to think like a lawyer. Scalia discusses how legal "canons and presumptions" impact judicial decision-making, for canon and presumptions guide one's reading of a legal text. Specifically, canons are general rules for reading; they could be construed as grammatical rules for textual construction. Scalia offers *expressio unius est exclusio alterius* (Latin for "expression of the one is exclusion of the other") as an example of a canon. According to this canon of construction, if one group is identified specifically, then we can assume that another group is excluded. When an applicable canon cannot be ascertained easily, presumptions should be employed. A presumption favors one result over another. Scalia offers the example of ambiguity in a criminal statute. When ambiguity exists, the issues should be resolved in favor of the defendant. Legal canons and presumptions explain why judicial opinions do not rely upon colloquial or contemporary meanings of language. Reasonable readings will apply the canons and presumptions that judges first learn about in law school to guide judicial decision-making. Reasonable readings of the law, therefore, are interpretations of the law by a legal authority trained in how to read the text of the law through the lens of legal canons and presumptions.

Legal training does not equip one to determine the intent of another person. Scalia rejects the use of legislative history, gleaned from legislative debates and committee reports, or of legislative intent, assembled through the personal communications of legislators, when deciding cases. The only artifacts from the lawmaking process that judges should take into consideration are statutes and amendments adopted by the states and the federal government. As discussed above, legislative history serves as a particularly bad resource for adjudication, because committee reports and legislative debates do not express the will of Congress. Most legislators do not read reports, nor are they present at debate. Thus, the expression of a few does not reflect the intent of the whole. Judges must, in other words, interpret the law as it was adopted; intent does not matter.

For the majority of his essay Scalia considers how statutory laws should be construed, not differentiating between statutory construction and constitutional construction, because the act of interpreting the text of a legal document does not differ per se. The process by which a judge reads the law does not vary; the only distinction is the document that is interpreted. When interpreting the Constitution, a judge applies "the usual principles . . . to an unusual text."[46] Scalia explains, "In textual interpretation, context is everything, and the context of the Constitution tells us not to expect nit-picking detail, and to give words and phrases an expansive rather than narrow interpretation—though not an interpretation that the language will not bear."[47] The Constitution establishes our government and explains citizen's rights and liberties; the Constitution does not regulate contemporary social problems. Unlike "new" textualists, who focus on the meaning of the Constitution within the context of modern linguistic meanings, Scalia's textualism focuses on the original meaning of the text for members of the founding generation.

For Scalia, hermeneutic insight comes from the original meaning of the text. Instead of looking to earlier judicial decisions, Scalia argues that interpretation should begin with the text being interpreted: the Constitution itself. And since he is trying to understand a constitution—a *written* document, resistant to change—there is no better place to look for original meaning than in the writings of persons who took part in the founding of the nation. Scalia explains that he uses the writings of founders "not because they were Framers and therefore their intent is authoritative and must be the law; but rather because their writings, like those of other intelligent and informed people of the time, display how the text of the Constitution was originally understood."[48] Original meaning, not original intent, is the objective of interpretation. Scalia appears to be able, as the colloquial phrase goes, to have his cake and to eat it too without any form of cognitive dissonance. If documentation from the founders can help clarify how the founding period understood the text, then it can be used. For Scalia, the difference between original intent and original meaning lies in the distinction between what an individual founder desired and what the founding generation writ large understood the text to mean.

Scalia calls judges back from the error of interpreting a living Constitution. He asserts that by expanding the meaning of the Constitution carelessly, loose interpretations have decreased, rather than increased, individual liberty. Citing as examples the ban on illegally obtained criminal evidence, the prohibition against invoking God at public school commencement ceremonies, and the government's inability to outlaw pornography unless it is "obscene," Scalia explains the judiciary has limited legislative responses to solving community problems. Instead of state or local communities being able to respond to local problems in a manner that might best suit the region, the communities are forced to respond in whatever manner the Supreme Court has determined to be appropriate.

Scalia contends that since judicial decision-making should be limited to interpreting the constitutional text as it is and not as the text should be, changes in the way society is governed should be left to the people themselves through the democratic process. A democracy is to be ruled by the people. If we allow ourselves to be governed by a small group of elites who believe the Constitution is living, then our system of government would be an oligarchy and our foundational principles would become unstable. As young schoolchildren are taught, the functions of the different branches are distinct; the legislature creates the laws and the judicial branch interprets the laws. Making laws subject to the people, rather than to five members of the Supreme Court, perpetuates our system of government.

As stated earlier, Scalia argues in "Common-Law Courts" that interpretation is a neglected science. As such, legal decisions regarding constitutional questions should be objective, predictable, and replicable. For Scalia, a legitimate Court decision is one that relies upon the text of the Constitution and the historical practices of the people. The judge is removed from the interpretation process; the text commands its own meaning, reasonably constructed in light of original meaning and judicial practices. The law exists *a priori* to any legal question; all a judge need do is determine the correct legal canon to apply to the case in question. Thus, the public needs to appoint judges who exhibit "impartiality, judgment, and lawyerly acumen."[49]

From Scalia's "Common-Law Courts in a Civil-Law System" essay, we understand that the political and the legal command separate spheres. The legal is established by the Constitution, statutory, and common law. The political is a question of values to which the law does not provide a response. Judges can resolve legal questions; elected officials need to settle political questions. Interpreting the law requires legal training to decide outcomes, whereas public policy is facilitated by elections and debates. According to Scalia, judges need to understand the original meaning of the Constitution when deciding cases. Legislators are under no such obligation; they can create whatever statutory laws they are inclined to adopt. Scalia advocates originalist forms of interpretation, although he never offers a prescription for how to apply textualism. Auditors can infer from Scalia's essay that the text should be the starting point. Specifically, judges should try to understand how the text was understood originally as they "reasonably" interpret the text according to legal canons and presumptions.

Reading Law

In *Reading Law: The Interpretation of Legal Texts*, Scalia and Bryan Garner, a law professor at Southern Methodist University, expound upon the ideas Scalia presents in his speeches and his "Common-Law Courts" essay. In a series of short essays collated into a 567-page tome, Scalia and Garner contend that judges should follow a series of suggested canons to interpret the law, as a means to avoid subjective interpretation.

In *Reading Law*, Scalia and Garner conflate Bobbitt's textual interpretation with historical interpretation, specifically, original meaning—so much so that constitutional scholar Judge Richard Posner refers to the form of interpretation they advance as "textual originalism."[50] Scalia contends, "In their full context, words mean what they conveyed to reasonable people at the time they were written—with the understanding that general terms may embrace later technological innovations."[51] The authors present original meaning as textualism—the title for the section is "Textualism and Its Challengers." Two sentences later they define textualism as "the exclusive reliance on text when interpreting text."[52] They insist that the text per se and its meaning for an attentive public are two distinct things within the realm of judicial interpretation, however. Agency in textualism resides in the text, whereas agency in original meaning is located within the reasoning public. In neither is agency located within the authoring justice.

The authors refer to textualism, defined two ways, as "commonsensical."[53] Commonsense appeals do not rely upon the persuasive appeal of a person, a cause, or an event—they stand outside of secular or public time, calling forth the sacred time of the founding.[54] By referring to judicial interpretation in such a fashion, Scalia and Garner imply that any thinking person who uses sound reasoning can interpret the Constitution and decide cases, irrespective of legal training. Agency is located outside the person of the judge; legal training is not a necessity for interpretation, but such training protects the process of saying what the law is. Such an antielitist form of decision-making is reminiscent of Hariman's "republican style,"[55] which Hogan and Williams describe as a "celebration of the spoken word, collective deliberation, and the articulation of consensus."[56] When judges adjudicate the law, they should celebrate the Constitution, which founded our government and represents the collective consensus of our founding principles, by following it.

Repeating Scalia's arguments in "Common-Law Courts in a Civil-Law System," in *Reading Law* the authors deny that textualism advances a particular ideological perspective:

> Textualism, in its purest form, begins and ends with what the text says and fairly implies. Its principal tenets have guided the interpretation of legal texts for centuries. To enable the reader to evaluate pure textualism with an open mind, we must lay to rest at the outset the slander that it is a device calculated to produce socially or politically conservative outcomes. Textualism is not well designed to achieve ideological ends, relying as it does on the most objective criterion available: the accepted contextual meaning that the words had when the law was enacted. A textualist reading will sometimes produce "conservative" outcomes, sometimes "liberal" ones. If any interpretive method deserves to be labeled an ideological "device," it is not textualism but competing methodologies such as purposivism and consequentialism, by which the words and implications of text are replaced with abstractly conceived "purposes" or interpreter-desired "consequences." Willful judges might use textualism to achieve the ends they desire, and when the various indications of textual meaning point in different directions, even dutiful judges may unconsciously give undue weight to the factors that lead to what they consider the best result. But in a textualist culture, the distortion of the willful judge is much more transparent, and the dutiful judge is never *invited* to pursue the purposes and consequences that he prefers.[57]

The above section lays out the clearest and most succinct explanation of Scalia's theory of textualism. Their first sentence supports a plain meaning of textualism. Meaning is derived from the words scripted on a page, gleaned from within particular textual boundaries or gestures of intent from those words (what the words could be taken to reasonably imply). Since the meaning of the text should be clear to a wide audience, interpretive abuse would be apparent. Thus, textualism guides constitutional meaning as well as acts as a watchdog against judicial activism. Or, in other words, textualism informs the process of interpretation while protecting the substance of constitutional meaning. The rest of the paragraph clarifies what textualism does not do and how reliance upon textualism brings into sharp relief non-textual forms of interpretation.

Setting aside the definitional confusion and ideological concerns the book presents, Scalia and Garner attempt to provide their readers with a set of authoritative guidelines for judicial interpretation. They begin with "fundamental principles," which include (1) all texts require interpretation, (2) the words of the text should guide the interpretation, (3) no one canon is absolute, (4) readings should advance the purpose of the text, and (5) readings that support the text are given more weight than those that invalidate the text. The authors then develop eleven semantic canons, seven syntactic canons, fourteen contextual canons, seven expected-meaning canons, three government-structuring canons, four private-rights canons, and six stabilizing canons. The first three types of canon apply to all legal language. The semantic canons insist upon a permissible range of meaning for words or phrases. The syntactic canons examine the context of a word or a phrase, using its grammatical surroundings to indicate meaning. The contextual canon considers the text within its larger structure or within its larger situational context. The last four canons apply to governmental laws (the authors cite statutes, ordinances, and regulations as examples). Although the authors acknowledge that the categories are somewhat arbitrary, they nevertheless group the canons by content, as the name of each suggests. The final substantive section of the book refutes thirteen fallacies of constitutional interpretation, such as the idea that the spirit of the law matters more than the letter of the law. The authors conclude that if the canons of the book were followed, "then over time the law will be more certain, and the rule of law will be more secure."[58] The process of judicial interpretation is important, Scalia and Garner emphasize; judges must adhere to textualism as a method to ensure the replicability of their findings.

Conclusion

In both his speeches and his extrajudicial writings, Scalia rejects the notion that the Constitution can respond to all social needs. He also refuses to accept a living Constitution. Quite the opposite, Scalia contends that the intent of the Constitution was to incorporate rigidity into the United States' governmental system, hence the United States' *written* Constitution. Scalia claims that the words of the constitutional text, not society's shifting needs, should be given primacy. Scalia affirms this message in his speeches and essays, maintaining that the Constitution has limited meaning and that legislatures should respond to the shifting needs of the people.

From his 1989 Sibley Lecture to his 2005 Woodrow Wilson remarks, Scalia begins each of his published speeches on the subject of constitutional interpretation by criticizing living Constitution theories of law. He characterizes the living Constitution theory as "an empty bottle which we feel free to fill up with whatever liquid seems to us passionately desirable."[59] Yet the Constitution cannot be empty, Scalia counters. The Constitution created the United States' system of governance and protects citizens' rights and liberties. The founding document has remained in effect for over two hundred years because its unalterable substance has stood the test of time.

Rather than a living Constitution, Scalia advances what he calls a "dead" or "enduring" Constitution. Maintaining that the Constitution should be interpreted as a statute is interpreted, Scalia claims that the Constitution's meaning was fixed at the time of the founding. Therefore, constitutional interpretation is, for Scalia, an easy exercise. When deciding a case, he would ask questions such as "What does the Constitution have to say about this matter?" and "Was this permitted or proscribed at the time of the founding?" Although the latter question does not support textualism (as it is an originalist question), Scalia uses it because it gives him an idea of what people at the time of the founding understood the text to mean. Thus, Scalia contends that he does not interpret the law per se but creates guidelines for how to understand the original meaning that guides his decision-making.

From his speeches and extrajudicial writings, Scalia's concept of judicial deference can be reduced to his belief that the Supreme Court can consider some issues and not others. The issues the court can consider are those mentioned expressly in the text of the Constitution. Those issues that are not mentioned should be left to legislative deliberation.

In his public address Scalia distinguishes between personal belief and judicial action. For example, in his "God's Justice and Ours" speech, Scalia offers capital cases as an area of law in which his personal views differ from his adjudication of the law. Although he never states his personal views—doing so could lead to him having to recuse himself from capital cases—since Scalia is a devout Catholic, we can assume his Catholicism means that Scalia-the-person disagrees with the death penalty. Scalia-as-justice, however, recognizes that the Eighth Amendment upholds the constitutionality of the death penalty. Based on this speech and others, we can infer that, for Scalia, there is a difference between a lawyer's work and a politician's work. A lawyer's work consists of interpreting statutes, while a politician's work consists of responding to the will of the people and trying to enact that will in legislation.

A division exists between "the political" and "the judicial" for Scalia. Although one might think the realm of "the judicial" falls within the larger realm of "the political," from Scalia's remarks we understand each realm to have distinct characteristics that make them mutually exclusive. Such boundaries should not be collapsed into the different branches of government, since both the executive and the legislative branches would be concerned with "the political." "The judicial," however, would be a smaller sphere that considers questions of fact and questions of law, not questions of public policy.

To distinguish between a judge's jurisdiction and a politician's jurisdiction, Scalia looks to the expressed laws of the Constitution. In his Pew Forum speech, he states, "For me, therefore, the constitutionality of the death penalty is not a difficult, soul-wrenching question. It was clearly permitted when the Eighth Amendment was adopted. . . . And so it is clearly permitted today."[60] Original meaning, in other words, and not personal predilection, determines judicial decision-making. The application of the law does not cause him any psychological anxiety, for the law is not an emotional venture. The law is not subjective; it is objective. Law is not an art; it is a science. Constitutional meaning does not evolve; constitutional meaning remains fixed.

Scalia contends that since judicial decision-making should be limited to interpreting the constitutional text as *it is* and not as the text *should be*, changes in the way society is governed should be left to the people themselves through the democratic process. A democracy is to be ruled by the people. If we allow ourselves to be governed by a small group of elites, such as the Supreme Court, our system of government would be ruled by an oligarchy. As schoolchildren are taught, the functions of the different branches are distinct; the legislature creates the laws and the judicial branch interprets the laws. Making laws subject to the people rather than to five members of the Supreme Court perpetuates our system of government.

In addition to observing how Scalia advocates textualism, we have gained in this chapter a clearer understanding of the form of Scalia's textualism. According to his three essays, for Scalia, (1) the text of the Constitution should be the starting point for interpretation, (2) interpretation should be "reasonable," and (3) "reasonable" should be understood in terms of the historical meaning of constitutional principles as well as modern legal principles and practices. Scalia makes no provisions for interpretation when the Constitution does not address a matter. In those cases, judges should leave the matter to popularly elected representatives.

At first glance, Scalia's assertion that texts should be construed "reasonably" would lead one to conclude that any person off the street could interpret the Constitution and that every citizen could access the meaning of the constitutional language because linguistic meaning can be found in contemporary usage of that language. Yet Scalia denies this possibility, emphasizing the importance of legal process, generally understood only by persons with legal training, in responding to legal questions. Moreover, to perform Scalia's textualism one must be a historian, mining the meaning of language at a time when the document's meaning may be uncertain, unknown, or conflicted.

The difference between common law and constitutional law, which Scalia emphasizes in "Common-Law Courts," would seem to give people voice in interpreting the Constitution. Common law is judge-made and constitutional law was adopted when the people ratified the Constitution. In principle, all Americans ratified the Constitution and continue to possess the right to interpret it. Therefore, for Scalia, the Constitution should be construed in as clear, open, and "democratic" (nonlawyerly) a way as possible. This interpretation will be easy in some cases and difficult in others, so the text must be supplanted by structural and doctrinal arguments.

As stated earlier, Scalia argues in "Common-Law Courts" that interpretation is a neglected science. As such, legal decisions regarding constitutional questions should be objective, predictable, and replicable. Scalia contends that the process of textual interpretation can further these aims better than any other form of constitutional interpretation, yet he never offers a clear picture of how to apply textualism. The three points above—that the text should be the starting point, that judges should "reasonably" interpret the text, and that "reasonably" should be understood in light of original meaning and judicial practices—are inferred from Scalia's writings. He never once clearly proffered them as a prescription for how to engage in textual interpretation.

Since Scalia's speeches and extrajudicial writings do not address how one would go about engaging in textualist readings of the Constitution, we must conclude that his purpose is not to instruct one in how it should be done, but simply to convince his audience that constitutional interpretation is an important issue. His entire corpus of extrajudicial work is concerned with advocating textualism and with refuting other forms of interpretation. This follows logical reasoning. If someone does not think the matter important or does not agree with your assertion, then you should not waste time telling them how to do something but rather focus on establishing the importance of doing it at all.

Some of the nation's leading legal scholars reject Scalia's assertions about his form of interpretation and doubt that his version of textualism could be actualized in practice. In their written commentaries of Scalia's "Common-Law Courts" essay, Gordon S. Wood, Laurence H. Tribe, Ronald Dworkin, and Mary Ann Glendon offer responses as varied as the scholars themselves. Professor Wood challenges the historical foundation upon which Scalia builds his form of textualism. Professors Tribe and Dworkin both agree that Scalia actually interprets the Constitution in an expansive fashion (and that the Constitution does not require a strict, narrow reading). Professor Glendon agrees with Scalia that a systematic form of interpretation is important but chooses to place the agency for reform in the law schools. Although their reasons differ—Wood finds the problems existed since our founding, Tribe supports expansive readings of the text, and Dworkin denies an original meaning ever existed for certain clauses—these three scholars agree that Scalia's interpretation is unworkable, although they rest their conclusions on different premises. Professor Glendon, on the other hand, agrees with Scalia's assertion that judicial decision-making has become subject to the popular will rather than to the constitutional text, which for her is problematic.

My analysis of Scalia's adjudication supports professors Wood, Tribe, and Dworkin's conclusion that Scalia's form of textualism does not abide by the aspirational purposes of textualism that he sets forth in his speeches and extrajudicial writings. I therefore turn next to a consideration of three areas of law—one in which the Constitution is explicit, one in which the Constitution is conflicted, and one in which the Constitution is silent—to see how Scalia uses textualism and how he advocates textualism in actual decisions. As we shall see, Scalia does little in his application of the method of textualism to clarify exactly how it is to be done. Rather, Scalia uses the textualism he speaks or writes about when it furthers the results he seeks; he alters reasonable textual constructions or uses other forms of interpretation when it does not.

3

Interpreting a Clear Clause

The Eighth Amendment's Cruel and Unusual Punishments Clause

> We must disregard the new reality that, to the extent our Eighth Amendment decisions constitute something more than a show of hands on the current Justices' current personal views about penology, they purport to be nothing more than a snapshot of American public opinion at a particular time.
>
> —Justice Antonin Scalia

The Eighth Amendment declares, "Excessive bail shall not be required, nor excessive fines imposed, nor cruel and unusual punishments inflicted." Eighth Amendment jurisprudence has a long and storied history. In more years than not, the court accepts cases challenging laws and practices as a violation of the Cruel and Unusual Punishments Clause. The court has struggled with the question of what constitutes cruel and unusual punishment and derived different doctrines to guide their thinking. In his survey of the clause's history, legal scholar Anthony F. Granucci concludes that the framers misunderstood the intent of the English drafters. The language of the Eighth Amendment can be traced back to the English Bill of Rights of 1689, written in protest of the sentencing practices of judges during the reign of King James II.[1] George Mason included the phrase "cruel and unusual punishments" in his 1776 Virginia Declaration of Rights.[2] The clause subsequently was adopted by eight other states and included in the 1787 Northwest Ordinance. James Madison introduced the clause as part of the Bill of Rights, and in 1871 the clause was adopted as the Eighth Amendment. The language of the Eighth Amendment follows the English Bill of Rights almost verbatim. Only one difference exists: "ought" was replaced by "shall."[3] The founders interpreted the clause to mean that particular methods of punishment were illegal. According to Granucci, "It is indeed a paradox that the American colonists omitted a prohibition on excessive punishments and adopted instead the prohibition on cruel methods of punishment, which had never existed in English law."[4] It was not until the twentieth century that the court resolved that the punishment should be proportional to the crime committed and that society has evolving stands of decency to regulate what amounts to an acceptable form of punishment.

The Supreme Court has a wide array of cases that take up issues presented by the Eighth Amendment. From the time the Constitution was adopted until the mid-twentieth century, the amendment applied to the federal government alone. In *Louisiana ex rel. Francis v. Resweber* (1947) the court held that it was not cruel and unusual punishment to impose capital punishment (via electrocution) on a convict after a failed first attempt.[5] Cruelty, the court explained, refers to the *method* of punishment—not any suffering that might be involved in ending life. In 1958 the court declared that evolving standards of decency must influence the meaning of the Cruel and Unusual Punishments Clause. When questioning the application of the death penalty, the Supreme Court has considered whether the punishment fits the crime, the competency of the accused, and discriminatory effects of sentencing. The court extended the clause to the states in 1962 in *Robinson v. California* (1962),[6] dramatically increasing the number of capital offense cases considered by the court. Over the years the court has upheld certain forms of punishment, banned others, and protected two classes of people from execution.

For more than a century the Supreme Court has agreed that the clause forbids "inhuman and barbarous" forms of punishment. In *In re Kemmler* (1890), Chief Justice Fuller declared, "Punishments are cruel when they involve torture or a lingering death," for the Cruel and Unusual Punishments Clause "implies there something inhuman and barbarous,—something more than the mere extinguishment of life."[7] The court has held that particular sentences and individuals are beyond the boundaries of constitutional penalties. For example, death by firing squad (*Wilkerson v. Utah* [1878]), death by electrocution (*In re Kemmler* [1890]), life imprisonment with the possibility of parole (*Rummel v. Estelle* [1980], *Harmelin* [1991]), and fifty years to life with the possibility of parole under California's three-strikes policy have all been held to be unconstitutional.[8] The court has determined that individuals cannot be tortured (*Weems* [1910]), have their citizenship revoked for wartime desertion (*Trop v. Dulles* [1958]), be jailed for being addicted to a narcotic absent an act of illegal drug use (*Robinson v. California* [1962]), be put to death for raping an adult woman (*Coker v. Georgia* [1977]), be sentenced to death for aiding and abetting a capital crime (*Enmund v. Florida* [1982]), be given life without parole for a nonviolent felony (*Solem v. Helm* [1983]), or be put to death for raping a child (*Kennedy v. Louisiana* [2008]).[9] The court also placed mentally handicapped persons outside the purview of capital punishment in *Atkins* (2002) and extended that prohibition to minors in *Roper* (2005).

The High Court has wavered with regard to what it deems cruel and unusual punishment. In *Furman v. Georgia* (1972) the court found that three sentences for capital punishment—one for murder and two for rape—constituted cruel and unusual punishment, but the per curiam opinion did not give an explanation as to the reasoning.[10] Rather, the justices offered five concurring opinions and four dissents, expressing concern about the application of capital sentences and characterizing them as arbitrary and discriminatory. *Furman* (1972) inaugurated a moratorium on capital punishment as thirty-seven states revised their laws to address the concerns of the *Furman* (1972) opinions. Four years later the court affirmed revised sentencing statutes in four states on the same day: *Gregg v. Georgia* (1976), *Proffitt v. Florida* (1976), *Jurek v. Texas* (1976), and *Woodson v. North Carolina* (1976).[11] In the Georgia, Florida, and Texas cases, the state statutes were upheld because their sentencing procedures were determined to be clear and consistent, as well as considerate of any "mediating factors." In the North Carolina case, the Supreme Court reversed and remanded the decision to the lower courts and declared that states could not impose automatic, mandatory death sentences for certain crimes. Cases following *Gregg* (1976) required courts to consider any mediating factors when sentencing—factors that work for or against a person—including attempting to escape apprehension (*Lockett v. Ohio* [1978]), kidnapping (*Bell v. Ohio* [1978]), an abusive family history (*Eddings v. Oklahoma* [1982]), and aiding and abetting (*Enmund v. Florida* [1982]).[12] Finally, the court determined that states do not have to cite a comparative proportionality review (i.e., previous similar cases) in every capital punishment case in order to impose a death sentence.

The Supreme Court first introduced the idea of proportional punishment in *Weems* (1910). Citing lower court cases from Massachusetts, Georgia, and Minnesota, the court indicated that certain punishments might be disproportionate to the crime committed.[13] More than half a century later, the court began to apply the doctrine of proportionality in a variety of contexts. In *Coker* (1977), the court held that a death sentence for rape is a "grossly disproportionate" punishment for the crime.[14] In *Hutto v. Finney* (1978), the court found that prison conditions could violate basic notions of "dignity, civilized standards, humanity, and decency."[15] In *Enmund* (1982), the court determined that a capital sentence could not be given for a noncapital crime. In *Solem* (1983), the court held that the Cruel and Unusual Punishments Clause "proscribes grossly disproportionate punishments"—in Helm's case, life in prison without parole for a petty crime.[16] The court declared, "We hold as a matter of principle that a criminal sentence must be proportionate to the crime for which the defendant has been convicted."[17] The court rejected the idea that the standard of proportionality was violated in *McCleskey v. Kemp* (1987) when the court refused to consider racial bias in capital punishment sentencing and executions.[18] Rather than offer sweeping proof of racial discrimination in capital trials, the petitioner would have to prove that his punishment was disproportionate to the punishment in other, similar murder cases. More recent court cases have held that proportionality decisions, to the greatest extent possible, should be informed by objective factors—specifically, legislation from the states—and the determination of justices of the court.[19]

In the mid-twentieth century the Supreme Court introduced a doctrine of evolving standards of decency. In *Trop* (1958), Chief Justice Earl Warren concluded that the Cruel and Unusual Punishments Clause "must draw its meaning from the evolving standards of decency that mark the progress of a maturing society."[20] The standard was not mentioned again for almost two decades, until *Gregg* (1976), when Justice Stewart synthesized earlier capital cases, concluding that an evolving standard of decency was a possible lens through which to evaluate the constitutionality of punishments. The court has issued a blanket ruling against state law following evolving standards of decency regarding the matter of who is executed, proscribing the execution of minors in *Thompson* (1988) and the mentally handicapped in *Atkins* (2002). In *Thompson* (1988), the court overturned the execution of a fifteen-year-old offender, citing a national consensus against executing minors under the age of sixteen.[21] The pathway to ending the execution of minors was not direct, however. The next year, in *Stanford v. Kentucky* (1989), the court determined that no national consensus existed against the execution of minors.[22] The court then reversed its *Stanford* (1989) decision in *Roper v. Simmons* (2005), characterizing the decrease in the number of states who execute minors as "significant"[23] and pointing to the consistency in the direction of change. In *Atkins* (2002), the court found the execution of mentally handicapped individuals to be "excessive"[24] and, citing the small number of states that have passed legislation outlawing their execution, opined that the actual number of states that banned the execution of the mentally handicapped was not important. Rather, "the consistency of the direction of change" mattered.[25]

Although death penalty advocates argue capital punishment should be abolished because all other Western societies' evolving standards of decency have led them to proscribe execution, the Supreme Court consistently has maintained capital sentences are constitutional.[26] Various justices have challenged the method of execution according to evolving standards of decency, but those who have done so have all been in the minority.[27] The court also has held that sentencing in capital punishment cases should be clear and consistent, that courts should consider any mediating circumstances particular to the case and the petitioner at hand, and that the punishment should be proportional to the crime.

Scalia on the Eighth Amendment

I begin my analysis of Scalia's jurisprudence by considering how the conservative justice interprets what could be considered a clear constitutional clause: the Eighth Amendment's Cruel and Unusual Punishments Clause. The Eighth Amendment declares, "Excessive bail shall not be required, nor excessive fines imposed, nor cruel and unusual punishments inflicted." In this chapter I focus on the last phrase of the amendment. I consider this a *clear* clause because the prohibition is stated directly and does not conflict with another clause. The clause presents an opportunity for a justice to engage the text directly, considering what the plain meaning of the text is.

My analysis of the Eighth Amendment focuses on Justice Scalia's use of the Cruel and Unusual Punishments Clause in all of Scalia's opinions that mention the Eighth Amendment. I do not include cases that consider a tangential issue (e.g., conviction and sentencing) but do not mention the amendment. Twenty-six opinions fulfilled my parameters: three majority opinions, eleven concurring opinions, ten dissenting opinions, and two opinions in which Scalia concurred in part and dissented in part.[28] Not all of Scalia's opinions are equally important. Some briefly state his disagreement with the majority opinion and one upholds a stay of execution for a person who committed a crime while a minor. Overwhelmingly Scalia's opinions reject that a violation of the Eighth Amendment has occurred.

Scalia's capital punishment narratives always support the constitutionality of capital punishment—including the execution of minors and the mentally handicapped—allowing for variances in public control. Scalia grounds his Cruel and Unusual Punishments Clause opinions in the same reasoning: the text of the Constitution does not prohibit the execution of certain individuals, a certain punishment was practiced at the time the Bill of Rights was adopted, the person committing the crime has moral culpability, and states should have the flexibility to administer the death penalty. In these opinions the narrative he tells focuses on the cruelty of the crime committed and ignores questions about the punishment for the crime. Scalia's approach to understanding unusual punishment is inconsistent; he offers multiple definitions that rely on both contemporary meanings of "unusual" and historical perspectives. He uses statistical evidence to deny a national trend against capital punishment. For Scalia, if a punishment exists in more than one state, it cannot be unusual.

The Text's Original Meaning

Regardless of Scalia's claim that his form of interpretation is "unusually clear and unequivocal,"[29] the original meaning of the Eighth Amendment text does not easily reveal itself. Should the original meaning of the amendment be set at the time of its adoption in the Bill of Rights or through its incorporation to the states through the court's interpretation of the Fourteenth Amendment? In his opinions Scalia refers to Blackstone's *Commentaries* (a frequent source of his), locating the meaning of the document in that derived from the British system upon which the US system is based. Regarding the execution of minors, Scalia offers the example that someone could be sentenced to capital punishment at age seven in 1769 (predating both the adoption and the incorporation of the Bill of Rights). Scalia turns again to Blackstone's *Commentaries* in the mental health cases to elucidate that "idiot" commonly referred to persons without any ability to distinguish between right and wrong. He reasons that since both minors and the mentally handicapped were executed at the time of the founding, they can be executed now. In these examples Scalia does not cite an American historical document to support his position; he relies upon a scholar of English law. One is left to wonder why someone who advocates a strict interpretation of the Constitution would use another country's legal history to justify his legal reasoning?

Scalia's analysis of "cruelty" in his capital cases is cursory at best. In *Atkins* (2002), he maintains that punishments deemed cruel have always been categorized thusly. Scalia states, "The Eighth Amendment is addressed to always-and-everywhere 'cruel' punishments, such as the rack and the thumbscrew."[30] For Scalia, new forms of punishment (e.g., gas chamber, electrocution, lethal injection) are not cruel; forms of torture in existence at the time of the founding (e.g., drawing and quartering, burning alive, disembowelment) are cruel. Scalia rejects the assertion that an excessive punishment is a cruel punishment. In *Harmelin* (1991), Scalia recognizes that some degree of proportionality is necessary in sentencing, but only to the extent that each sentence is determined according to its own merits. Scalia states, "We have held that a capital sentence is cruel and unusual under the Eighth Amendment if it is imposed without an individualized determination that that punishment is 'appropriate'—whether or not the sentence is 'grossly disproportionate.'"[31] Sentences should be appropriate—and appropriateness is not determined by the level of excess.

Sçalia's measure for "unusual" is how many states *allow* the executions, not how many *implement* the sentences. For Scalia, the execution of minors and the mentally handicapped could be unconstitutional if only one state allowed either.[32] The infrequency of the punishment does not detract from its constitutionality. According to Scalia, "It appears that actual executions for crimes committed under age 18 accounted for only two percent of the total number of executions that occurred between 1642 and 1986."[33] Although states may have used the capital offense to execute minors infrequently, such executions nevertheless occurred. Consequently, states should be allowed to maintain the option to use it if they want to do so.

Constructing the Meaning of Cruel and Unusual Punishments

Scalia presents his most textual argument in *Stanford* (1989), one of his first cruel and unusual punishment cases. A textualist reading of the clause would require a justice to consider whether a punishment is both cruel and unusual since the coordinating conjunction "and" links the two adjectives "cruel" and "unusual." In *Stanford* (1989), Scalia explains, "The punishment is either 'cruel *and* unusual' (i.e. society has set its face against it) or it is not" (emphasis in original).[34] He claims that his interpretive approach "is dictated . . . by the language of the Amendment—which proscribes only those punishments that are both 'cruel and *unusual*'" (emphasis in original).[35] I will disregard for the moment Scalia's emphasis on unusual (a stress I take up shortly) to focus first upon his previous stress on the conjunction "and." In these cases Scalia underlines the fact that a punishment must be both. Since a punishment cannot be cruel *or* unusual, one must ask, If the punishment is cruel, is it also unusual? Or if it is unusual, is it also cruel? To respond to these questions, a justice would also need to understand what constitutes cruel punishment as well as unusual punishment, since those adjectives explicate the boundaries of appropriate punishment. Importantly, the two adjectives are linked, so both elements must fail to meet the standard set forth for a punishment to be unconstitutional.

Scalia's Eighth Amendment opinions turn on his understanding of unusual. The cruelty of the punishment does not really matter for Scalia, because the punishment being cruel does not matter if the punishment is not unusual. In his *Penry* (1989) opinion, Scalia characterizes "unusual" as "if any objective examination of laws and jury determinations fails to demonstrate society's disapproval of it."[36] Scalia's use of a double negative in the preceding quote can be confusing, but his message is that the burden of proof rests with the challenger, who must prove the punishment is unusual; the presumption is that the punishment is unnoteworthy. Scalia repeats the sentiment that "unusual" is the determining adjective in his *Walton* (1990) concurring opinion: "When punishments other than fines are involved, the Amendment explicitly requires a court to consider not only whether the penalty is severe or harsh, but also whether it is 'unusual.' If it is not, then the Eighth Amendment does not prohibit it, no matter how cruel a judge might think it to be."[37] He repeats his emphasis of unusual in *Harmelin* (1991): "Severe, mandatory penalties may be cruel, but they are not unusual in the constitutional sense, having been employed in various forms throughout our Nation's history." Scalia expounds: "The drafters of the Declaration of Rights did not explicitly prohibit 'disproportionate' or 'excessive' punishment. Instead, they prohibited punishments that were 'cruell and unusuall.' The *Solem* Court simply assumed, with no analysis, that the one included the other. . . . As a textual matter, of course, it does not: a disproportionate punishment can perhaps always be considered 'cruel,' but it will not always be (as the text also requires) 'unusual.'"[38] Cruelty, for Scalia, is not a quality upon which a punishment may be deemed unconstitutional. Consequently, regardless of how often Scalia mentions the terms in conjunction with one another, the dominance of "unusual" over "cruel" in Scalia's constitutional determination separates the two terms. "Unusual" is given primacy within the clause as the determiner of constitutionality. His opinion in *Harmelin* (1991) also emphasizes that proportionality—the idea that the punishment should fit the crime—does not need to be taken into consideration. Certain punishments, proportionality tells us, are too severe for the crimes that elicit them. According to Scalia, the Constitution does not demand that proportional considerations be taken into account.

Unlike the meaning of "cruel," Scalia attempts to define the meaning of "unusual," although he offers three different meanings in three different cases. "Unusual," according to the *Oxford English Dictionary*, means "Not usual; uncommon; exceptional." Scalia uses the plain meaning as elucidated in the *OED* in several of his cases. In his survey of capital punishment for minors and the mentally handicapped, Scalia quantifies "unusual" as one state alone having laws allowing a particular punishment that no other states have. Scalia maintains that the rarity of implementation can speak to the *offense/offender* more than the *punishment*. For example, in *Thompson* (1988) he contends, "The statistics of executions demonstrate nothing except the fact that our society has always agreed that executions of 15-year-old criminals should be rare, and in more modern times has agreed that they (like all other executions) should be even rarer still."[39] According to Scalia, the United States does not want to be a society that frequently executes its minors. Such executions should be rare events but not proscribed entirely. In *Walton* (1990), Scalia offers a second meaning, shifting the definition of "unusual" from "rare" to "nontraditional": "The text did not originally prohibit a traditional form of punishment that is rarely imposed, as opposed to a form of punishment that is not traditional."[40] Rare is infrequent; nontraditional is new. Scalia offers a third definition of unusual in *Harmelin* (1991). In this case he cites the history of the word as meaning "illegal," rather than rare or new. Relying upon the British common law for evidentiary support, Scalia proclaims that "the phrase 'cruell and unusuall,'" in the common law tradition, "is treated as interchangeable with 'cruel and illegal.'"[41] At that time, "'illegall' and 'unusuall' were identical for practical purposes."[42] Consequently, for Scalia the plain meaning of the term "unusual" is muddled—the word could mean "rare" or "infrequent," "new" or "unconventional," or "illegal." With each evolution, the word moves farther away from its plain meaning ("rare"), until it adopts a usage that might have been consistent with colonial times but is unfamiliar to contemporary auditors.

In *Harmelin* (1991), Scalia offers his most in-depth consideration of what constitutes "unusual," which he argues does not pertain to judges but to legislatures. His understanding of British common law leads him to conclude that "the provision must have been meant as a check not upon judges but upon the Legislature."[43] He explains:

> Wrenched out of its common-law context, and applied to the actions of a legislature, the word "unusual" could hardly mean "contrary to law." But it continued to mean (as it continues to mean today) "such as [does not] occur in ordinary practice." . . . According to its terms, then, by forbidding "cruel and unusual punishments," . . . the Clause disables the Legislature from authorizing particular forms or "modes" of punishment—specifically, cruel methods of punishment that are not regularly or customarily employed. . . . The language bears the construction, however—and here we come to the point crucial to resolution of the present case—that "cruelty and unusualness" are to be determined not solely with reference to the punishment at issue ("is life imprisonment a cruel and unusual punishment?") but with reference to the crime for which it is imposed as well ("Is life imprisonment cruel and unusual punishment for possession of unlawful drugs?").[44]

In other words, the legislature should not pass laws legalizing forms of punishment that have not been used historically. If they do, they authorize illegal forms of punishments (although the legislature, by nature of its function as the creator of laws, cannot create illegal laws). Moreover, this interpretation lends itself to two meanings: punishment on its own merits and punishment in conjunction with the crime committed. Following this segment, Scalia reminds his auditor that the Cruel and Unusual Punishments Clause does not regulate *proportionality* but particular *forms* of punishments. To be certain, Scalia's reasoning in *Harmelin* (1991) is convoluted, extending far beyond the boundaries of the plain meaning of the text and justifying his examination of the crime committed. To wit, in *Harmelin* (1991) we do not have a plain meaning of the law; cruel punishments are allowed and we must look to legal history to tell us how to understand what constitutes "unusual."

In *Stanford* (1989), cited also in *Penry* (1989), Scalia rejects an additional means by which to understand the meaning of the Cruel and Unusual Punishments Clause: evolving standards of decency. In *Stanford* Scalia maintains: "The punishment is either 'cruel *and* unusual' (*i.e.*, society has set its face against it) or it is not. The audience for these arguments, in other words, is not this Court, but the citizenry of the United States. It is they, not we, who must be persuaded. For, as we stated earlier, our job is to *identify* the 'evolving standards of decency'; to determine, not what they *should* be, but what they *are*" (emphasis in original).[45] In his discussion of evolving standards of decency, Scalia uses the abbreviation *i.e.* for the Latin phrase *id est*, which translates to "that is" and which we frequently understand to mean "in other words" in English. Importantly, although Scalia presents the phrase as analogous with the constitutional protection against cruel and unusual punishments, nowhere in the Constitution is the phrase "society has set its face against it." The phrase is a biblical reference and is typically used in Jewish law to signify God's punishment for his people's sin. Leviticus 17 states, "I will set My face against that person who eats blood and will cut him off from among his people," and chapter 26 proclaims, "I will set My face against you so that you will be struck down before your enemies; and those who hate you will rule over you, and you will flee when no one is pursuing you."[46] Ezekiel 15 makes a similar claim: "and I set My face against them. Though they have come out of the fire, yet the fire will consume them. Then you will know that I am the Lord, when I set My face against them."[47] To "set my face" signifies one's resolve. Such a resolve was present in the Hebrew Bible as well as in the New Testament when the person of Jesus Christ travels to Jerusalem to be crucified. Luke 9 reports, "When the days drew near for him to be taken up, he set his face to go to Jerusalem."[48] These examples indicate two possible constructions: a positive toward (e.g., Jesus committed to suffering the cross) and a negative against (e.g., God determined to enact a form of punishment). Scalia's use of the phrase "set its face," rich in its grounding in the biblical text, lends righteous indignation to his view of sentences, including the death penalty. Scalia imparts a religious framing not included in the Cruel and Unusual Punishments Clause.

Importantly, as the biblical examples demonstrate, a singular entity can set its face. For Scalia, that entity is society as a whole. Yet as he explains in his capital cases, if one state allows for capital punishment, then that punishment is not unusual. Society will not set its face against the execution of the accused until all states proscribe such punishment. So no evolving standards of decency exist by which to proscribe capital punishment.

Moreover, incidental suffering as part of a sentence does not constitute cruel and unusual punishment. If a prisoner experiences what one might consider such punishment, the occurrence would have to have been inflicted upon the prisoner intentionally to be unconstitutional. Scalia explains that "some mental element must be attributed to the inflicting officer before it can qualify."[49] Thus, the inmate would need to show that the guard *intended* to harm the prisoner. Cruel and unusual punishment thus becomes an active penalty rather than a passive consequence. In addition to being intentional, the violation also must be "wanton"—a requirement mitigated by the conditions in the prison at the time of the incident.[50]

Scalia offers a reading of the Cruel and Unusual Punishments Clause that is different from what the plain meaning of the text supports. For a punishment to be unconstitutional, it must violate both qualifiers. Yet for Scalia, a cruel and unusual crime has a specific meaning, fixed at the time of the founding. Moreover, "cruel" does not equate to a punishment that is not proportionate to the crime. Rather, Scalia focuses cruelty on the crime committed by the accused rather than on the punishment to which the accused is sentenced.

Agency as Determiner of Cruelty

In his Eighth Amendment capital cases Scalia frequently focuses his concern about cruelty on the agent of the person convicted of committing the crime rather than on the cruelty of the punishment. By doing so, Scalia constructs the accused as a monstrous, violent person deserving of death. Scalia employs additional rhetorical strategies to emphasize the guilt of the accused. He details previous criminal convictions, suggesting that the impulse toward violence and lawlessness is innate within the person committing the crime. The intrinsic cruelty of the defendant spills out into criminal acts, which will continue to be repeated if the defendant is released from prison. He also offers a description of the victim, juxtaposing someone guilty with someone innocent. Within such logic, no punishment can mitigate the terrible act or rehabilitate the defendant.

Unlike many other descriptions of facts in capital punishment cases, which can be sterile and straightforward (emphasizing trial and appellate court proceedings), Scalia's description of the facts highlights the cruelty of the crime committed by framing the *convicted person as wicked* and the *victim as laudable*. The clearest example of Scalia's differentiation between the defendant and the victim is in *Atkins* (2002). Scalia's statement of facts affords a critic the opportunity both to examine how Scalia constructs the defendant differently than the majority opinion and to observe how he distinguishes the defendant from the victim. Thus, I first turn to the statement of facts from the majority opinion. In *Atkins* (2002), Justice Stevens recounts: "At approximately midnight on August 16, 1996, Atkins and William Jones, armed with a semiautomatic handgun, abducted Eric Nesbitt, robbed him of the money on his person, drove him to an automated teller machine in his pickup truck where cameras recorded their withdrawal of additional cash, then took him to an isolated location where he was shot eight times and killed."[51] Majority opinions must offer a brief restatement of facts as part of the genre. Although at first glance it may appear we have learned everything we need to know about the crime, seeing as how the who, what, when, where, and how of the case are reported, Stevens's opinion does not answer the question of why. Moreover, Stevens makes sure his statement of facts describes what happened in as brief a fashion as possible. It is difficult to imagine, in fact, how Stevens could have portrayed the crime in a more efficient manner. Scalia agrees, offering "a brief restatement of facts that are abridged by the Court but important to understanding this case."[52] The facts abridged, according to Scalia, are all of the details associated with who, what, when, where, and how. Moreover, the court's majority omits the why, which Scalia includes in his restatement. Scalia writes: "After spending the day drinking alcohol and smoking marijuana, petitioner Daryl Renard Atkins and a partner in crime drove to a convenience store, intending to rob a customer. Their victim was Eric Nesbitt, an airman from Langley Air Force Base, whom they abducted, drove to a nearby automated teller machine, and forced to withdraw $200. They then drove him to a deserted area, ignoring his pleas to leave him unharmed. According to the co-conspirator, whose testimony the jury evidently credited, Atkins ordered Nesbitt out of the vehicle and, after he had taken only a few steps, shot him one, two, three, four, five, six, seven, eight times in the thorax, chest, abdomen, arms, and legs."[53] The majority's statement of facts, housed in one difficult to read sentence, expels the facts of the case as quickly as possible. Scalia's description of facts, on the other hand, slows down the movement of the scene. Scalia's auditor can envision the crime taking place, hear the victim beg for his life, hear the gunshots, and see the bullets hit different parts of Nesbitt's body—as if they are bearing witness to a true-life Quentin Tarantino film. The auditor also has insight into the perpetrators of the crime—drunken potheads who loaf around as unproductive members of society until they decide to engage in petty and violent crime to continue their miscreant ways. Since Atkins is the focus of the case, he is named; the person with whom he committed the crime remains nameless, constructed merely as a "partner in crime." Atkins thus becomes consubstantial with crime. We also learn the "why": "intending to rob a customer." The crime did not just happen accidentally or in the heat of the moment; it was planned and executed. Moreover, we learn that the victim is not just any person but a military man. For some reason, the fact that Nesbitt is a serviceman increases the pathetic appeal of Scalia's restatement—the life of a serviceman is more valuable than that of a nonmilitary person. Nesbitt's military identity throws into sharp relief the sad fact that a life was valued so little by Atkins and his partner. To murder someone for only $200 is a tragedy; to murder a military man for only $200 is an outrage. We learn as well that Nesbitt begged for his life. He did not threaten or warn; he begged the perpetrators to take the money and not to end his life. But, again, as wicked persons, Atkins and his partner set out to rob someone and then, for whatever reason, decided to escalate their criminal activity from robbery to murder. The very act of the murder does not occur as quickly as Stevens portrays it. Nesbitt was not "shot eight times and killed" but was shot "one, two, three, four, five, six, seven, eight times in the thorax, chest, abdomen, arms, and legs." Whereas Stevens's description does not give his auditor time to envision the action, Scalia's dramatic depiction slows down the act of murder, allowing his auditors to visualize each shot, as the bullets pierce Nesbitt's flesh one at a time.

In case after case, Scalia repeats the idea that *certain types of crimes* are worthy of death. In *Thompson* (1988), Scalia characterizes the murder as "brutal"[54] and "especially heinous, atrocious, or cruel."[55] In *Walton* (1990), he contends, "the murder was committed in an 'especially heinous, cruel or depraved' manner."[56] Scalia brings up the phrase "heinous, cruel or depraved" again to describe the murder in *Lee* (1992). Then in *Simmons* (1994), he talks about the "sheer depravity"[57] and "the gruesome grotesque handiwork"[58] of the crime committed, referring to it as a "brutal" murder.[59] In *Atkins* (2002), he uses "brutal,"[60] "exquisite torture-killing,"[61] "heinous,"[62] and "extreme"[63] to describe the murder. In *Atkins* (2002), he advocates that the "depravity of the crime"[64] should be considered when determining the defendant's culpably. He again characterizes a murder as "brutal"[65] in *Moore* (2002). In *Roper* (2005), "heinous crimes deserving of death"[66] are ones that "involve truly monstrous acts."[67] In *Baze* (2008), he asserts, "Certain crimes are themselves so grievous an affront to humanity that the only adequate response may be the penalty of death."[68] A cruel crime, according to Scalia, does not happen by accident but involves the intentional enjoyment of someone else's pain and agony; it is an event that shocks the moral conscience of a community. The terms Scalia uses to describe the crimes in these cases assume almost a doctrinal quality owing to their frequent repetition. To Scalia, a crime is worthy of death if it is "heinous," "cruel," "depraved," "brutal," "gruesome," "extreme," "torture," or "monstrous." These terms derive, in large part, from the Model Penal Code, as suggested by the American Law Institute (ALI). The Model Penal Code suggests that capital sentences be awarded in cases in which "the murder was especially heinous, atrocious or cruel, manifesting exceptional depravity."[69] Although some states interpret these terms as having distinct meanings,[70] for Scalia these adjectives mean essentially the same thing: The crime committed was cruel.

In each of these cases, Scalia characterizes crimes broadly as heinous, cruel, depraved, or some derivative of the same idea. Yet he also gives *specific examples* to clarify what constitutes a capital crime. In his examples, criminal acts worthy of death include premeditated acts of violence, repeated and varied acts of violence, acts against protected classes of people (e.g., the elderly, mentally retarded, women), acts in which multiple people are murdered, and acts in which bodies are desecrated. In *Simmons* (1994), the accused vividly described the murder he intended to commit, revealing malice aforethought. Most of Scalia's examples bear witness to repeated and varied acts of violence, which points to malice innate within the person committing the crime. In *Atkins* (2002), Scalia describes the defendant as having "violent tendencies,"[71] as exemplified by the defendant hitting "one over the head with a beer bottle; . . . he slapped a gun across another victim's face, clubbed her in the head with it, knocked her to the ground, and then helped her up, only to shoot her in the stomach."[72] Violent people commit violent acts. In the case of *Moore* (2002), "One victim was stuffed in the trunk of a car, shot, doused with gasoline, and lit afire. The second victim was driven to his girlfriend's home, where he and the third victim, the girlfriend, were shot dead."[73] Repeated and delayed violence are evidence of inherent wickedness. Also in *Moore* (2002), "The mentally retarded victim was found in his ran-sacked apartment with a swastika drawn on his abdomen and 11 stab wounds to his neck, chest, abdomen, and back."[74] Only malevolent people take the time to draw a hate symbol on the body of a mentally handicapped victim after they brutalize his body. In *Roper* (2005), the defendant "broke into the home of an innocent woman, bound her with duct tape and electrical wire, and threw her off a bridge alive and conscious."[75] Humane individuals do not capture, bind, and send to death an innocent person. Also in *Roper* (2005), Scalia recounts how the accused "picked up a female hitchhiker, threw bottles at her, and kicked and stomped her for approximately 30 minutes until she died."[76] The crime did not end with the beating, however. "They then sexually assaulted her lifeless body and, when they were finished, threw her body off a cliff. They later returned to the crime scene to mutilate her corpse."[77] Only wicked people brutally murder, sexually violate, and mutilate other people. The narratives that Scalia recounts do not describe people who can be redeemed. Rather, they describe monstrous people who engage in inhumane acts of violence. These offenders cannot be rehabilitated; they should be exterminated.

For Scalia, people who commit violent crimes are depraved individuals who engage in *habitual* criminal activity. Depraved individuals plan to kill their victims and to brutalize their bodies. In his opinion Scalia describes how the murder in the *Thompson* (1988) case involved Thompson cutting Keene in the throat and chest, kicking and shooting him in the head, and dumping his body in the river.[78] Importantly, for Scalia, a string of earlier crimes offers evidentiary support that the criminal acts are an outpouring of the person's nature, not a random individual act. Thompson had previous arrests, which include assault and battery, burglary, and assault with a knife and with a deadly weapon—violent acts that Scalia emphasizes were repeated in the case at hand. In *Lee* (1992), Scalia reports that the defendant had a previous conviction for a felony. In *Simmons* (1994), the defendant was found guilty of a crime similar to one he had committed before: "the brutal murder of a 79-year-old woman in her home, and three prior crimes confessed to by the petitioner, all rapes and beatings of elderly women, one of them his grandmother."[79] Criminal activity begets criminal activity, Scalia contends, and typically in a fashion similar to earlier unlawful acts. Criminals favor weapons and acts of violence, and they repeat offenses. Consequently, if prisoners are released (early), "inevitable murders, robberies, and rapes to be committed by the released inmates"[80] will follow. Prison does not rehabilitate criminals; crime is innate in their person or being.

Scalia's description of the facts revivifies the act, so the judicial decision cannot be distanced from the criminal event. In an interesting interpretive move, Scalia shifts the weight of interpretation from the cruelty of the punishment, which the Eighth Amendment was created to address, to the cruelty of the crime. His detailed statement of facts often creates a vivid scene for his auditors, placing the personal accountability of the defendant and the harm to the victim in the forefront of his opinion and thereby justifying execution.

States as Arbiter of Death

Scalia maintains that states should be the arbiter of death. He supports this position by giving agency to states, advocating the separation of powers that the federal system affords, pointing out inconsistencies in judicial decision-making by certain justices, and citing case precedent that asserts repeatedly that states have the right to determine how they administer capital punishment.

States have the power to determine what constitutes a constitutional use of the death penalty. In *Walton* (1990), Scalia argues that states "must administer [the death] penalty in a way that can rationally distinguish between those individuals for whom death is an appropriate sanction and those for whom it is not."[81] The power should reside within the states, because they are the entities that penalize their citizens most frequently.[82] Within a democratic system, the decision to enact a capital punishment is the will of the people.[83] States have the "discretionary" power to construct whatever laws they think best serve the people of their state regarding criminal procedures.[84] States can determine their criminal processes and select experts to evaluate the fitness of state denizens to stand trial in a state court to receive the state's judgment.[85] A prisoner is an entity of the state.[86] States house prisoners, administer the death penalty, and stand before the court to respond to appeals instigated by the accused. States can address issues of proportionality in sentencing as well as vary how they punish different activities—or even whether they find certain behaviors illegal.[87] States have the liberty to determine what they want their criminal sanctions to be. States can use sentences other than capital punishment, including life imprisonment without the possibility of parole.[88] Since the Eighth Amendment guarantees states the right to administer death but requires very little in the way of considerations outside that basic allowance, states can determine how best to administer capital punishment.

Since states have the power to administer the death penalty, it stands to reason that the federal government should not intervene. In his Eighth Amendment dissents, Scalia criticizes the court for violating the separation of powers. The Supreme Court, as a representative of the federal government, should not intrude upon powers reserved for the states. States regulate the health, safety, and wellness of their citizens and punish any members of their population who violate the well-being of other citizens. When the court upheld a maximum population limit in prison in *Brown* (2011), it interfered with the state's ability to rehabilitate its population. "It seems that the Court's respect for state sovereignty has vanished," Scalia contends, "in the case where it matters most."[89] Scalia repeats his criticism in *Baze* (2008), wherein he claims it is not the court's responsibility to stipulate that state legislatures must use empirical studies to fashion criminal sanctions.[90] In a series of previous cases, the court overstepped the separation of powers, taking on legislative functions. The court did so, specifically, by: "effectively requiring capital sentencing proceedings separate from the adjudication of guilt, . . . dictating the type and extent of discretion the sentencer must and must not have, . . . requiring that certain categories of evidence must and must not be admitted, . . . undertaking minute inquiries into the wording of jury instructions to ensure that jurors understand their duties under our labyrinthine code of rules, . . . and prescribing the procedural forms that sentencing decisions must follow."[91] Through such judicial legislating, the court governs sentencing in ways not intended by the Constitution. Scalia offers similar criticisms in *Thompson* (1988), *Gathers* (1989), *Booth* (1987), *McKoy* (1990), *Espinosa* (1992), *Richmond* (1992), *Simmons* (1994), *Atkins* (2002), *Moore* (2002), *Tennard* (2004), *Roper* (2005), and *Abdul-Kabir* (2007). Although the court may disagree with a state's capital policies, the court does not have the right to mandate particular actions. Or as Scalia argues in *Atkins* (2002), "There is no justification for this Court's pushing them into the experiment—and turning the experiment into a permanent practice—on constitutional pretext."[92] When the High Court mandates legal procedures and evidentiary burdens, it assumes legislative functions better left to state legislatures.

In addition to functional breaches of power, the Supreme Court violates states' rights in a wholesale fashion by proscribing the punishment of two categories of people: minors and the mentally handicapped (now characterized as "mentally incapacitated"). Regarding the execution of minors, Scalia maintains that most states do not have a minimum age at which a minor can be found culpable for a capital crime.[93] Moreover, in *Thompson* (1988), Scalia disagrees with the majority's position that a "national consensus" exists to proscribe the sentencing of minors to death. A national consensus should represent a majority of states. "Words have no meaning if the views of less than 50% of death penalty States can constitute a national consensus," Scalia maintains.[94] Since a majority of states that have the death penalty do not prohibit the execution of minors, states should be allowed to execute minors. Even more importantly, however, the national consensus that exists contradicts the majority's assertion. In other words, more states than not are of the opinion that minors can be executed if the crime warrants such action. "Turning to legislation at the state level," Scalia explains, "one observes the same trend of *lowering* rather than raising the age of juvenile criminal liability."[95] Questioning the information the majority uses in support of its position, Scalia states that evidence for his opposition's position is not "discernable in the legislation of *this* society."[96] Society, he tells us, thinks the execution of minors should be a rare occurrence, but it does not seek to ban it outright.[97] Thus, Oklahoma's sentencing a minor to death is consistent with other state positions.

Scalia's arguments about whether states can execute the mentally handicapped/incapacitated follow the same line of reasoning he presents in his minor cases: the majority of states support execution. In *Atkins* (2002), Scalia notes that eighteen states have laws that ban the execution of mentally handicapped people, and only seven states retroactively ban the execution of those persons already sentenced. The percentage of laws banning such executions "is not a statement of absolute moral repugnance," Scalia asserts, "but one of current preference between two tolerable approaches."[98] If other states agree that this classification of people should not be executed, then those states can pass laws prohibiting their execution. States can choose to ban execution for certain individuals; the Supreme Court, however, should not proscribe death for certain groups of persons if the states want to execute them.

Although it is not unusual for a justice to rely upon legal precedent in cases to support their argument, Scalia offers thorough recitations of precedent to support his claim that the state has the power to administer punishment, including death. Scalia varies in how he cites precedence, however. Sometimes he merely cites the case. At other times he quotes from the case and cites the case name. At yet other times he quotes the case and identifies the author of the quote in addition to the case name. When he cites his colleagues' former opinions to support his claim in the issue in question, he does so to highlight what he perceives to be an inconsistency in their jurisprudence. For example, in his *Baze* (2008) opinion, Scalia quotes the joint opinion given by Justices Stewart, Powell, and Stevens in *Gregg* (1976). He cites this opinion to show that Stevens's current opinion violates Stevens's earlier way of thinking. Scalia writes: "But even if we grant Justice Stevens his 'uncontroversial premise,' his application of that premise to the current practice of capital punishment does not meet the 'heavy burden [that] rests on those who would attack the judgment of the representatives of the people.' . . . That is to say, Justice Stevens' policy analysis of the constitutionality of capital punishment fails on its own terms."[99] According to Scalia, a liberal justice such as Stevens knew at one time that states were the unit of control over capital punishment; his contemporary position is not consistent with his earlier belief. Scalia also cites the *Gregg* (1976) opinion in *Walton* (1990), *McKoy* (1990), *Roper* (2005), *Thompson* (1988), and *Atkins* (2002). He makes a similar move in *Payne* (1991), quoting Justice Marshall to argue against Marshall's criticism of the majority's failure to follow stare decisis. Although I could offer more examples, these two are sufficient to establish Scalia's point: Justices who disagree with him are inconsistent. In earlier cases these justices recognized the importance of allowing states to implement capital punishment as they saw fit. Since justices do not always adjudicate in a consistent fashion, they should not be the ones who decide what constitutes a capital offense and who is culpable under the law.

As I have already established, Scalia relies upon case precedent to support the right of states to execute their citizens throughout his opinions. He uses previous cases to highlight discrepancies between decisions. In many of his dissents he disagrees with the court's finding that a state cannot implement capital punishment. For example, in *Atkins* (2002), he argues: "Before today, our opinions consistently emphasized that Eighth Amendment judgments regarding the existence of social 'standards' 'should be informed by objective factors to the maximum possible extent' and 'should not be, or appear to be, merely the subjective views of individual Justices.'"[100] Chaining a series of previous cases offers credibility to Scalia's argument by showing that the preponderance of evidence supports his claim that the justices do not have the power to dictate whether states can execute their citizens. At other times he surveys previous decisions to show how the court has given guidance to states about proper capital punishment protocols. In *Walton* (1990), he proclaims: "Since the 1976 cases, we have routinely read *Furman* as standing for the proposition that 'channelling and limiting . . . the sentencer's discretion in imposing the death penalty' is a 'fundamental constitutional requirement,' . . . and have insisted that States furnish the sentencer with 'clear and objective standards' that provide 'specific and detailed guidance,' and that 'make rationally reviewable the process for imposing a sentence of death.'"[101] As it has for decades, the Supreme Court can provide states with direction about legal procedure. But the important point is that the entity that acts, again, is the state. Scalia's survey of precedent shows that in earlier cases the court upheld capital punishment laws that were clear, consistent, and considered any mitigating factors. The underlying idea was that if a state fully considered any mitigating factors—age, mental ability, upbringing—it would deliberate upon each case in turn and no person would be quickly and summarily executed without due process. Although the court can offer guidance, states must be allowed to differ in judgment and in practice.

Scalia uses several rhetorical strategies—traditional powers of the states, the federal system, inconsistent judicial stances, and previous case precedent—to support the idea that states should be able to determine the punishment for crimes. Since most of the crimes committed violate state rather than federal law, states more frequently have the ability to enact punishment. States decide punishment procedures and protocols via legislative act and judicial guidelines set forth in case precedent. Since judges can alter their opinions, the power to terminate life should not rest within their hands. Case precedent provides guidelines regarding sentencing protocol, but the court should not place certain individuals outside the reach of capital sentences. Thus, the states must have the power to govern criminal sentencing.

Conclusion

In his Eighth Amendment Cruel and Unusual Punishments Clause cases, Scalia argues that the death penalty has to be both cruel *and* unusual for it to be deemed unconstitutional. Scalia concludes that while society might agree that the execution of minors or the mentally retarded is cruel, such a punishment was not unusual at the time of the amendment's adoption. The underlying standards that guide Scalia's Eighth Amendment jurisprudence are: (1) who was allowed to be put to death at the time of the adoption of the Eighth Amendment, (2) what forms of execution were used, and (3) the fact that society has not "set its face" against the death penalty. Throughout his opinions Scalia makes interesting rhetorical choices that support capital punishment. First, Scalia quantifies "unusual" as one; the execution of individuals would be unusual only if just one state allowed such executions. Second, he gives agency for "cruel" to the person committing the crime rather than to the punishment itself. Third, he leaves the ability to use the death penalty to the states, refusing to establish a national standard.

First, according to Scalia's standards, for a punishment to be determined "unusual," it would have to be allowed by only one state. If that were the case, the death penalty, for all purposes and effects, would be null and void without the court needing to declare it so. This has implications for the forms of capital punishment. If, as Scalia argues, a punishment must be *both* "cruel" and "unusual" to be unconstitutional, one might ask whether any form of execution would be beyond the boundaries of cruelty, so long as more than one state used that form.

Second, from his opinions we can infer that the cruelty of the act the convicted person committed outweighs the cruelty of the death penalty. Scalia begins his opinions in his first-degree murder cases with an explicit consideration of the facts of the case, emphasizing the cruelty of the act committed by the person sentenced to death. His detailed description of facts slows down the scene of the crime to offer a horrible reenactment of the crime. His description also highlights the personhood of the criminal and of the victim. People who read his statement of facts feel as if they have a firsthand account of the crime rather than a third-person account. The sense of being present at the crime scene enhances moral outrage and decreases objectivity, encouraging auditors to seek execution.

Third, Scalia denies the judiciary power to proscribe execution, instead locating that power in the states. If the people of a state hold the accused culpable for a crime, Scalia does not see fit to deny them that right. Although he shifts the notion of "cruel" to apply to a person rather than a punishment, he rejects the court's ability to characterize as cruel sentencing someone to death. According to Scalia the judiciary should, in areas of capital punishment, defer to the states and their representatives. Scalia contends that proscribing execution would decrease liberty rather than increase it. Although current social mores may have shifted away from widespread use of capital punishment, future societies may desire to execute their criminals. National mandates, such as those put forth in Supreme Court decisions, encourage a totalitarian state. When *Furman* (1972) was handed down, states could not choose to implement capital punishment even if they wanted. Supreme Court decisions, therefore, can have a totalizing effect on governmental policy choices; they can limit states' freedom to experiment with democratic solutions to social problems.

The Eighth Amendment clearly states that "cruel and unusual punishments" should not be inflicted upon someone. While the Constitution does not give guidelines as to what is "cruel" and what is "unusual," the Constitution's Fourteenth Amendment, which allows for the taking of life (after a person has received due process of the law), means that execution is permissible. Nevertheless, the interpretation of this "clear" clause can be disputed. The adjective "cruel," which Scalia devalues to the extent that it has no role within the constitutional clause, describes practices outside the boundaries of acceptable suffering of convicted persons and injects into the clause a sense of biblical righteousness. The adjective "unusual" depicts punishments not frequently occurring, punishments rare or nontraditional, or punishments illegal. In Scalia's textual story the meaning of both words could be fixed at the point in time the amendment was adopted or the meaning of cruel and unusual could be understood in light of modern understandings. Also according to Scalia's narrative, the court does not have the ability to adjudicate this area of law. The court's strongest advocate of textualism offers rhetorical challenges to this explicit amendment. The clear clause turns out not to be clear in Scalia's textual tale.

4

Interpreting Competing Clauses

Mediating Religion between the Establishment and Free Exercise Clauses

> If the Religion Clauses demand neutrality, we must enforce them, in hard cases as well as easy ones.
>
> —Justice Antonin Scalia

The First Amendment begins, "Congress shall make no law respecting an establishment of religion, or prohibiting the free exercise thereof." Although the Establishment Clause comes first in the text, notable constitutional historians argue that the Establishment Clause was ratified to protect the free exercise of religion.[1] In fact, the first draft proposed by James Madison to the House of Representatives declared, "The civil rights of none shall be abridged on account of religious belief or worship, nor shall any national religion be established, nor shall the full and equal rights of conscience be in any manner, or on any pretext, infringed."[2] The language of the religion clauses would go through several revisions before it would assume language similar to the final version that the House proposed to the Senate: "Congress shall make no law establishing Religion, or prohibiting the free exercise thereof, nor shall the rights of conscience be infringed."[3] Multiple versions of the clause were also considered and rejected by the Senate before the Senate proposed its version to the House for consideration: "Congress shall make no law establishing articles of faith or a mode of worship, or prohibiting the free exercise of religion."[4] A conference committee produced the final version of the language as it was adopted in the First Amendment.

Adjudicated as two separate clauses, the Establishment Clause and the Free Exercise Clause present a unique interpretive challenge, as two possibly competing clauses exist in tension with one another. In his essay "Two Concepts of Liberty," Isaiah Berlin explains that individuals have positive rights and negative rights.[5] Positive rights grant people the *freedom to* engage in certain activities, and negative rights ensure people have the *freedom from* participating in others. The Free Exercise Clause represents a positive liberty right—allowing US citizens to practice whatever religion they desire. The Establishment Clause represents a negative liberty right, requiring the government not to institute a religion. The line between freedom *from* and freedom *to* can be blurred and messy, as religion law struggles to mediate the dichotomous tension between these two clauses. How does a nation enable its citizens to practice religious freedom within the public sphere without demonstrating a preference for one religion over another?

In this chapter I separate the two religion clauses. Although doing so may appear to create an artificial distinction to anyone not familiar with religion law, the two clauses are considered separately when taken up by the courts, and each has produced different case precedents. I summarize interpretative approaches to each of the clauses, offer a brief survey of case precedent created by Supreme Court rulings for the clause, and then consider the two clauses separately. I find that these competing clauses challenge Scalia's textual tale.

Presently, three approaches can be used to adjudicate the Establishment Clause: strict separation, nonpreferentialism, and accommodation. Strict separationists contend that the Constitution demands there be no interaction between church and state; religion should not be favored over nonreligion. Nonpreferentialists assert that religion is a positive good in society and that religion should be preferred over nonreligion but that no one religion should be preferred over another religion. Accommodationists maintain that the Constitution supports the inclusion of religion in the public sphere.

Most constitutional questions concerning the establishment of religion focus on the issue of school funding. Generally, the court has upheld funding to students and denied funding to parochial schools. Although the Supreme Court has decided that schools cannot receive funding directly from the federal government, students can be supported by publicly funded transportation (*Everson v. Board of Education* [1947]) and textbooks (*Mueller v. Allen* [1983]).[6] The court is more favorably disposed to giving grant money to institutions of higher education, believing that college students will be less inclined to be influenced by religious doctrine than younger students (*Tilton v. Richardson* [1971]).[7] Outside the realm of education, the court's decision-making has been inconsistent. The court has determined that nativity scenes (*Lynch v. Donnelly* [1984]) and menorahs (*Allegheny County v. American Civil Liberties Union* [1989]) can be displayed in public arenas but has rejected the right to offer nondenominational prayer before football games (*Santa Fe Independent School District v. Jane Doe* [2000]) and at graduations (*Lee v. Weisman* [1992]).[8] The court also has held that displays of the Ten Commandments cannot remain within courtrooms (*McCreary County v. American Civil Liberties Union* [2005]) but are acceptable when displayed outside on public property amid other statues (*Van Orden v. Perry* [2005]).[9]

In their efforts to make sense of the Establishment Clause, judges have developed multiple doctrinal tests to determine whether an establishment exists: *Lemon*, coercion, endorsement, and neutrality. Set forth in *Lemon v. Kurtzman* (1971), the *Lemon* test requires that a law pass a three-prong test to be constitutional: first, the law must have a secular purpose that neither endorses nor unnecessarily burdens religion; second, the law must neither advance nor inhibit religion; and third, the law must not result in an excessive entanglement between religion and government. The *Lemon* test was revised in the court's *Agostini v. Felton* (1997) opinion, which combined the last two prongs, resulting in a purpose prong and an effects prong.[10] The court also outlined the following as what constitutes an unconstitutional advancement of religion: 1) government indoctrination, 2) defining recipients of benefits by reference to religion, or 3) excessive entanglement. The coercion test claims that a law does not present an unconstitutional violation of the Establishment Clause unless it: 1) provides direct aid to religion or 2) coerces people to support or to participate in religion.[11] In *Lynch v. Donnelly* (1984), Justice O'Connor proposed the endorsement test, which requires the courts to ask whether a law amounts to an endorsement of religion.[12] The neutrality test, developed through a series of cases, finds that government can support initiatives so long as they do not help or harm religion.

Case precedent and doctrinal reasoning is somewhat simpler in the realm of free exercise case law. Scholars and jurists have not adopted different ideological perspectives regarding free exercise, as they have for establishment questions. Although both areas of law have used doctrinal tests to assess the validity of different laws and practices, the free exercise test has been abandoned, while the establishment test limps along. Scholars critique both areas of law, finding that the court's adjudication is not consistent and that it thus provides little guidance for lower courts and legislators.

Constitutional questions pertaining to the free exercise of religion largely have centered on whether a person is excused from complying with a law based upon that person's religious beliefs. In *Reynolds v. United States* (1878), the court rejected the practice of Mormon polygamy.[13] Declaring a difference between belief and action, the court determined that government could regulate a person's activity so long as it has a rational basis for doing so. The division between belief and action means a person can believe whatever he wants, but government can regulate his actions. Nevertheless, at times the court has ignored the distinction between belief and action, favoring the accommodation of religious practices to protect minority rights. Specifically, the belief/action divide was abandoned in the mid-1960s when the court increased accommodation for religious differences. In *Sherbert v. Verner* (1963), the court ordered a state to pay unemployment compensation to a woman who had been fired for refusing to work on Saturday, her Sabbath.[14] Also in *Sherbert* (1963), the court determined that a state must have a compelling interest that does not significantly infringe upon a person's free exercise of her religion. Then, in *Wisconsin v. Yoder* (1972), the court concluded that the Amish did not have to send their children to public schools beyond the eighth grade.[15] In contrast to *Sherbert* (1963), in which the state had to show a compelling interest to make someone comply with a state law, in *Yoder* (1972) the state had to prove that its compelling interest (in educating youth) would be hindered significantly by granting an exemption to the Amish. The 1980s saw the end of the *Sherbert-Yoder* accommodations to religious exercise. In *United States v. Lee* (1982), the court denied an Amish man exemption from paying social security taxes.[16] Then, in *Bowen v. Roy* (1986), the court rejected the request that a Native American's daughter not be assigned a social security number.[17] In *Goldman v. Weinberger* (1986), the court rejected a Jewish man's request to wear his yarmulke while in military dress.[18] And in *Lyng v. Northwest Indian Cemetery Protective Association* (1988), the court allowed a highway to be built through Native American land, even though it would prohibit worship on that land.[19] In *Employment Division v. Smith* (1990), the court held that religious beliefs or practices would not be exempted from generally applicable laws. Centering its free exercise jurisprudence on the separation between belief and action, the High Court began prohibiting actions that could lend to widespread challenges to governmental control.

Only one doctrinal test has been used in free exercise cases: the three-prong *Sherbert* test. The first prong asks if the government has burdened an individual's free exercise of religion. If they have, the government must prove that it had a compelling interest to do so (second prong) and that it used the least restrictive means by which to burden his/her religion (third prong). The Supreme Court rejected the *Sherbert* test in *Employment Division* (1990), contending the government did not need to require religious exemptions from generally applicable laws. Disgruntled with the *Employment Division* (1990) decision, the US Congress codified the *Sherbert* test into statutory law by passing the Religious Freedom Restoration Act (RFRA) of 1993. In *City of Boerne v. Flores* (1997) four years later, the Supreme Court struck down RFRA as a violation of constitutional separation of powers. Since the judicial branch is tasked with interpreting the law, the legislative branch cannot pass laws requiring a rejected judicial doctrine. In the intervening years since *Employment Division* (1990) and RFRA, the court largely has neglected to use the *Sherbert* test in its free exercise cases.

The division between belief and action is an interesting choice of interpretation, for one would think "free exercise" would mean "an action without constraint." "Exercise" most often refers to some form of practice or action. The *Oxford English Dictionary* tells us, with respect to religion, that "exercise" has been understood to mean "to celebrate, perform (a ceremony, religious service, etc.); to perform the observances of (a religion)" since the fifteenth century. Therefore, the Free Exercise Clause would seem to mean that there can be no division between belief and action. "Exercise," a verb, would be preceded by its adverb, "free," meaning "without restraint." The court, however, largely has refused to define free exercise in this manner; precedent recognizes "free thought" or "free belief" (modern renditions of John Locke's "freedom of conscience")[20] but not "free *exercise*" (emphasis mine).

In this chapter I examine fourteen of Scalia's religion law opinions. As with his Eighth Amendment cases, not all of these cases present equally important sites of analysis. I do not consider his *Arizona Christian School Tuition Organization v. Winn* (2011) concurring opinion, because Scalia does not mention the question of an establishment.[21] I consider his reading of each of the clauses in turn, starting with the Establishment Clause.

Scalia on the Establishment Clause

Scalia has written opinions in twelve of the court's Establishment Clause cases. In each case Scalia furthers the interests of religion and denies that the presence of religious symbolism or the allowance of religious discourse or ideology in the public sphere constitutes an establishment of religion. In this section I consider most, but not all, of Scalia's religion clause opinions.

In *Edwards v. Aguillard* (1987), the Supreme Court determined that the Louisiana law requiring creation science to be taught in conjunction with evolution violated the establishment clause. Scalia dissented, arguing that the *Lemon* test is invalid. In *Weisman* (1992), the court decided that it was unconstitutional to have members of the clergy offer prayers at high school commencement services. Scalia dissented, declaring that the longstanding tradition of public prayer at ceremonial occasions was not unconstitutional. In *Capitol Square* (1995), a board rejected the Ku Klux Klan's request to display an unattended crucifix in the statehouse square, claiming that a cross on statehouse grounds would be an endorsement of a particular religious viewpoint—even though they allowed a Christmas tree and a menorah. The

Ohio District Court rejected the board's argument, and the Supreme Court, with Scalia writing the majority opinion, affirmed its judgment. In *Good News Club* (2001), the court held that a religious club could use school property, a limited public forum, for their meetings. Scalia wrote a concurrence, arguing that denying the club use of the space would amount to viewpoint discrimination. In *Van Orden* (2005) the court upheld a Ten Commandments display on Texas state property. Scalia wrote a concurrence, maintaining that the Establishment Clause does not prohibit government from favoring religion generally. In *Hein* (2007), the High Court rejected taxpayers' standing to sue the government. In his concurrence Scalia contends that whether the founders meant for the Establishment Clause to restrict the taxing and spending power of the government is irrelevant to the case. In *Pleasant Grove City* (2009), the court denied the Summum church the right to erect a permanent monument carved with its Seven Aphorisms on public property. In his concurrence Scalia argues that the Ten Commandments statute does not violate any aspect of the First Amendment (speech or establishment). In *Salazar* (2010), the High Court held that the Establishment Clause did not require all religious symbols to be removed from the public sphere. Scalia agreed but wrote separately to state that the petitioner did not have standing to sue. In Scalia's dissents, he argues that legislators can use their religious convictions when passing laws (*Edwards* [1987]), that making religious publications tax-exempt does not constitute an establishment (*Texas Monthly* [1989]), that prayer can be said at public school graduation ceremonies (*Weisman* [1992]), that school boundaries can be drawn using cultural characteristics as boundaries (*Kiryas Joel* [1994]), and that religious displays can be exhibited on public property (*McCreary* [2005]).

I turn now to a consideration of Scalia's establishment cases. In his opinions Scalia constructs establishment questions as free speech issues to validate religious expression within the public sphere. Scalia also uses the original intent of the founders and the original meaning of the text to support his claim that strict separation of church and state is neither required nor expected in order to create the sort of governmental system the founders intended. Government should accommodate religion, allowing for demonstrations of religious faith in the public sphere to the greatest possible extent. Scalia concludes that the historic practices of the people are consistent with such public expressions of religious belief. Scalia dresses his originalism argument in the cloak of historic practices. Each of Scalia's rhetorical strategies leads him to conclude that religious practice should be allowed in the public sphere. Largely absent from his establishment opinions is a consideration of the constitutional text.

Establishment as Free Speech

Frequently in his Establishment Clause opinions, Scalia combines religion law and free speech law. In *Good News Club* (2001), Scalia contends, "The private right to exert and receive that compulsion (or to have one's children receive it) is protected by the Free Speech and Free Exercise Clause."[22] Scalia's claim that a case involves two fundamental rights requires that the courts bring additional strict scrutiny elements to bear on the case at hand. It is not enough to demonstrate that the government has not established a religion; they must also prove they have not infringed upon a citizen's ability to express herself. The enactment of religion in the public sphere, therefore, is a form of speech—religious speech. As such, religious activity deserves the protection guaranteed to speech. Religious expression deserves free speech protection, Scalia contends, because it is the type of speech that historically has been threatened most often. The existence of one clause necessitates the need for the other clause.

Scalia uses a method of interpretation to connect free speech to establishment. In his one mention of a textualist approach to his religion law cases in *Capitol Square* (1995), Scalia merely states, "By its terms that Clause applies only to the words and acts of government."[23] Thus, the words and acts of private individuals cannot denote an establishment of religion—only the words and actions of government officials can do so. Scalia does not offer an in-depth analysis of the textual meaning of the Establishment Clause, however. Rather, he shifts the argumentative framework from textualism to originalism, which allows him to consider the act as a free speech issue rather than as an establishment issue. According to Scalia, the Establishment Clause "was never meant, and has never been read by this Court, to serve as an impediment to purely private religious speech connected to the State only through its occurrence in a public forum."[24] Starting with original intent, an interpretative move that Scalia frequently rails against, he then shifts to a broader form of interpretation—how the court has "read" the amendment. He repeats the idea that the founders never intended religion to be banned from the public sphere and further maintains in his *McCreary* (2005) dissent that historical tradition has never supported such an approach. "Religion is to be strictly excluded from the public forum. That is not, and never was, the model adopted by America," Scalia asserts.[25] It stands to reason, Scalia concludes, since the founders did not intend for religion to be banned from the public sphere, as evidenced by their use of religious language and activity, that religion expression should be allowed.

Scalia does not distinguish between private and public speech within a public forum in his establishment cases. He maintains that both forms of speech deserve the same protections. Central to much of Scalia's Establishment Clause jurisprudence is the idea that private speech can occur within a public forum. The distinction between types of public spaces was set forth in the Free Speech Clause case *Perry Educational Association v. Perry Local Educator's Association* (1983). In *Perry* (1983), the court identified three forums for expression: traditional (e.g., public streets, parks, town halls, and sidewalks), designated/limited (e.g., spaces not typically public but set aside for a specific, limited governmental purpose), and nonpublic (e.g., either private or restricted areas).[26] According to *Perry* (1983), each forum invites a different level of judicial scrutiny, with the traditional forum requiring the highest level of scrutiny (and therefore the greatest protection for the individual), and the nonpublic having the lowest level of scrutiny, with legislation merely needing to be reasonably related to its goal. Most frequently Scalia refers to "the public forum," blurring the lines between traditional and designated/limited spaces.

Within his establishment opinions, Scalia modifies the meaning of establishment from the idea of a legal status to a geographic space. His uniting of establishment and free speech facilitates this change. In *Capitol Square* (1995), Scalia explains, "Religious expression cannot violate the Establishment Clause where it (1) is purely private and (2) occurs in a traditional or designated public forum, publicly announced and open to all on equal terms."[27] Although Scalia does not engage in formal reasoning, the logic used appears to follow this line of thinking: religious speech is private speech; private speech does not require governmental sponsorship; therefore, religious speech does not present an establishment issue within the public forum. Thus, in *Capitol Square* (1995), Scalia relies upon place arguments to claim that if the space in which someone wants to communicate traditionally has been held as a public forum, then individuals can use that space for private expression.

For Scalia, speech and establishment exist on a continuum, and speech should be favored over establishment. According to Scalia, if the court gives preference to the exclusion of religion from the public sphere, then the court creates a free speech violation. Using a slippery slope argument, Scalia asserts: "Every proposed act of private, religious expression in a public forum would force officials to weigh a host of imponderables. How close to government is too close? What kind of building, in what context, symbolizes state authority? If the State guessed wrong in one direction, it would be guilty of an Establishment Clause violation; if in another, it would be liable for suppressing free exercise or free speech."[28] The court should not start down the slippery slope of trying to parse out what geographic space would constitute an establishment. Scalia concludes that government cannot afford to restrict religious expression within the public sphere. Doing so violates another fundamental liberty—and the one most valued in our contemporary society.

Establishment and free speech become so entangled for Scalia that he questions whether the freedom of expression has been violated when evaluating an establishment question. In *Pleasant Grove* (2009), Scalia insists that the existing "park displays do not violate *any* part of the First Amendment."[29] We can infer from Scalia's emphasis on "any" that the practice does not violate the Free Speech Clause. The entanglement of the two clauses also leads Scalia to evaluate religious expression bans as a form of content regulation. Time and time again within Free Speech Clause jurisprudence, the High Court has determined that government cannot regulate the content of speech. Thus, if the government does not allow religious expression, then the state engages in unconstitutional restrictions. "From no other group does respondent require the sterility of speech that it demands of petitioners," Scalia maintains.[30] Moreover, the right to speak is a fundamental aspect of the right to protest. In *Edwards* (1987), Scalia recounts: "Political activism by the religiously motivated is part of our heritage. . . . We do not presume that the sole purpose of a law is to advance religion merely because it was supported strongly by organized religions or by adherents of particular faiths. . . . To do so would deprive religious men and women of their right to participate in the political process."[31] As a fundamental right, free speech is necessary to the enactment of the free exercise of religion. Allowing for religious speech, therefore, does not constitute an establishment of religion. Free speech, rather, guarantees that other fundamental rights can be celebrated and upheld.

From his opinions we can infer that Scalia considers religious speech to be public speech, that the public and government should have "a toleration —no, an affection"[32] for religion, and that the Constitution approves the general endorsement of religion in the public sphere—all for the betterment of "public virtue." In his opinions Scalia considers the ways in which "the public" and "the public sphere" have changed with respect to religion. Religious speech (including speeches, prayer, signs, and symbols) has been banned from public schools—from their classrooms, football stadiums, and graduation ceremonies. Yet religious speech in other settings has flourished. The Pledge of Allegiance has been altered to include "under God." Public settings, open to religious displays, have increased the variety of religious symbolization—from nativity scenes to menorahs. Challenging the trend toward relegating religion to the private sphere, Scalia claims that exposure to different religions can create a greater toleration of difference among the people and that religious speech is an essential element of this.

When an establishment question becomes an issue of free speech, that right shifts from a negative liberty directed at the government to a positive liberty guaranteed for the people. One is hard-pressed to imagine a scenario in which religion could not be allowed, as no content-based regulations could be used to proscribe free speech. Scalia insists that his establishment-cum-speech philosophy is consistent with the intent of the founders and the original meaning of the clause, as well as with the historic practices of the people. The connection emphasizes the belief aspect of religion, as realized through speech or expression.

The Intent of the Founders and the Original Meaning of the Text

Although Scalia denies in his extrajudicial speeches and writings that the original intent of the Constitution can be known, advocating that judges instead seek to understand the original meaning of the text, in his Establishment Clause opinions he nevertheless refers to the original intent of the founders. In fact, in Scalia's Establishment Clause opinions it becomes very difficult to parse out original intent from original meaning. Although the terms indicate a difference between how the founders intended the document to be understood and how the public understood the document, the evidence Scalia presents reinforces the idea of original intent rather than original meaning.

According to Scalia, the founders were well aware of the possible negative consequences of allowing religious expression in the public sphere, yet they thought the benefits outweighed the possible costs. Since they did not intend for religion to be excluded from the public sphere, public religious expression must be allowed. In *Weisman* (1992), Scalia professes to know the thoughts and will of the founders without providing any evidentiary support as to how he has come by such knowledge, a rhetorical move he repeats in several cases. Scalia asserts that the founders were well aware of the possible difficulties that could arise from allowing religious expression in the public sphere. Yet, he contends, they also knew the benefits of allowing people to join together in public expressions of faith. In *Lamb's Chapel* (1993), he proclaims that the Constitution allows for "preferential treatment," favoring religion over nonreligion. The founders supported religious expression because the virtues fostered by religion benefit society as a whole. Then in *Capitol Square* (1995), he argues that the Establishment Clause was not meant to restrict private religious speech from occurring in the public sphere. And in *Kiryas Joel* (1994), he contends that the founders would be shocked to know that the Establishment Clause would prohibit the practice of a minority religion. In each of these cases Scalia contrasts the court's majority position with what he understands the founders' intent to be. The High Court misconstrues the original intent of the clause, Scalia claims, when they take it to mean that religion cannot be expressed in the public sphere.

Scalia makes an effort to discuss original meaning in *Weisman* (1992). In that opinion he develops a detailed consideration of the original meaning of the Establishment Clause. He tells us that scholars would agree the First Amendment prohibited a national religion and adds that public taxation with intent of financial support to religion was also considered a form of "establishment" by 1790. While such actions would be unconstitutional, Scalia concludes that any practice initiated by the public is acceptable and does not constitute an establishment of religion. Establishments can occur only when state or national units of government impose, by law, mandates to support religious beliefs or practices. In other words, not all support or toleration of free exercise constitutes an establishment of religion, and by so holding the court has gone too far. By fearing the establishment of religion at the expense of free exercise, the court denies the public a means by which to increase national unity. Scalia falls back on original intent by asserting that the founders intended multiple sects to thrive, thereby creating communal respect for different forms of worship.

Scalia's most thorough discussion of original intent—albeit the original intent of the statutory law rather than of the Constitution—can be found in his *Edwards* (1987) dissent, in which he considers the text of the law and the legislative debates to prove the intent of the Louisiana legislators. Oddly, Scalia advances a doctrinal argument to support the notion that Louisiana's law has "a secular purpose," thus satisfying the first prong of the *Lemon* test. Although Scalia frequently criticizes the use of doctrinal tests, expressing a preference for textual readings of the law rather than doctrinal reasoning, he nevertheless uses doctrinal arguments to explain what he perceives to be the court's incorrect reasoning. Essentially, Scalia strives to show that even under the court's doctrinal test, the statute in question fails. Scalia agrees with the majority that the opinion should consider "academic freedom," which fulfills the secular-purpose prong of *Lemon*'s test, yet he provides an alternative explanation. In contrast to the majority construction of "academic freedom" as the freedom of teachers to teach what they want without restriction, Scalia understands "academic freedom" to mean "freedom from indoctrination."[33] Seen in this light, by passing a law that mandated that teachers teach creation science in addition to evolution, Louisiana protected the *students'* academic freedom rather than the *teachers'* academic freedom.

Scalia extends his understanding of original meaning in *Edwards* (1987) to include a textual analysis of the Establishment Clause. He cites a segment of the First Amendment and then makes the argument that the advancement-of-religion prong does not follow from the plain meaning of the text. According to Scalia, the plain meaning of the text does not allow for a reading of the clause that goes beyond official state-church establishment. Thus the clause cannot be given an elasticity that its textual meaning does not support. Since the Louisiana law was implemented to protect the students, and since Scalia does not interpret the Constitution in such a way as to make the state statute invalid, the act is constitutional.

In *McCreary* (2005), Scalia develops a detailed list of religious practices established by early political leaders to support his understanding that the Constitution does not ban religious activity in the public sphere. He cites George Washington's addition of "so help me God" to the presidential oath, the Supreme Court's and the First Congress's opening of their sessions with prayer, the creation of legislation by the First Congress to support paid legislative chaplains, as well as that same legislative body's request that the president proclaim a national day of thanksgiving and prayer. Scalia continues his historical survey, offering as examples of original intent the prayer of Washington at his First Inaugural and Jefferson at his Second Inaugural, a letter from Adams to the Massachusetts Militia about the morality and religiosity of the American people, and Madison's reference to the Divine in his First Inaugural. These examples help Scalia understand how the founding generation understood the clause—a rhetorical maneuver he sees as an extension of his textualist philosophy. The purpose of such religious practice, Scalia tells us, was to foster a moral people that would, in turn, encourage the well-being of the nation. The founding evidence demonstrates the pervasive role of religion in the nation's history and practices. The majority opinion in this case, Scalia opines, has gotten the intent of the religion clauses so wrong that the founders "would surely regard it as a bitter irony that the religious values they designed the Clauses to protect have now become so distasteful to this Court that if they constitute anything more than a subordinate motive for government action they will invalidate it."[34] As Scalia's earlier examples attest, the founders did not mean for religion to be ostracized from the public sphere; thus, religious practice should be allowed.

The founders' inclusion of religious practice in public life leads Scalia to conclude that little distinction exists between accommodation and establishment. In *Weisman* (1992), he claims that unconstitutional establishments of religion involve "coercion of religious orthodoxy and of financial support *by force of law and threat of penalty*."[35] Scalia maintains concern for the boundary lines of what constitutes an unconstitutional establishment of religion if a citizen faces criminal charges. He asserts that the Establishment Clause was adopted to prohibit a national religion and to protect state religions from national intrusion. Consequently, longstanding traditions do not equate to a violation of the Establishment Clause. Religious expression can occur within the public sphere, but the government cannot charge for it or force it to occur.

Scalia's original intent and original meaning arguments repudiate a complete rejection of religious discourse and practice in the public sphere. Scalia's examples in multiple establishment cases reflect his understanding of the founders' original intent for the clause and the clause's original meaning. Importantly, he maintains that his arguments do not reflect his own views of the religion clauses. Rather, Scalia would have us believe he merely is the historical archivist, recounting the intent of the founders and the original meaning of the clause for the founding generation. And, time and time again, Scalia repeats originalist, rather than textualist, arguments to support his claim. According to Scalia, neither the intent of the founders nor the original meaning of the clause nor the traditions of the American people support strict separation; accommodation and nonpreferential treatment are to be preferred.

Just as Scalia uses the original intent of the legislators and the founders and the original meaning of the founding generation to support constitutional approaches to religion in American life, he does the same with historical reasoning. The first is embodied in the meaning of the text and the second within the traditions of the people.

The Historic Practices of the People

One of Scalia's primary arguments in favor of allowing the accommodation of religion is that the historic practices of the people either support or challenge the law in question. Most of his examples, however, do not support the historic practices of the *people* per se, even though Scalia frames them as such. Rather, they offer additional examples of what the founders appeared to believe constituted permissible religious activity in the public sphere, thus reinforcing his claim that the original intent and original meaning of the text allow for religious activity in the public sphere. In a few cases Scalia gestures to the historic practices of the people themselves, but he does not linger long enough to establish a significant body of evidence that the historic practices of the people support public religious activity.

Scalia's *Texas Monthly* (1989), *Weisman* (1992), and *McCreary* (2005) opinions, more than the rest of his Establishment Clause opinions, rest upon key historic moments for evidentiary support. What his examples highlight, however, are how institutions have the power to enact religious expression, not that the historic practices of the people reflect a desire for public religious expression. Specifically, the founders, each branch of government, and school districts employ theistic language and symbolism. The court incorrectly decided in its *Texas Monthly* (1989) opinion, Scalia asserts, because its decision goes against the historic practices of the people. His broad survey of events, customs, and items invoking a higher power lists historic practices with which the average person would be familiar. They are not uncommon; they occur daily and annually. Each and every person in the nation will have participated in many of them, from celebrating Thanksgiving and handling money to saying the Pledge at the start of the school day. "The history and tradition of our Nation are replete with public ceremonies featuring prayers of thanksgiving and petition," Scalia proclaims in *Weisman* (1992).[36] Citing as examples of the nation's rich history of religious displays in the public sphere the Declaration of Independence, the inaugural prayers of George Washington, James Madison, and George H. W. Bush, Thomas Jefferson's creation of Thanksgiving (as a day of national prayer and thanksgiving), the opening of congressional and judicial sessions with prayer, and the use of prayer at the first public high school commencement in 1868, Scalia maintains that these occurrences also are examples of historical practices of the people. He does the same in *McCreary* (2005). None of these examples, however, present grassroots illustrations of religious activity. The layperson does not initiate the practice. Each and every one offer a control group—be that the national government or the local school board—that utilizes religious language.

In a couple of his opinions, Scalia mentions historic practices of the people that could possibly be understood as generating from the people themselves. In *Capitol Square* (1995), for example, Scalia uses historical surveys to establish the traditions of Columbus, Ohio, as well as those of America in general. He does not develop this point any further. At a moment that appears ripe for Scalia to offer a list of specific instances wherein religious practices have occurred within the park, he engages in an abrupt shift to a different argument line. His suggestion that the public space has hosted individual's actions of religiosity remains unsubstantiated, merely hinting at the historical evidence of public religious activity. Then in *Weisman* (1992), Scalia argues that a person's mere presence at a ceremonial demonstration of religion does not necessarily constitute acquiescence or indoctrination of religious views and beliefs. Scalia appears to assume that prayers at graduation ceremonies are a result of the will of the community; the community seeks to mark such a momentous occasion, one can infer, with prayer. Again objecting to the majority's supposition that any religious demonstration results in an establishment of religion, or that public exhibitions of religion, such as prayer, force religious compliance upon nonreligious spectators, Scalia compares public prayer to reciting the Pledge of Allegiance. Religious expression thus becomes a ritualized activity used by a governmental agent to engender patriotic adherence to American values.

His use of the historic practices of the people suggests that America is a religious nation and that the adjudication of religion law should reflect that aspect of our character. In fact, religion is such a part of our history that all of our major civil ceremonies (e.g., inaugurals and commencements) include religious acts (e.g., prayer, references to a deity); our coinage is embossed with our faith in God; we pledge our allegiance to a nation we craft as under the authority of God; we begin our legislative and judicial sessions with appeals to our higher power for wisdom, guidance, and blessings; and we display religious texts and symbols in public spaces. According to Scalia, the essence of what it means to be an American integrally is tied to public religious expression and practice.

Yet Scalia's use of the phrase "historic practices of the people" rings hollow, devoid of any meaning other than the original intent of the founders or the original meaning of the text (as assumed based upon the accepted practices at the time). Although the phrase would seem to indicate that American customs since the founding of the nation have reflected grassroots initiatives to allow for vernacular religious practices, Scalia's exposition about the historic practices of the people do not reflect such an idea. To wit, while his claims may be historical practices, as they cite examples from American history, they are not historical practices of *the people* but merely a restatement of the practices adopted by early *governmental leaders*. Within such a scenario, the distinction between original intent and original meaning is indistinguishable. Scalia's use of institutional practices relies, rather, upon a logical assumption that such practices evidence the people's desire for religious accommodation. Thus, the historic practices of the people reinforce Scalia's claim that the Supreme Court should allow the maximum accommodation of religion.

In his extrajudicial speeches and writings, Scalia favors strict forms of interpretation. Consequently, it should come as no surprise that he advocates the originalist forms of interpretation or that his "historic practices of the people" rely upon originalist examples for support. Yet Scalia repeatedly comes back to doctrinal arguments in his Establishment Clause cases. Although Scalia would prefer to overturn doctrinal reasoning, he nevertheless finds that it provides a somewhat systematic way to understand the clause and can give consistency to this area of law.

Doctrinal Arguments

Scalia's discussion of the *Lemon* test in his Establishment Clause cases presents an interesting site for commentary about Scalia's philosophy of interpretation. The casual observer would expect Scalia to favor overturning doctrinal precedent in favor of stricter methods of constitutional interpretation. Yet in the area of establishment law, Scalia advocates overturning only the secular-purpose prong of the *Lemon* test. He understands that the other two prongs—that laws must neither advance nor inhibit religion and that laws must not encourage excessive entanglement with religion—were developed through a general understanding of the constitutional language and the historic practices of the people, although he merely gestures to such an argument and does not develop it through the use of any examples. He repeatedly summarizes what precedent the *Lemon* test has created, advocating the use of doctrinal arguments to give this area of law some consistency. Rather than reject *Lemon* (1971), he overwhelmingly encourages the use of its doctrinal test, because he fears that to overturn it would be to invite the justices to use their own reason to decide establishment questions.

In *Edwards* (1987), Scalia argues that the court should make more of an effort to evaluate legislator's secular purpose for creating laws. According to Scalia, the court does not offer much guidance about establishing a secular purpose of a legislative act. In fact, time and time again, the court "effortlessly discovered a secular purpose for measures challenged under the Establishment Clause, typically devoting no more than a sentence or two to the matter."[37] Only three times in the court's history, Scalia tells us, have they invalidated a law because it fails to establish a secular purpose. And in this case, he argues that the majority errs in finding that no secular purpose exists, because the Louisiana legislature stated a secular purpose in the bill. Scalia then criticizes the inconsistency of the court's establishment opinions, referring to them as "a maze."[38]

Part of the difficulty, Scalia contends, is in knowing how to determine legislative intent. Should the court consider legislative histories? Individuals' beliefs? The strength of their beliefs? None of these are reliable, Scalia argues. As set forth earlier in this chapter, in his Establishment Clause cases Scalia repeatedly points to the acts of governmental agents as evidence of founding intent. In his survey of "historic practices," Scalia recounts actions already taken by governmental officials. They are not the unexpressed will of a person; they have achieved material reality. They also represent an institutional will rather than an individualized will. These distinctions offer a justification for why Scalia frames public religious gestures as "historic practices" rather than as "legislative intent."

At the end of his *Edwards* (1987) and his *McCreary* (2005) opinions, Scalia calls for the rejection of the *Lemon* test's secular-purpose prong but upholds the rest of the test. He does not call for a complete rejection of the *Lemon* test—just its secular-purpose prong. In his *Kiryas Joel* (1994) dissent,

Scalia states that the religion clauses demand neutrality and that the majority would have to demonstrate that the legislative act was crafted either to "disadvantage or to benefit a religious group."[39] The court needs something to guide its decision-making. He concludes, "To replace Lemon with nothing is simply to announce that we are now so bold that we no longer feel the need even to pretend that our haphazard course of Establishment Clause decisions is governed by any principle."[40] In *McCreary* (2005), Scalia repeats the idea that discarding the *Lemon* test would have negative repercussions. The court errs, specifically, by heightening the secular-purpose prong. Rather than merely determine that the law has to advance a secular purpose, the secular purpose has to "'predominate' over any purpose to advance religion."[41] For Scalia, a secular purpose for any law can be assumed and the court should not require legislatures to prove a secular purpose that significantly outweighs any religious benefit. The fact that a law might "foster or assist religious practice is not necessarily invalidating," Scalia contends.[42] For, as his arguments about the original intent, original meaning, and historic practices of the people attest, the founders did not mean for, nor have the people understood, government to be hostile to religious expression in the public sphere.

My analysis of his Establishment Clause opinions shows that Justice Scalia does not rely upon textual analysis to decide such questions. Most frequently, he offers examples of the original meaning, as understood through the practices of governmental agents. The historic practices of the people are not based on religious practice by the average person but by national leaders, several of whom were Founding Fathers. In a sense, Scalia employs a tautological appeal. The founders meant to allow for religious expression in the public sphere, and the use of religious discourse by the founders indicates their intent. Trapped within the cycle of founding intent/original meaning, Scalia claims that the legal test created in *Lemon* (1971) reflects historic practices. Moreover, Scalia does not consider what the contemporary layperson would consider to be an establishment and only once considers what the actual text says.

Scalia on the Free Exercise Clause

Scalia has written three Free Exercise Clause opinions: the majority opinion in *Employment Division v. Smith* (1990), a concurring opinion in *Church of the Lukumi Babalu Aye v. City of Hialeah* (1993), and a dissenting opinion in *Locke v. Davey* (2004). In *Employment Division* (1990), the court upheld the state of Oregon's right to limit the ceremonial use of peyote in religious ceremonies for the Native American church. In *Lukumi Babalu Aye* (1993), the court invalidated a law that outlawed the sacrificial killing of animals as an unconstitutional violation, because the laws were not neutral or generally applicable. And in *Locke* (2004), the court upheld the state of Washington's right to deny scholarship benefits to persons majoring in religious studies.

Of greatest interest to my study of Scalia's forms of constitutional interpretation is his textualist analysis of "free exercise" in *Employment Division* (1990) and in *Locke* (2004). In the former Scalia distinguishes between belief and action, and in the latter he maintains that persons with a deep sense of religious conviction are a protected minority class of people. A consideration of these two cases quickly reveals that Scalia's reasoning in these cases conflict. In his majority opinion, he claims that religious belief and religious practice can be separated; in his dissenting opinion, he asserts that the fusion of belief and practice forms a protected class of individuals.

Scalia's *Lukumi Babalu Aye* (1993) opinion also offers interesting insights into his use (or lack thereof) of textualism. In contrast to his Establishment Clause cases, in which Scalia repeatedly asserts the intent of the founders, in this case Scalia maintains that original intent cannot be known. Hidden within his assertion, however, is an appeal to the doctrinal test set forth in *Sherbert* (1963). I turn now to how Scalia separates belief and action.

The Separation of Belief and Action

In his free exercise cases, Scalia offers a textual reading of the clause. At first blush his analysis appears to assert a textual reading, but a deeper analysis shows that even his textual analysis is used to support and to maintain a doctrinal argument.

Asserting a division between belief and action, Scalia's *Employment Division* (1990) opinion relies upon the doctrinal argument set forth in *Reynolds* (1878). "The free exercise of religion means, first and foremost, the right to believe and profess whatever religious doctrine one desires," Scalia declares.[43] Scalia links the religion clauses to the Free Speech Clause; for Scalia the exercise of religion primarily resides in one's ability to profess one's belief. He also acknowledges that the exercise of religion may involve enacting one's belief. Scalia drafts a list of possible religious acts, recognizing corporate and individual acts of faith employed by commonly accepted religious traditions, beginning with the religious exercise most widely practiced (e.g., gathering for worship) and ending with a less common practice (e.g., the Amish refusal to use motorized vehicles). He does not include minority sects whose practices are not widely accepted by contemporary culture. In fact, he finds that minority practices do not have to be accepted by the community in which they occur and can be proscribed. For Scalia, a practice is acceptable so long as it is not deemed illegal for other reasons—

in this case, the recreational use of drugs. The free exercise of religion does not exist on its own merits but is linked to other laws.

One can ask, then, what does the "free exercise of religion" mean? Does it mean the ability to practice one's religion without restraint? After considering the facts in the *Employment Division* (1990) case, Scalia concludes, "As a textual matter, we do not think the words must be given that meaning."[44] Free exercise, in *Employment Division* (1990), means a person can practice his or her religion so long as it is a practice not deemed illegal by the community. Scalia's separation of religious practice from religious belief, first instituted in *Reynolds* (1878), means that government may not regulate *belief* but may regulate *action*. We can infer, as well, that government may not regulate what a believer has to *say* about his or her faith. In fact, religiously minded actions are deemed acceptable so long as they mirror religious action engaged in by majority faith traditions. Members of the Native American Church can gather together to worship, they can pray, and they can consume certain sacrificial foods—but they cannot ingest the hallucinogenic drug peyote during a religious ceremony.

Scalia also considers the meaning of the Free Exercise Clause in his *Locke* (2004) dissent. Rather than characterize "free" as a liberty without restraint, Scalia quantifies "free." "The First Amendment, after all, guarantees free exercise of religion," he avows, "and when the State extracts a financial penalty of almost $3000 for religious exercise—whether by tax or by forfeiture of an otherwise available benefit—religious practice is anything but free."[45] Scalia alters the meaning of the term. Although "free" can mean "available without pay," neither early definitions of the term nor any former court cases used "free" in such a fashion. His rhetorical sleight of hand highlights the negative consequences of construing the term in a negative fashion rather than as the positive liberty it was meant to be.

Scalia's characterizations of the Free Exercise Clause in *Employment Division* (1990) and *Locke* (2004) are in tension. In *Employment Division* (1990), he distinguishes belief from action and thus determines that while the state cannot regulate belief, it can regulate action. Fourteen years later he determines that "free" means "available without financial cost." If Scalia had followed his *Locke* (2004) reasoning in the *Employment Division* (1990) case, he would have reached a different conclusion. He would have reasoned that petitioners in *Employment Division* (1990) could practice their religious beliefs regardless of the criminality of the action. Ingesting peyote in Oregon is a Class A felony, which can result in up to $300,000 in fines and up to twenty years in prison.[46] Such would seem to fall within the purview of Scalia's rejection of fiscal penalties for religious practice.

Scalia upholds Oregon's ability to proscribe peyote use in *Employment*

Division (1990) because the state has classified peyote as an illegal drug and has not made an exception for religious use. He denies that an otherwise generally applicable law needs to be construed as a denial of free exercise. He states the law's repudiation of religious liberty to the petitioners is an "incidental effect" of the law.[47] Scalia ignores the textual placement of the clause and the fact that the first part of the Amendment states, "Congress shall make *no law* . . . denying the free exercise of religion" (emphasis mine). Although his reasoning as to the general applicability might withstand other textual challenges, in this instance the "no law" qualifier challenges his interpretation. The agent who acts in the clause is the legislative body, not the citizen.

Moreover, the separation between belief and action that Scalia maintains is justified is a doctrinal argument, established in an earlier case without textual grounding in the Constitution. As discussed earlier, the separation of belief and action doctrine was introduced in *Reynolds* (1878). In that case, the court decided that, although a polygamist might believe that he needed to engage in plural marriage to fulfill the call of God in his life, the state nevertheless could deny him that right. And in the more than a century since, the court has upheld the distinction between belief and action time and time again.

Scalia is not consistent in his Free Exercise jurisprudence. Whereas he denies a minority a right to practice their religious beliefs in *Employment Division* (1990), in *Locke* (2004) Scalia maintains that religious action cannot be separated from religious belief. Moreover, in *Locke* (2004), he concludes that religious minorities should be protected under the Free Exercise Clause, while in *Employment Division* (1990), he denies a different religious group protection for a less orthodox religious practice.

A Religious Minority

In his two most important Free Exercise cases, Scalia sets forth different constructions of identity. In *Locke* (2004), Scalia portrays the petitioner as a member of a religious minority; in *Employment Division* (1990), he portrays the petitioners as merely individuals. Ironically, the *Locke* (2004) petitioner professes Christianity as his religious affiliation, which Scalia characterizes as a member of a religious minority. The petitioners in *Employment Division* (1990), on the other hand, are members of the Native American church and thus members of a religious minority. In his *Locke* (2004) opinion, Scalia constructs the majority member as a minority and does not grant minority status to the minority member.

In the *Locke* (2004) case, Scalia chastises the court majority for refusing to protect a religious minority and upholding a law intentionally hostile to those with religious faith. In his dissent he proclaims, "This case is about discriminating against a religious minority."[48] One would think a religious minority would have few members or, at the very least, be smaller than a religious majority, examples of which include Judaism, Islam, Hinduism, Buddhism, and Paganism in the United States. Since Christianity claims more than 70 percent of the American population, it would not be considered a religious *minority* in any sense of the term.[49] Yet Scalia does not construct "religious minority" according to number of persons who practice the faith tradition. Rather, a religious minority is an individual within a majority religion who enacts his faith in a way that Scalia argues few others enact. According to Scalia's reasoning, the majority includes anyone professing any faith. Religious minorities are persons who devote their professional career to advance a religious calling. Never mind that hundreds of religiously affiliated institutions of higher education exist in the United States, many of whom offer degrees in pastoral studies. Scalia's minority is a subset within the dominant cultural set. In this case his protected minority is a young man who desired to study religion to enter into full-time vocational ministry as a pastor. According to Scalia, most Americans have a "tepid, civic version of faith," which implies either that a large number of persons have a belief but do not put that belief into practice or that most Americans simply use the language of civil religion without the belief.[50]

Throughout his dissent Scalia equates the persecution of a religious minority as analogous to discrimination against a racial minority. Since one cannot separate his faith from his actions, just as one cannot separate his race from the color of his skin, laws must be neutral—they can neither favor or disfavor any particular race nor benefit or hinder religious groups or individuals. Religion laws demand neutrality in their application. Thus, legislatures cannot single out religious minorities—persons who practice their beliefs—while allowing everyone else to benefit from a piece of legislation, in this case a scholarship program. Since the true believer cannot separate belief and action, to enact harm against him based upon his belief system is unacceptable.

In *Employment Division* (1990), the drug rehabilitation officers are not constructed as members of a minority sect—the Native American Church—but as individuals. In the opinion, Scalia refers to "an individual's religious beliefs"[51] and "an individual's religion,"[52] asking, "can a man excuse his practices to the contrary because of his religious belief?"[53] Scalia concludes no, "an individual's obligation to obey" the law does not depend upon his religious beliefs, because to do so would make him "a law unto himself."[54] According to Scalia, the individual does not have the power to violate communal norms—only a collection of persons identified as a religious minority does. Although Scalia could have placed the drug rehabilitation offers within the Native American Church community, tribal law, not by US law, regulates Native American property. Therefore, the community of believers within the Native American Church tradition, who may ingest peyote as part of their religious ceremony, largely exists outside the boundaries of US law; their religious practice is not subject to US restrictions. Scalia thus leaves the rehab officers as individuals with a personal faith who violate a generally acceptable law. Importantly, a textual reading of the Free Exercise Clause does not support a separation between the individual and the community; nor does it point to the person (or community) of faith as a modifier of legislative action. Rather, the clause mandates that *Congress* make no law, not that Congress allows majority religions to practice their faith tradition but refuses to grant the same right to religious minorities. The agent in the clause is the legislative branch, not the individual *or* the community.

It is important, as well, to clarify how Scalia distinguishes *Employment Division* (1990), in which he rejected the petitioners' free exercise claim, from *Locke* (2004), in which he rejected the majority's denial of free exercise, regarding the criminality of the act and the general applicability of the law. In *Employment Division* (1990), Oregon's criminal prohibition against peyote use, a generally applicable law, applied to every individual. In *Locke* (2004), Washington's clause, which exempted religious studies majors from benefiting from the scholarship, singled out religious faith as an unacceptable exception.

Original Intent

In his extrajudicial writings and speeches Scalia rails against the use of legislative intent, advocating instead for the use of original meaning. Scalia offers no arguments in the way of original intent/meaning in the two free exercise cases discussed above. Yet he raises the matter of original intent in *Lukumi Babalu Aye* (1993), when he claims the court cannot determine legislative intent. "The First Amendment does not refer to the purposes for which legislators enact laws, but to the effects of those laws enacted," Scalia proclaims.[55] Scalia is, in fact, wrong. His statement suggests that a textual reading tells us that we do not need to pursue intent but should be attuned to the results of the law. The text merely tells us that an agent (Congress) should not use its constitutional function (law-making) to create an object (a law prohibiting the free exercise of religion). By claiming that the courts should be attuned to the effects of a law, Scalia invokes the specter of the *Sherbert* test, which asks whether the government has burdened an individual's free exercise of religion (and, if it has, whether the government can prove it has a compelling interest to do so and, if so, that it did so in the least restrictive manner possible). To better reflect the logical move Scalia has made in *Lukumi Babalu Aye* (1993), one would need to revise his statement to read, "The First Amendment, as interpreted by previous Courts, does not refer to the purposes for which legislators enact laws but must apply the *Sherbert* test by asking if the government had a compelling interest to burden one's free exercise rights and, if so, did so in the least restrictive fashion possible." Although he suggests a textual reading of the clause, the underlying interpretive strategy he uses is doctrinal. We see, in this one sentence, Scalia suggest textualism, reject originalism, and use doctrinalism—a rhetorical move he would criticize in his extrajudicial speeches and writings.

In his free exercise cases we see, once again, that Scalia does not rely upon the plain meaning of the text to craft his legal opinion. In one case he relies upon doctrinal reasoning, in another he contorts a textualist reading into the form he wants the law to take, and in another he purports to use textualist reasoning while in fact using a doctrinal argument.

Conclusion

As expected, the Establishment Clause and the Free Exercise Clause create problematic sites of analysis for Scalia. They do not do so because the clauses themselves are in tension; they do so because Scalia does not rely upon the strict forms of interpretation that he advocates in his extrajudicial speeches and writings. As a result, Scalia struggles with how to interpret the religion clauses and relies upon forms of reasoning that he would reject if he were to identify them as such. Scalia's rhetorical fiction that a textualist reading of the religion clauses would produce a better result cannot be tested, because Scalia neglects to use textual interpretation in this area of law.

As a textual matter, one religion clause easily provides a plain meaning, whereas the other does not. The court treats the Establishment Clause as problematic, because the judiciary cannot determine what constitutes an establishment of religion. If the court were to read the clause as merely prohibiting legislation respecting a religion—as the text sets forth—the court would allow for accommodation and nonpreferential religious displays on public property. But the court worries about perception, for if a religious display were to be on public property, would an auditor understand that artifact to represent an establishment of religion, even if no law has been passed? Rather than employ the plain meaning of the text, which would allow for a wide variety of religious expression on public property, Scalia blends the Establishment Clause with free speech (another fundamental right), creating a convoluted reading of the clause that does not allow it to stand on its own textual merit; rather, it must rest upon the foundation of free speech. On the other hand, the court regards the Free Exercise Clause as easy to interpret, because the justices do not have to determine the sincerity of belief but merely ensure that individuals are able to pursue their freedom of conscience. Scalia again does not rely upon the plain meaning of the text but transforms the plain meaning from "without restraint" to "without financial cost." Although the founding generation understood the free exercise of religion to prohibit taxation upon churches, Scalia extends the meaning from a protection of *churches* to a protection of religious *individuals*. Doing so employs a contemporary twist on the language of the clause, violating the textual trust supposedly established through strict readings of the law. The language of the text does not mean what one would understand it to mean within the textual boundaries of the clause but allows for alternative connotative meanings of a term or a phrase. Although a self-declared textualist, Scalia utilizes few textualist arguments in his religion law decisions and offers textual interpretations that do not rely upon a plain reading of the law. Consequently, textualism is not advanced as a necessary method of constitutional interpretation.

The Establishment Clause continues to be a complicated matter to adjudicate. When the Constitution was adopted in 1788, all states, except Rhode Island and Pennsylvania, supported established state religions. The clause therefore did not apply to the states; it applied to the national government. The incorporation of the clause to the states thus violated the original intent and the original meaning of the document. Scalia thus attempts to construct a version of originalism that is not faithful to the founding generation. Citing references to God from national leaders, upon our money, and in our Pledge, Scalia's references to the traditional practices of the people are an attempt to locate original meaning. Ultimately the examples he offers do not point to original *meaning* so much as they indicate original *intent*. Scalia's reference to the founders' intent directly refutes his argument against intent in his "Common-Law Courts" essay. "It is the *law* that governs, not the intent of the lawgiver," Scalia asserts.[56] Yet Scalia repeatedly points to the intent of the founders to support the interpretive angle he chooses to advance.

Although Scalia criticizes doctrinal arguments as loose readings with little fidelity to the constitutional text, within his religion clause cases he repeatedly returns to doctrinal arguments. In his Establishment Clause cases, he supports two out of the three prongs identified in the *Lemon* test. According to Scalia, the test provides some semblance of a method for interpreting this area of law, other than as the personal preferences of the persons who sit on the bench. His acquiescence to the test indicates that textualism and originalism do not provide sufficient means by which to understand this area of law. It stands to reason that if they did, Scalia would not use the doctrinal test. The same applies to his free exercise cases. He advances doctrinal arguments from the *Sherbert* test in his *Lukumi Babalu Aye* (1993) free exercise opinion, even though he does not name the test (most likely because he refused to use the doctrine in his majority opinion in *Employment Division* [1990]).

In the end, Scalia's religion law opinions do little to stabilize religion law. Because the Establishment Clause is joined with the Free Speech Clause, few actions or displays constitute an establishment of religion for Scalia. The original intent and historic practices mean religion should be welcome in the public sphere. If the religious expression, icon, or practice represents a generally accepted expression of faith, then Scalia allows for its use on public property. Perhaps the only limitation would be to name an official national or state religion. In free exercise cases, Scalia offers competing notions of what "free exercise" means. In one case he determines that a separation exists between belief and action, and in another case he claims that to engage in free exercise makes one a protected minority. His contradictory explication of "free exercise" gives no guidance to lower courts attempting to predict how the court will decide future cases. He rejects—in part or in full—doctrinal arguments in both areas of law, yet he nevertheless employs them in his own legal justification. Scalia maintains certain divisions and parameters that earlier religion cases set forth, divisions that even he does not fully believe are consistent with "reasonable" interpretations of the constitutional text's language. Although the religion clauses might demand neutrality, as Scalia opines in *Locke* (2004), he does not apply neutral principles to his adjudication of this area of law. These clauses, which are in tension with one another, again fail to illuminate how Scalia's textual tale can be told in his appellate jurisprudence.

5

When the Constitution Is Silent

Rejecting the Right to an Abortion

> I continue to believe . . . that the Constitution contains no right to abortion. It is not to be found in the longstanding traditions of our society, nor can it be logically deduced from the text of the Constitution—not, that is, without volunteering a judicial answer to the nonjusticiable question of when human life begins.
>
> —Justice Antonin Scalia

The Constitution does not mention a right to an abortion. How, therefore, did the Supreme Court reach its decision in *Roe v. Wade* (1973) that the US Constitution guarantees a woman a right to an elective abortion? Although few people other than constitutional scholars are aware of its genesis, the right to an abortion did not begin with the human body or reproductive rights but with a technological innovation. In 1928 the Supreme Court handed down *Olmstead v. United States* (1928). In *Olmstead* (1928) the majority held that the US government's use of wiretaps against private citizens was not a violation of the Fourth Amendment's prohibition against illegal searches and seizures (an opinion overturned almost forty years later in *Katz v. United States* [1967]). In Justice Louis Brandeis's landmark dissent in *Olmstead* (1928), he famously asserted that individuals have the "right to be let alone."[1] He wrote, "The makers of our Constitution . . . sought to protect Americans in their beliefs, their thoughts, their emotions and their sensations. They conferred, as against the government, the right to be let alone—the most comprehensive of rights and the right most valued by civilized men."[2] For Brandeis, information obtained via an illegitimate wiretap violated the Fourth Amendment. Furthermore, when information unlawfully obtained subsequently was used during a trial as evidence of wrongdoing, that information unconstitutionally violated the Fifth Amendment by forcing an individual to bear witness against himself.

In *Olmstead* (1928), Brandeis set forth the doctrine of privacy implicit in two earlier cases. Both *Meyer v. Nebraska* (1923)[3] and *Pierce v. Society of Sisters* (1925)[4] consider the ability of parents to make decisions regarding the education of their children. In *Meyer* (1923), the court overturned a law that banned the teaching of foreign languages to children before the ninth grade, and in *Pierce* (1925), the court rejected a law that required students to attend a public, rather than a parochial, school. In both cases Justice James Clark McReynolds relied upon the Due Process Clause of the Fourteenth Amendment to substantiate his claim. Specifically, when considering the meaning of liberty, McReynolds employed substantive due process (rather than procedural due process). Substantive due process protects the materiality of human rights (e.g., privacy), whereas procedural due process guarantees courses of action (e.g., a quick and speedy trial). Under substantive due process, the Fourteenth Amendment protects a wide variety of rights, as individuals have the right to seek self-actualization in any form that does not violate the general laws of the state or the rights of another human being. Within *Meyer* (1923) and *Pierce* (1925), a right to be let alone within the realm of the home and the family can be inferred. Brandeis's negative liberty, the "right to be let alone" (free from governmental intrusion), shifted into a positive liberty, the "right to privacy" (free to engage in whatever behavior you desire within the seclusion of your home), in Justice William O. Douglas's *Griswold v. Connecticut* (1965) opinion.

Griswold (1965) took up the issue of marital privacy when it overturned a state law prohibiting the possession, sale, and distribution of contraceptives to married couples. In his majority opinion, Douglas states that earlier cases indicate that the specific guarantees of the amendments to the Constitution "have penumbras, formed by emanations from those guarantees that help give them life and substance."[5] In other words, the specific protections found within the amendments to the Constitution cast shadows of other rights. For Douglas, several of the amendments of the Bill of Rights come together to create a general "right to privacy." Following Douglas's line of reasoning, Justice Harry Blackmun in *Roe* (1973) extends the "right to privacy" to a woman's ability to abort a fetus, detailing the amendments that come together to guarantee the right.

In 1973 the Supreme Court handed down *Roe v. Wade*, which held that a "zone of privacy" could be gleaned from the First, Fourth, Fifth, Ninth, and Fourteenth Amendments to the Constitution.[6] In his majority opinion, Blackmun reasons that, although the Constitution does not mention privacy, multiple amendments protect, and a line of cases support, an individual's right to privacy. The right to privacy pervades a wide range of areas, from the right to consume pornography and be protected against unreasonable searches and seizures to decisions about procreation and conception, marrying a person of a different race, and rearing your children. At issue in these cases, Blackmun explains, is the question of whether the issue at hand represents an aspirational right that would need to be protected to secure the rights enumerated. Rights not enumerated include those rights that protect the person himself or herself. Blackmun's reasoning leads him to conclude that the right to privacy extends to a woman's decision to terminate her pregnancy. Privacy has no meaning, Blackmun contends, if the court does not allow for technological advances that alter how an individual's privacy can be breached beyond those traditionally understood by the founders.

When the court decided *Roe* (1973), the judiciary attempted to remove the controversy from the political realm to the legal realm. Their efforts failed. In the years since *Roe* (1973), the potential for compromise has diminished, moral extremes have become prominent, abortion rights have expanded judicially, and rational public discourse on abortion issues has all but disappeared. Frequently abortion is considered a "closed" area of law; *Roe* (1973) established the precedent that a woman has a "right to privacy," a decision most legal scholars doubt will soon be overruled by the judicial body that created it. Nevertheless, prolife advocates in the states continually have sought to limit the incidence of abortion within their borders. These attempts have resulted in cases before the court that consider location for the procedure, waiting periods, spousal and parental notification and consent, judicial bypass for minors, and different procedures.

Later Court decisions considered constraints on the right to an abortion as well as the state interest in protecting potential life. In *City of Akron v. Akron Center for Reproductive Health* (1983), the court found Akron's ordinance that all second-trimester abortions be performed in a hospital to be a violation of the woman's due process.[7] The court also found the ordinance's parental consent, informed consent, twenty-four-hour waiting period, and fetal remains disposal requirements to be unconstitutional. In *Webster* (1989), the court upheld states' ability to limit abortion funding to indigents, claiming that the use of funds to encourage childbirth and to discourage abortions is a constitutional use of state power. In *Hodgson* (1990), the court held a Minnesota statute requiring parental notification of both parents, even with judicial bypass, to be an unconstitutional violation of a minor's due process right to seek an abortion. In *Casey* (1992), the court upheld the decisional liberty of a woman to terminate a pregnancy but abandoned the trimester framework, adopting stronger "viability" language instead. *Casey* (1992) also maintained that the woman had to give her informed consent twenty-four hours before the procedure and that a minor had to receive both parental informed consent and judicial bypass, except in cases of "medical emergency." The case also overturned the spousal consent requirement of the

Pennsylvania statute, declaring it to be an unconstitutional violation of the woman's due process. In *Bray* (1993), the court rejected a claim that abortion clinic protesters obstructing the entrance to clinics violated a woman's right to an abortion. In *Carhart* (2000), the court found a prohibition against intact dilation and extraction procedures to be an undue burden on a woman's right to abort. In *Whole Woman's Health* (2016), the court determined that a Texas law requiring doctors to have admitting privileges and abortion clinics to have facilities comparable to an ambulatory surgical center constituted an undue burden on the right to an abortion.[8]

In 1992 the Supreme Court attempted to right the perceived wrong of *Roe* (1973) in *Planned Parenthood v. Casey*. Constitutional scholars and political commentary had criticized Blackmun's support of abortion since the decision was handed down, challenging the idea that the penumbras and emanations derived from a collection of constitutional amendments created a right to privacy. Advancing a substantive due process argument, the *Casey* (1992) plurality abandoned the right to privacy in favor of a decisional liberty to obtain an abortion. Grounded in the Fourteenth Amendment's Due Process Clause, the *Casey* (1992) plurality argued that a woman's right to an abortion was a substantive due process right—a decisional liberty, to be specific. By locating its holding in the language of the Fourteenth Amendment, *Casey* (1992) found firm footing for the right to an abortion as a decisional liberty right to an abortion.

Since *Roe* (1973), the court has struggled with where to draw the line in abortion cases. In general, the court has upheld state laws if the statutes or ordinances do not violate the decisional liberty of a woman to seek an abortion, yet the court has acknowledged that the right to an abortion is a conditional right. The court recognizes the state's interest in fetal life as the fetus approaches viability and can craft legislation that gives preference to childbirth over abortion in public funding determinations.

Scalia on Abortion

The question arises as to how Scalia justifies a textual interpretation when the Constitution is silent with regard to a particular issue. Interestingly enough, Scalia's clearest example of what a textualist approach to constitutional interpretation should "look like" occurs in his abortion opinions. In each of these opinions, Scalia argues that the Constitution does not protect a woman's right to an elective abortion. He reasons that because the Constitution is "silent" on (i.e., does not mention) abortion, the courts should not adjudicate the issue. Scalia maintains that abortion is not a legal issue. Rather, abortion is a moral question and elected officials answerable to the public at the ballot box should determine abortion policy. According to Scalia, when the High Court passes judgment on abortion issues, it is overreaching its sphere of influence, creating bad law that harms its credibility.

In this chapter I examine all six of Scalia's abortion opinions.[9] His first three abortion opinions are relatively brief, mostly asserting his objection to adjudicating abortion law. His *Casey* (1992) opinion, however, is an extended analysis of the majority's reasoning, critiquing the majority's use of the phrase "undue burden." His *Bray* (1993) opinion offers an in-depth examination of legal principles brought forth by the parties in the case regarding access to abortions. His *Stenberg* (2000) dissent returns to a relatively brief objection to abortion decisions, with prolife objections included. Before I examine Scalia's arguments against the right to an abortion, however, it is important to address Scalia's point about the Constitution being silent in regard to abortion.

Absence and Silence

Scalia repeatedly argues that the Constitution does not contain the right to an abortion and that the document is silent about the controversial topic. To make this argument about abortion, Scalia uses two metaphors: a container metaphor and an organic metaphor. The container metaphor conjures a static constitution that is fixed and unchanging, a hermeneutic approach consistent with his public lectures and extrajudicial writings. The organic metaphor implicates a living Constitution, which Scalia rails against in his lectures, writings, and judicial opinions. Scalia's personification of the Constitution as "silent," "speaking to," and "protecting" certain rights suggest that the Constitution is an independent, organic entity that has the capacity for judgment.

Linguists George Lakoff and Mark Johnson explain that metaphors guide our lives by organizing our thinking in their landmark work, *Metaphors We Live By*.[10] The metaphors we use determine the reality we experience. This statement is not news; Lakoff and Johnson's work, which argues that metaphors are "pervasive in everyday life, not just in language but in thought and action," is widely accepted.[11]

For Scalia, the Constitution is a container filled with enumerated laws that lays out the structures, procedures, guarantees, and propositions judges are to read and to interpret. The metaphor of Constitution as container asserts that the Constitution does not contain a right to an abortion because it does not directly *list* abortion as a right. In his most direct use of the metaphor, Scalia contends, "the Constitution contains no right to an abortion."[12] Since the text does not mention such a right, the constitutional container does not hold such a right. In another case Scalia explains, "One will search in vain the document we are supposed to be construing for text that provides the basis for the argument over these distinctions."[13] Digging around through the barrel of the Constitution will not produce a right that has no material reality within its textual frame. Since the Constitution does not contain a right to abort, Scalia concludes that the court should not adjudicate abortion law—abortion should be left to the legislatures.

For Scalia, activist judges are the villains of our national narrative. Judges may have to decide cases in a manner not supported by the public. But that is why justices on the Supreme Court are appointed without term—they are put on the High Bench to do the right thing (by following and implementing the law) regardless of context. Scalia explains that justices appointed to the Supreme Court are granted "extraordinary, undemocratic characteristics precisely in order that we might follow the law despite popular will."[14] Judges should not be swayed by popular opinion; they exist outside of the political process to interpret the law as it is written. In case after case, Scalia repeats the idea that judges are not to *draft* law; they are to *interpret* the law. Within the area of abortion law, specifically, Scalia criticizes justices who rely upon their personal proclivities rather than refuse to adjudicate an area of law about which the Constitution is silent. Within the area of abortion law, the majority has invented its own tale—the story that women have a right to abort the unborn. In his opinions Scalia indicates that the court has overstepped its constitutional function of interpreting the law to reach into the realm of the legislature by drafting and amending law. In *Casey* (1992), he maintains the justices attempt to adjudicate the law based upon the "social consensus" of its readership.[15] Within our system of separation of powers, judicial functions and legislative functions are distinct. And, according to Scalia, judges are not equipped with the skills needed to draft legislation.

For Scalia, the Constitution is the hero of our national narrative. The Constitution determines the fundamental rights and liberties guaranteed to individuals. According to Scalia's organic metaphor, the Constitution, not the judge/justice, is the active agent in constitutional interpretation. The organic Constitution follows other organic metaphors used to enhance public understanding of political systems and dominates current metaphoric constructions of political structure in the United States (e.g., the president of the United States as "head of state," citizens as the "body politic," the "birth" of our nation, the United States as "Uncle Sam," and liberty as a "lady").[16] That Scalia draws upon the organic metaphor is telling; it indicates that, try as he might, even he has difficulty escaping the organic metaphor. For, as Lakoff and Johnson tell us, metaphors influence Scalia's thinking—even the organic metaphor he detests.

In his more recent abortion opinions Scalia portrays the Constitution as both silent and having the capacity for voice, as well as for prohibiting action and protecting rights. In these opinions the Constitution is personified in different ways, including as an authority figure requiring acquiescence, a bodyguard securing safety, and an educator informing the public. The authority figure first shows up in *Casey* (1992): "The State may, if they wish, permit abortion on demand, but the Constitution does not *require* them to do so."[17] It is also present in *Carhart* (2000): "The notion that the Constitution of the United States . . . *prohibits* the States from simply banning this visibly brutal means of eliminating our half-born posterity is quite simply absurd."[18] Scalia presents the Constitution as protector in *Casey* (1992) and in *Bray* (1993): "The issue is whether it is a liberty *protected* by the Constitution of the United States. I am sure it is not";[19] and "It would be most peculiar to accord [abortion] that preferred position, since it is much less explicitly protected by the Constitution, than, for example, the right of free speech."[20] He grants the constitutional agent voice to instruct the public in *Casey* (1992)—"The Constitution *says* absolutely nothing about it"[21]—and *Carhart* (2000) —"It has been arrived at by precisely the process *Casey promised*—a democratic vote by nine lawyers, not on the question whether the text of the Constitution has anything to *say* about this subject (*it obviously does not*)."[22] The Constitution fulfills many roles in our national narrative; it commands us, protects us, and guides us. What we need to realize, however, is that personifying the Constitution suggests that the Constitution is self-determining and hides the role of the judge in the judicial decision-making process.

Scalia's uses of the container metaphor and the organic metaphor work toward opposing ends. The Constitution-as-container is passive; it does not change on its own nor have the ability to influence others (unless used toward that end by judges or the executive branch). The Constitution-as-organic-person is active; rather than interpreted by an external agent—in this case the justices of the Supreme Court—the text assumes agency to express its own will. The Constitution-as-container embodies a philosophy of strict interpretation. In other words, the Constitution cannot mean more than it means. The Constitution-as-organic-person represents a philosophy of loose interpretation. For justices who support expansive readings of the constitutional text, the organic metaphor results in a "living" Constitution. Not so for Scalia. His organic metaphor grants agency to the document without allowing it to evolve. The authorizing Constitution, for Scalia, speaks (or is silent) about its provisions, protects rights, and calls (or does not call) for action. The constitutional persona is less an evolving entity and more of an autocratic automaton. Nevertheless, Scalia's use of the organic metaphor indicates the powerful force the metaphor has within contemporary society: a justice who disagrees with the idea of an organic document and yet cannot escape its prevailing reach.

Textualism and Historicism

In his abortion opinions Scalia tells a story of justices crafting their own legislative code, regardless of separation of powers. His passion to protect the integrity of the constitutional text rests on two factors: the Constitution's silence about abortion and the historical practice of allowing states to proscribe or to restrict the practice. Unlike his Eighth Amendment jurisprudence, which bases its decisions mostly on the historic practices of the people, in *Casey* (1992), Scalia does not turn to the historic practices of the people until after he addresses the Constitution's "silence," although the two arguments frequently go hand in hand.

Scalia crafts a narrative of competing voices: his voice against those of activist judges. Whereas the plurality argues that abortion is a liberty protected by the Constitution, Scalia disagrees. Since the Constitution does not address abortion rights, a woman does not have a fundamental right to abort a fetus. Scalia does not deny that abortion could be constructed as a liberty right, but such a right is a lesser right, not a fundamental one. Fundamental rights include the freedom of speech, the freedom of religion, the freedom of association, procedural due process of the law, and the equal protection of the law—rights without which our system of government would not be able to function. For Scalia, citizens have many rights in addition to their fundamental rights; yet these supplemental rights are limited. They can be restricted—or completely proscribed—by the states. In his narrative of competing perspectives, Scalia portrays himself as protecting the integrity of the Constitution while the plurality bastardizes the document.

Scalia argues that if abortion were protected by the Constitution, then legal decisions regarding abortion would be stable. According to Scalia, the court erred when it created a right to privacy that protected the right to an abortion and the court extends its mistake in *Casey* (1992). For although the court has changed its reasoning, the new legal reasoning it adopted (substantive due process) is no more valid than the right to privacy doctrine established in *Roe* (1973). Moreover, *Roe* (1973) allowed a state to proscribe abortion in the third trimester, because of the state's interest in protecting the life of a fetus. Therefore, the *Casey* (1992) plurality is wrong to conclude that any law that might discourage abortion would constitute an "undue burden" on the right to an abortion.

Brief Responses

With the exceptions of *Casey* (1992) and *Bray* (1993), Scalia crafts brief responses in his abortion cases. His *Webster* (1989) and *Carhart* (2000) opinions span four full pages in the United States Reports, and his *Hodgson* (1990) and *Akron* (1990) opinions cover one full page each. He uses these opinions to express his disagreement with the court's use of stare decisis—precedence from an earlier opinion—to support abortion. Since Scalia contends that the court should not decide abortion cases, it follows that his opinions are short; he needs merely to state that he disagrees with the court's findings. He contends that a bad decision (*Roe* [1973]) should not be upheld merely because it serves as precedence. According to Scalia, the court should correct its past errors by overturning *Roe* (1973) and refusing to adjudicate abortion. The brevity of Scalia's opinions, combined with his lack of response to the majority opinion (instead of, for example, expressing disfavor for the "political" nature of the decision and highlighting the lack of a clear message to lower courts and other levels of government), corresponds with his belief that the court should not be adjudicating abortion. Form follows content in this case. If the Constitution is silent on the matter of abortion, then it does not require much prose to say that the Constitution does not consider the issue. If Scalia were to construct arguments discussing previous case history, a woman's "right to choose," or the constitutionality of state laws policing abortion, he would undermine his entire argument by validating his opposing justices' reasoning. For Scalia, *Roe* (1973) was decided incorrectly. Thus, Scalia rhetorically is restricted to declaring that the court should not adjudicate abortion. Because the court mistakenly stepped into the political world of abortion, it follows that its decisions have been fragmented.

Scalia refutes the argument that abortion needs to be upheld simply because it has been the law for so long. His primary opponent is Justice Sandra Day O'Connor, who asserts *Roe* (1973) should not be overthrown—even if it is "bad law"—because it has been the law of the land for decades. Scalia cites examples of recent decisions, joined by O'Connor, in which a new rule of constitutional law has replaced an earlier rule. In *Webster* (1989), Scalia does not see fit to discuss the merits of the case at hand, nor does he consider the majority opinion's reasoning (with which he does not agree). Rather, he writes a separate concurrence to respond to O'Connor's *concurring* opinion, which argues that the constitutionality of *Roe* (1973) does not have to be reconsidered at the present time. Scalia disagrees. Frustrated by what he perceives as the court's insistence upon overturning *Roe* (1973) in an incremental fashion, rather than in one fell swoop, Scalia chastises his fellow justices for their judicial legislating.

Scalia uses his short opinions, such as his one in *Hodgson* (1990), to highlight the court's confused thinking caused by trying to adjudicate a political issue. Portraying himself as a common person trying to understand the court's decision, Scalia explains the decision and opinions as he understands them. Scalia's summary of the court's fragmented decision highlights its political nature. Since the Constitution does not provide any direction in abortion, the justices base their decisions upon how they think this case should be decided, not upon how the Constitution commands it to be. The splintered decision leads Scalia to assert, "One will search in vain the document we are supposed to be construing for text that provides the basis for the argument over these distinctions; and will find in our society's tradition regarding abortion no hint that the distinctions are constitutionally relevant, much less any indication how a constitutional argument about them ought to be resolved."[23] Since one purpose of Supreme Court decisions is to give direction and guidance to lower courts in decision-making, Scalia wonders how the convoluted decision can offer guidance? If one of the greatest legal minds cannot understand the decision, how can the lower courts, the legislators, or the people themselves understand the decision? Scalia's summary highlights the increased fragmentation of the court concerning the constitutionality of abortion law and emphasizes the fact that this area of law confuses, rather than clarifies, states' ability to legislate abortion.

Abortion Is a Political Issue, Not a Legal Issue

Unlike the majority of the court in most abortion cases, Scalia wants to remove himself from the legal narrative about abortion by shifting abortion questions from the judicial branch back to the political arena. From his first opinion to his last, Scalia contends that abortion is a political issue, not a legal quandary, and should be treated as such. The justices should not act as legislators, crafting law and rewriting the Constitution. Rather, popularly elected representatives, persons accountable to the public at the ballot box, should determine abortion legislation. From his opinions we learn that Scalia thinks shifting abortion back to the legislative realm would create discursive space for public debate and policy variation.

A fundamental issue for Scalia is the proper role for members of the judiciary as opposed to the proper role for members of the legislature. In *Webster* (1989), Scalia argues that the majority has co-opted legislative functions and powers. They exhibit "judicial statesmanship," granting themselves a "self-awarded sovereignty."[24] The term "statesmanship" typically refers to someone who governs over the political realm. "Sovereignty," moreover, is the ability of a nation-state to govern itself. The judicial branch, the "least democratic branch" of government, was not created to be responsive to the people. Judges do not concern themselves with being "statesmen" or protecting the "sovereignty" of the nation-state per se.

Scalia repeats the idea that abortion is a political issue and not a legal one in all of his abortion opinions. He addresses the issue through two means: first, through claiming that the judicial branch should not decide abortion issues and, second, through affirming that the judicial process circumvents the democratic process. Some of his remarks are brief, pithy one-liners, whereas others offer more extended commentary on the ill effects of the court's actions. His remarks are, by turns, straightforward, sarcastic, biting, impassioned, and resigned. In *Akron* (1990), Scalia avers, "Leaving this matter to the political process is not only legally correct, it is pragmatically so."[25] His short remarks characterize him as a prim and proper justice, willing to adjudicate only what the law allows. In *Hodgson* (1990), he remarks, "I continue to dissent from this enterprise of devising an Abortion Code, and from the illusion that we have authority to do so."[26] He portrays himself as someone with long-suffering opposition to adjudicating abortion. In *Casey* (1992), he chastises, "It is difficult to maintain the illusion that we are interpreting a Constitution rather than inventing one, when we amend its provisions so breezily."[27] The interpreter-justice expresses disdain for the wayward practices of his colleagues. He passionately continues: "By foreclosing all democratic outlet for the deep passions this issue arouses, by banishing the issue from the political forum that gives all participants, even the losers, the satisfaction of a fair hearing and an honest fight, by continuing the imposition of a rigid national rule instead of allowing for regional differences, the court merely prolongs and intensifies the anguish. We should get out of this area, where we have no right to be, and where we do neither ourselves nor the country any good by remaining."[28] Scalia calls his peers to repent from their sinful ways. In *Bray* (1993), he declares, "If only for the sake of its own preservation, the court should return this matter to the people—where the Constitution, by its silence on the subject, left it—and let them decide, State by State, whether this practice should be allowed."[29] Finally, in *Carhart* (2000), Scalia appears resigned, as he contends that the decision in this case is the logical result of the court's previous adjudication: "The most that we can honestly say is that we disagree with the majority on their policy-judgment-couched-as-law. And those who believe that a 5-to-4 vote on a policy matter by unelected lawyers should not overcome the judgment of 30 state legislatures have a problem, not with the application of *Casey*, but with its existence."[30] In each of these statements, Scalia identifies a division between "the political" and "the judicial." Although one might think that the realm of the judicial falls within the larger realm of the political, one can infer from Scalia's remark that each realm would have distinct characteristics that make them mutually exclusive from one another. Such boundaries should not necessarily be collapsed into the different branches of government, since both the executive and the legislative branches would be concerned with the political.

How, then, could one identify the judicial realm? The distinction cannot rest on the fact that judges are not elected but appointed, for many judges at the state and local levels are elected. The distinction would seem to rest upon the law, as the judicial seems to deal with law and the political with political issues. Yet the legislature has no such limitations. The legislature creates law that the executive branch implements, legislative law commonly referred to as statutory law. Again, what then distinguishes the judicial? For Scalia, in the realm of abortion, it would seem that the judicial is relegated to the textual lines of the Constitution, which do not contain such a right. Abortion belongs to the political realm. And since the two realms are mutually exclusive, the judicial has no jurisdiction in the question of the constitutionality of abortion.

The story Scalia tells is one of wayward justices decreeing social policy from the High Bench. Scalia uses the phrase "abortion code" in several of his opinions, implying that the Supreme Court has drafted legislation. Codes are created by legislatures, not by the courts. National codes regulate every aspect of the political process, from the election of elected officials to the rules of lobbying. National codes also direct the functioning of bureaucracy. State codes regulate criminal behavior, and municipal codes regulate anything from animals to zoning. The enactment of codes systematizes and standardizes the functioning of government and the life of its citizens. Scalia's protest against the crafting of an abortion code is his way of saying that the court has stepped into the legislative domain. The court has the power to determine the constitutionality of national, state, and local codes, but the court does not have the power to craft new codes.

Scalia provides two reasons why judges should not legislate: judicial training and separation of powers. First, judges are trained in the law, not practiced in politics. Scalia writes in *Hodgson* (1990), "The tools for this job [legislating] are not to be found in the lawyer's—and hence not in the judge's—workbox."[31] Second, public opinion should not influence the court, since the court frequently has to protect individuals and the rights of minorities. Justices are appointed for life, their terms of office extending beyond that of the person who appointed them. Within this undemocratic branch of government, the public will encourage justices to enact social policy; justices should resist. By handing down decisions that should be determined by the legislative branch, the court opens itself up to political pressures from which it should be insulated.

Scalia's abortion decisions, more than his other judicial opinions, underscore his belief that there is a separation between what is political and what is judicial. The boundary line between the two means that while politicians can act upon what they believe to be the communal good, judges cannot. Judges act upon what is the law, not what they think the law should be.

Abortion's Dialogue: The Court's Misguided Taneys

Scalia's *Casey* (1992) opinion differs from all of his other abortion opinions. In this opinion, Scalia creates a dialogue between himself and the plurality opinion. While most concurrences and dissents are a dialogue between the justices, with the authoring justice responding to the majority's arguments, Scalia's opinion stylistically differs from most minor opinions. In *Casey* (1992), Scalia quotes and then responds to the plurality opinion. He creates a Socratic dialogue between the two opinions, instead of a general discussion of points that characterizes most dissents. Since the aim of dialogue is truth, Scalia uses this format to attack the plurality and to bolster his position. Scalia begins by denying the constitutionality of a liberty argument in the abortion issue. He rejects any notion that his own predilections direct his decision-making. Instead he argues that the Constitution does not contain a right to an abortion. He then begins his simulated dialogue with the majority opinion.

Scalia denies the majority opinion's assertion that it used "reasoned judgment" in deciding *Roe* (1973). He rejects this claim on the grounds that no one can determine whether a fetus is human life or "merely potentially human"—such a question is a "value judgment." He then challenges the majority's argument that abortion is a fundamental liberty. According to Scalia: "The emptiness of the 'reasoned judgment' that produced *Roe* is displayed in plain view. . . . The best the Court can do to explain how it is that the word 'liberty' *must* be thought to include the right to destroy human fetuses is to rattle off a collection of adjectives that simply decorate a value judgment and conceal a political choice."[32] For Scalia, these rattled off words are expressions of individual ideology, not the values of the Constitution. Abortion can be compared to polygamy, incest, sodomy, and suicide—all of which the court has determined can be banned.

Next Scalia turns to the majority's bold opening statement, "Liberty finds no refuge in a jurisprudence of doubt," countering the idea that *Roe* (1973) was, if anything, clear. Technological advances challenged the trimester system upon which *Roe* (1973) was based. The decisions that followed *Roe* (1973) left lower courts with little clear direction. The *Casey* (1992) decision, with its provision that any legislation to regulate abortion should not prove to be an undue burden on the right to an abortion, basically leaves lower courts with the power to overturn any state regulations of abortion. An undue burden on a right to an abortion, as the plurality opinion presents the doctrine of undue burden, has no limits. Any law that constrains a woman's ability to have an abortion could constitute an undue burden on the right. The court's opinion therefore would not allow for any law protecting fetal life.

Paralleling the majority's opening declaration, Scalia concludes this section's comments with the remark, "Reason finds no refuge in this jurisprudence of confusion."[33] Rather than focus on liberty, which he sees as a limited, conditional right, Scalia focuses upon reason. A play upon the majority's assertion that they are engaged in reasoned judgment, Scalia's turn of the phrase emphasizes the confusion the court's abortion decisions create for lower courts. The judicial workbox's most important tool would be the judges' use of reason. Law schools teach students to think differently, to approach situations and problems from a legal perspective. Students are encouraged to apply different forms of reasoning to a situation to determine the logical outcome of a scenario. Yet students should not create law or extend the fixed boundaries of the Constitution, as Scalia contends the plurality justices have in the *Casey* (1992) decisions.

Next Scalia briefly considers the plurality's insistence upon upholding *Roe* (1973) for the sake of legal consistency. For Scalia, the court should admit its mistake in deciding *Roe* (1973) and cease adjudicating abortion decisions. He confesses confusion as to how *Casey* (1992) supports stare decisis, the practice of upholding precedent in an area of law. The plurality purports to affirm *Roe*'s (1973) central holding that a woman has a right to obtain an abortion. The rest of *Roe* (1973), however, has been overturned and abandoned by the court. "I confess never to have heard of this new, keep-what-you-want-and-throw-away-the-rest version," Scalia remarks.[34] Judicial opinions should be maintained in their entirety—or disposed of completely. He then proceeds to list how the present decision does not adhere to the precedent of *Roe* (1973), highlighting the "arbitrary" nature of judicial decision-making.

Scalia challenges the plurality's assertion that its *Roe* (1973) decision provided resolution in the abortion controversy. He refers to their version of history as "unrecognizable." "Not only did *Roe* not, as the court suggests, *resolve* the deeply divisive issue of abortion; it did more than anything else to nourish it, by elevating it to the national level where it is infinitely more difficult to resolve."[35] The Supreme Court's decision in *Roe* (1973) had a totalizing effect. Rather than grant states the flexibility to respond to the abortion issue in a manner that state legislatures deem best reflects the beliefs and values of its denizens, the Supreme Court mandated the legality of abortion. Scalia maintains that the *Roe* (1973) decision increased hostilities and division on this controversial issue rather than resolved them.

Lastly, Scalia compares the court's decision-making in abortion to the court's *Dred Scott* (1857) opinion. In an extended description of Taney that is itself the length of (if not longer than) most of his other abortion opinions, Scalia personifies the error of the court. The *Dred Scott* (1857) decision, which denied black individuals personhood and citizenship, led both to the demonizing of Taney and to damage to the court's prestige. Taney and *Dred Scott* (1857) have become simplified archetypes: Taney as "evil" and *Dred Scott* (1857) as "a mistake."[36] In his description, Scalia focuses upon the person of Taney rather than on the *Dred Scott* (1857) decision, because Taney represents all of the justices (with the exception of Scalia, Rehnquist, and Thomas) who adjudicate in favor of abortion. These justices sit in chairs, penning their decisions. Their hands, however, may become limp and lifeless, as Scalia describes Taney's, because of the calamity their opinions wreak on the nation. *Roe* (1973) divides the nation into prolife and prochoice camps, just as *Dred Scott* (1857) divided the nation into proslavery and antislavery advocates in the era of the Civil War. Earlier in his *Casey* (1992) opinion, Scalia discusses how, before *Roe* (1973), states legislated abortion in accordance with the will of their citizens. The national mandate of *Roe* (1973) that abortion must be legal resulted in a rent nation with no hope of a solution that can satisfy all communities.

Scalia's discursive turns in his *Casey* (1992) dissent highlight the logical fallacies in the majority's opinion, and his discussion of Taney underscores the potential damaging result of the opinion. What constitutes reason in a Supreme Court decision? Not something that is based on an idea absent in the Constitution. Reason also is not challenged by a criterion such as an undue burden, which is, for Scalia, overly broad. Moreover, the fact that *Roe* (1973) has been case law for over a quarter of a century is no reason to perpetuate bad law. The court's insistence upon upholding *Roe* (1973) serves as evidence of the court's misguided attempts to legislate, leaving the court vulnerable to political attack. What can be inferred from Scalia's opinion is that the only way to have clarity in the law is to abide by the words of the Constitution.

Writing for the Majority: Rights Not in Conflict

Scalia has penned six abortion opinions, only one of which is a majority opinion. Since all of Scalia's previous abortion opinions assert that the Supreme Court should not adjudicate abortion opinions, at first glance it appears ironic that Scalia would pen the *Bray v. Alexandria Women's Health Clinic* (1993) decision. This case, however, does not focus on the right to an abortion per se, but on *access* to that right. The court does not construct the legal basis for the right (as did *Roe* [1973] and *Casey* [1992]) or question the validity of state statutes that regulate abortion (as did *Webster* [1989], *Akron* [1990], *Hodgson* [1990], *Carhart* [2000], and *Casey* [1992]); rather, the court determines whether the actions of other citizens can unconstitutionally *prohibit* women from obtaining an abortion.

In *Bray* (1993), demonstrations outside of abortion clinics by members of Operation Rescue restricted women who sought abortions from entering an abortion clinic. The case was framed as a question of whether Operation Rescue's protest activities thus present a "private conspiracy" by group members to "interfere with the rights" of a protected "class" of persons. As author of the majority opinion, Scalia determines, "Neither common sense nor our precedents support this."[37] In his opinion Scalia broadly considers the question at hand and then accounts for each element of the legal issue in turn. First, if people were allowed to seek redress when other persons interfere with activities they want to pursue, too many people would seek legal remedy. Second, the activity is engaged in not because the protesters maintain "animus" toward women as a group but to stop the practice of abortion, which they understand to end human life. Men and women both advocate prolife and prochoice positions; women are not the only persons who advocate for or against abortion. Regardless of the fact that women are the only persons who can *seek* an abortion, regulations that affect women alone do not need to be viewed as sex-based discrimination. Scalia explains in a footnote: "The characteristic that formed the basis of the targeting here was not womanhood, but the seeking of abortion—so that the class the dissenters identify is the one we have rejected earlier: women seeking abortion. The approach of equating opposition to an activity (abortion) that can be engaged in only by a certain class (woman) with opposition to that class leads to absurd conclusions."[38] Third, no conspiracy exists to halt the interstate travel of women; the purpose merely is to stop women from receiving an abortion not to impede their travel. Fourth, the laws as set forth protect persons from official state encroachment, not from private infringement. (The only right Scalia would acknowledge is prohibited by private infringement is involuntary servitude.) Each of these arguments rejects the claim that Operation Rescue's organized protests unconstitutionally interfere with women's right to abortion. Scalia denies that the actions of Operation Rescue represent a private conspiracy or interfere with interstate travel, that women seeking abortions are a protected class of persons, and that women's right to an abortion has been denied unconstitutionally.

Scalia presents this case not as a conflict between equally valid constitutional rights—the right to an abortion and First Amendment rights to assemble and to speak—but as an inquiry into whether a private conspiracy has transpired intentionally to interfere with the rights of women. Consistent with his criticisms of earlier Supreme Court abortion decisions, Scalia frames abortion as "the *asserted* right to abortion."[39] His qualification of abortion as "asserted" calls into question the right, for to assert something is to state it without proof. His use of the past participle also allows him to distance himself from abortion while nevertheless allowing him to author the *Bray* (1993) opinion. He does not support the right to an abortion as determined by a previous Court. Furthermore, although this case was decided one year after the Supreme Court abandoned the privacy justification for abortion established by *Roe* (1973), Scalia declares, "The right to abortion has been described in our opinions as one element of a more general right of privacy."[40] The right to privacy, which Scalia contends in earlier opinions has no textual basis in the Constitution, in this case serves as part of his defense of the actions of Operation Rescue—private persons are protected only from official governmental intrusion. He does not use the most recent precedent governing abortion law, which legal analysts agree has a better grounding in the Constitution than the infamous right to privacy, but instead relies upon the much-criticized, defunct legal doctrine. His decision to do so makes sense in conjunction with his establishment cases. An individual has the right to express a religious opinion. The protesters outside the abortion clinic are protected, as private citizens, in their expression of their religious opposition to abortion. Thus, protesters have the free speech and privacy right to protest abortion clinics.

In his majority opinion, Scalia's judicial ethos gives credence to the arguments of prolife advocates in the *Bray* (1993) opinion. "Whatever one thinks of abortion, it cannot be denied that there are common and respectable reasons for opposing it," Scalia opines.[41] Although Scalia assumes a stronger stance against abortion in his *Carhart* (2000) dissent (in which he states, "The method of killing a human child—one cannot even accurately say an entirely unborn human child—proscribed by this statute is so horrible that the most clinical description of it evokes a shudder of revulsion."[42]), he takes a stronger prolife stance in this case than in previous opinions in which he merely asserted that this is a political issue that should be resolved through democratic channels of deliberation. Scalia adopts the moral position that the unborn are persons and therefore should be protected by law.

In the *Bray* (1993) opinion, Scalia demonstrates that the law, set forth in statutory law and case precedent, can be applied regardless of the context. This opinion presents Scalia with an opportunity to enact the legal fiction that the law is objective and not subjective. He does so by exploring different legal concepts and the legal burdens of proof necessary to support the claims made by petitioners. For Scalia, the fact that this case involves women seeking abortion is not important per se. Scalia does not strengthen the right to abortion in this opinion; in addition to questioning it as a right, he does nothing to recognize efforts to impede women from obtaining an abortion. On the contrary, in *Bray* (1993), he supports prolife efforts to discourage women from seeking abortions.

Conclusion

Scalia's abortion opinions advance the argument that the judicial branch has no power to determine the constitutionality of abortion. The Constitution's silence on the issue of abortion means that states should have the power to decide for themselves whether they want abortion to be legal in their state. What becomes interesting about his abortion opinions, therefore, are their other rhetorical elements. Since no hermeneutic needs to be explained, most of his abortion opinions are short; style and substance reinforce one another. His absence of legal decision-making bolsters his argument that abortion is a political issue, not a legal matter. Unlike his other four opinions, Scalia offers an extended analysis of the law in *Casey* (1992) and in *Bray* (1993). In *Casey* (1992), Scalia offers an extended dialogue between himself and the majority in order to explicate his reasoning against the adjudication of abortion. In *Bray* (1993), he applies the law in what appears to be an impartial fashion.

Since his argument indicates an absence of right, Scalia does not spend much time discussing how to interpret abortion. The brevity of most of Scalia's abortion opinions supports his argument that abortion should not be adjudicated. Since the Constitution does not address abortion, Scalia does not have to construct a detailed argument to support his claim. The Constitution does not mention abortion; therefore, the High Court should not. States historically have been able to ban or police abortion, so they should be able to continue doing so. Scalia's lack of legal reasoning enables him to use his opinions for other ends: for criticizing his peers for being "judicial statesmen," crafting laws they feel are in the best interest of the public rather than interpreting laws in a manner the Constitution supports.

Scalia's textual argument purports that if the constitutional text does not directly address an issue, then it is not a matter to be adjudicated. For Scalia, no right to an abortion exists. He rejects both Blackmun's structural argument that several amendments taken together can constitute a right to privacy and the *Casey* (1992) plurality's doctrinal argument that abortion is a substantive due process right. Nowhere in the Constitution is the right to an abortion found. Moreover, abortion was not illegal at the time of the founding. Therefore, if one was looking to clues as to popular understanding about abortion, one could conclude that the matter, again, should be left to the states to decide, as it was left to the states to decide when they passed the Constitution and adopted the Bill of Rights.

His lengthy *Casey* (1992) opinion responds to the court's changing its justification for abortion. Although most constitutional scholars would agree that liberty is a better justification for abortion than privacy (and the reasoning that the public uses—that idea that a woman has a right to choose, a decisional liberty to an abortion), Scalia criticizes the court's shift. Concerned with the consequences of their decisions for lower courts and legislatures, Scalia contends that the abortion decisions confuse, rather than clarify, the law.

In the *Bray* (1993) opinion, Scalia does not take up the question of the legality of abortion (which was not at issue in this opinion) but demonstrates how the court should remain silent on the validity of abortion law. If one were to erase Scalia's inclusion of "asserted" before the phrase "right to abortion," *Bray* (1993) would present an example of how lower appellate courts could decide issues tangential to abortion rights, if states legalized abortion within their boundaries. Judges would vary in their interpretation of legal texts and precedents, but their decision-making would have established legal grounding.

Rather than use the Constitution's silence to constitute a right that it does not contain, Scalia advocates that the court remove itself from this area of law. Framing *Roe* (1973) as a mistake, he criticizes the court for continuing to adjudicate. For Scalia, abortion is a political issue that legislators, not jurists, should decide. Scalia maintains that the Constitution does not consider the issue of abortion; therefore, since the Constitution is silent, abortion is not a legal issue but a political one. Politically elected legislators who are responsive to the populace should decide abortion. The three themes in his abortion narrative are the Constitution does not discuss abortion, abortion is a political issue, and the court should not decide such cases.

Thus, the silent area of law proffers Scalia's clearest example of what a textualist reading of the law would look like. Unfortunately, we do not have a positive example of textualism to work from—meaning, an example in which Scalia unpacks the plain meaning of a material text. Rather, we have a negative example, offered from a textual absence. Scalia's textual tale therefore remains incomplete.

Conclusion

Scalia's Opportunistic Textualism

I set out in this book to consider what a textualist reading of the law would look like in different areas of the law. To that end, I offer here a brief thought experiment. I propose a summary of what a textualist reading of the three areas of law might look like and then offer a brief summary of the interpretive moves Scalia makes in his opinions.

At its most simplistic, a textualist reading of the Cruel and Unusual Punishments Clause would prohibit *punishments* that are *cruel* and *unusual.* The first focus would be on sentences, which would mean that proportionality would have to be considered. Does the punishment fit the crime? Interpreters would then need to agree upon what constitutes "cruel" as well as "unusual" and then ensure that the punishment doled out did not violate either parameter. A plain reading would also mean that cruel and unusual punishments would need to be considered in light of what constitutes such punishment *now*, not what constituted punishment more than two hundred years ago, although punishments that were unconstitutional then would probably be unconstitutional now.

Rather than assume that cruelty, as put forth in the Eighth Amendment, refers to the punishment being implemented, Scalia extends the meaning of the clause to the cruelty of the crime perpetrated against the victim. He infuses the defendants in capital punishment cases with the agency to be cruel. In doing so, he expands the clause beyond the usual textual interpretation and removes the language of the Constitution from its linguistic surroundings. This understanding of the text is not its original meaning, nor is it what the common person would understand the clause to mean today. Therefore, while Scalia criticizes the majority of the court for making the Constitution mean whatever five votes on the Supreme Court determine it to mean, he nevertheless engages in the same interpretive move by altering constitutional provisions to mean what he wants them to mean.

A plain reading of the Establishment Clause, even understood broadly, would seem to indicate that government, via the lawmaking body, should not pass laws about religion. Hugo Black's mantra "Congress shall make no law respecting a religion. . . . No law means *no* law" rings in my head. The First Amendment's proscription against an establishment does not necessarily have the totalizing effect that Black encourages. We are left to ask what constitutes an establishment of religion. Scholars differ on this account. A textualist reading of the Establishment Clause therefore does not easily present itself.

The *Oxford English Dictionary* explains that in the seventeenth and eighteenth centuries, an "establishment" denoted the "granting of legal status" to religious bodies recognized by the state. The sentence structure of the clause identifies an actor (Congress), an action (shall make), and an object (no law respecting an establishment of religion). Yet what constitutes an establishment of religion was contested at the time of the founding. According to Harvard Law professor Noah Feldman, the founding generation did not use the term in a consistent fashion; rather, establishment "was used in both narrow and expansive ways in the debates of the time,"[1] allowing for both preferential and nonpreferential support of religion. What is certain is the founders meant that the United States could not adopt a single national religion; anything beyond that becomes fuzzy. Does the clause restrict itself to the federal government or can it be applied to the states? Does the Establishment Clause mandate strict separation or allow for the inclusion of one or more religions in the public sphere? Judges and legal experts disagree when responding to these questions. One would need, at the very least, to make sure that a specific religion is not implemented in law or supported via financial means.

A plain reading of the Free Exercise Clause would grant citizens the right to practice their religion. The prohibition against interfering with the free exercise of religion appears to be totalizing—regardless of religious affiliation, theists should be allowed to participate in their religious rituals. Both of the clause's elements should be considered; what constitutes "free" as well as what constitutes "exercise"? "Free" would seem to connote without restraint or cost and "exercise" would mean a ritual or practice.

Scholars contend that the Free Exercise Clause was adopted to protect the right of conscience for religious citizens. In his survey of the genesis of the Establishment Clause, Natelson quotes constitutional ratification debates wherein founding luminaries such as Patrick Henry and Thomas Jefferson advocated for an explicit free exercise protection.[2] Natelson recounts how some, James Madison not included, worried that other constitutional powers (e.g., Necessary and Proper Clause, Supremacy Clause) would give the federal government power over religion unless explicitly denied the power to do so. Scholars maintain that the founders intended free exercise to apply to all theists; the clause did not apply to the freedom from religious practice of atheists and agnostics.[3] Nevertheless, little evidence from the clause's drafting gives direction as to the meaning of the clause, as no representative discussed what the clause meant to him, and the body as a whole did not debate the clause.[4] Thus, no definitive answer can be given as to what it means to protect this right. At a minimum the clause would allow theists to practice their religion, and the court's separation between belief and action would be deemed unconstitutional.

Scalia stretches his interpretation of the constitutional text even further in an area of law that is ambiguous, refusing to use textualist reasoning to justify his decision in church and state questions. Rather, he turns to the forms of interpretation he most often criticizes, and he abandons accepted legal doctrine for legislative control by the states. His opinions further confuse case law and do not provide a compelling justification for reliance upon original meaning or the historic practices of the people. Moreover, the tension between the competing religion clauses means that Congress, as well as the court, increasingly has become hostile to religious practice, giving the Establishment Clause preference over the Free Exercise Clause. Few are persuaded by Scalia's claim that the religious should be a protected minority group in America, and even Scalia himself cannot seem to determine whether religious belief can be separated from religious action. Textualism and originalism thus offer little relief as judges and scholars battle over the "correct" meaning of the text, the best ways to understand original intent and meaning, and whether to abandon—or to alter—doctrinal tests.

A plain reading of abortion is challenged by the Constitution's silence on the issue. The Ninth and Tenth Amendments would indicate that the issue may be a right reserved to the people or that the states have a right to regulate abortion. Abortion was *not illegal* at the time of the founding, so one might think that the practice is constitutional. Although the previous sentence may appear convoluted, laws regulating abortion did not exist until the 1820s. Some scholars argue that abortion was not outlawed at the time of the founding because the procedure was so dangerous that few women attempted to abort their fetus.[5] As the trend reversed, and abortion became safer than live birth, states began passing laws proscribing abortion. Abortion laws remained in effect for approximately the next 150 years. In 1962 the American Law Institute published the Model Penal Code, recommending that abortion be made legal in instances where the mother had been raped or the child would be born with a birth defect.[6] States ignored the Model Penal Code's suggestion until 1967, when Colorado legalized abortion in cases of rape, incest, or the disability of the fetus. Within five years thirteen states had passed abortion laws similar to Colorado's law. In 1972 New York passed a more liberal abortion law, allowing women to seek an elective abortion for any reason until the twenty-fourth week. Three additional states modeled their law after New York's law. By 1972 thirty-one states allowed abortions to protect a woman's health.[7] So the issue of abortion cannot be resolved via a textualist reading; one would have to use a different form of reasoning to resolve this controversial issue.

Scalia's clearest use of textual reasoning nevertheless occurs in his abortion law cases. Since the Constitution does not mention abortion, the courts should not adjudicate the issue. Scalia contends that as justices hand down abortion opinions, the judicial branch crafts a legislative code—an action outside of the purview of their functional powers. Scalia views abortion as a political, rather than a legal, issue and recommends judicial restraint. Unlike his rhetorical choices in Eighth Amendment cases and religion law cases, his decision and reasoning in his abortion opinions is consistent with his advocacy of textualism in his speeches and his law review articles.

My examination of Scalia's use of textual interpretation in three different areas of law—where the Constitution is clear, where the Constitution is ambiguous, and where the Constitution is silent—leads me to conclude that Scalia is an opportunistic textualist. I classify him as "opportunistic" because he uses textualism to achieve particular legal results rather than to limit judicial interpretation to the textual parameters of the Constitution. In my three case studies Scalia applies textualism, as he outlines it in his speeches and law reviews, only in the area of law the Constitution does not mention: abortion. Since the Constitution does not mention abortion, the Constitution is silent with regard to how to adjudicate abortion law. Therefore, the lack of an abortion clause or a right to privacy empowers Scalia to reject judicial activism. Yet when confronted with the question of whether a punishment is cruel and unusual, an area of the law in which the Constitution is clear, Scalia twists the meaning of "cruel" to his purposes. Then, in the area of religion law—one of the most confused areas of law because of the tension between the Establishment Clause and the Free Exercise

Clause—Scalia abandons textualism and originalism altogether in favor of the very forms of judicial interpretation that he criticizes in his speeches and extrajudicial writings.

In the three areas of law that I consider—clear, ambiguous, and silent—Scalia uses three different approaches to textualism and constitutional interpretation. In the clear area of law (cruel and unusual punishment), Scalia changes the linguistic meaning of the clause. In the ambiguous area of law (religion law), he uses other forms of interpretation. And in the silent area of law (abortion), he refuses to interpret the law because he claims that no textual justification empowers him to do so. Therefore, while his speeches and law review articles suggest a clear form of interpretation that can be applied in a somewhat systematic fashion to different areas of law, his actual judicial opinions reflect a more flexible approach.

Textualism, as Justice Scalia practiced it, was as rhetorical as any other form of interpretation, including loose forms of interpretation. When Scalia wrote in one of his religion law opinions that a distinction between belief and action exists—and that one may believe whatever she chooses but may not be able to act upon that belief—he made a rhetorical choice. When Scalia argued, in a separate religion law opinion, that belief and action cannot be separated, he made a rhetorical choice. These two contrasting religion law cases illuminate how Scalia crafted his judicial reasoning to achieve a particular result. The text of the religion clauses did not change in the time between these two cases; Scalia's strategic aim changed.

The variations in Scalia's application of textualism to different areas of law underscore the inherent problems with textualism as a form of interpretation. Earlier scholars have criticized textualism on three grounds: first, the constitutional text is not self-determining but rather has its meaning constituted through judicial interpretation; second, no other texts should be necessary to understand the text's plain meaning; and third, understanding the Constitution in light of fixed principles chains modern society to archaic customs and practices. My analysis reinforces the first criticism—that the Constitution is not self-determining—by demonstrating the ways in which Scalia himself interacts with the text to achieve a particular outcome, despite his advocacy of strict textual interpretation and judicial restraint. My analysis also troubles the notion that a plain meaning can be derived from the text of the Constitution at all. The Constitution contains competing values—such as the Free Exercise Clause and the Establishment Clause, or individual rights and states' rights—that have to be prioritized or balanced in any given case. These competing values necessitate judicial interpretation of the text; the text itself does not have intrinsic meaning.

Scalia's shifts in interpretation also highlight his opportunistic use of textualism. Earlier commentary about his jurisprudence attempted to reclassify Scalia's interpretation as originalist or as based upon the principles of originalism, traditionalism, and judicial restraint. Legal scholar David Zlotnick criticizes Scalia's opinions for using interpretations other than textualism, identifying Scalia's use of the historical practices of the American people as an example. These criticisms of Scalia are not as far-reaching as they could be, for they fall within the boundary of strict forms of interpretation. My analysis, however, shows that when textualism does not offer sufficient justification for his legal opinions, Scalia employs other forms of interpretation. He justifies his decisions using the same forms of interpretation that he criticizes in his public speeches and law review articles.

To wit, observers of Scalia's advocacy and his jurisprudence are presented with a disjunction between Scalia-as-perceived and Scalia-as-lived. Scalia-as-perceived was a strict interpreter who remained faithful to his juridical philosophy regardless of the results. Scalia-as-lived used whatever means would facilitate the outcome he desired. In the cases analyzed, we witness Scalia twist the meaning of terms beyond their plain meaning into a convoluted historical exploration of a position that supported his thinking. Law professor Carolyn Shapiro concurs. In an editorial published by CNN on the occasion of Scalia's death, Shapiro proclaims: "But even Scalia could not live up to the absolutist position he espoused. And his rhetoric created a false view of law as always having objectively correct answers even to difficult questions that the Supreme Court regularly decides. . . . He pretended that the gray areas do not exist. And his rhetoric of the subject was so insistent, so compelling, so flamboyant, so quotable, that he led not only his ideological compatriots, but numerous ordinary Americans, down the garden path. He painted a picture of reassuring certainty. If only judges do their job right, the objectively correct answers will emerge. But that promise of neutrality is absurd."[8] So a discrepancy exists between Scalia's theory of constitutional interpretation as presented in his speeches and extrajudicial writings and Scalia's jurisprudence, between Scalia-as-constitutional theorist and Scalia-as-constitutional practitioner, between Scalia-as-perceived and Scalia-as-lived.

Although one might argue that the blame for Scalia's lack of consistency lies within the man, constitutional law scholar Michael Gerhardt argues that textualism itself cannot accurately reflect constitutional meaning. In his article, "A Tale of Two Textualists," Gerhardt delves into the similarities and differences between the textualisms of "liberal" Hugo Black and "conservative" Antonin Scalia. In his analysis Gerhardt finds that both men agree on questions of the Commerce Clause, substantive due process rights, equal protection, separation of powers, freedom of speech, and searches and seizures. He finds that they disagree on religion law cases and the use of tradition in constitutional decision-making. Gerhardt concludes that the difference between the two men and their forms of constitutional interpretation is not textualism itself but the different political and personal predilections of the two justices. Gerhardt maintains that Justice Black favors judicial activism, while Justice Scalia prefers judicial restraint. Specifically, Scalia deferred to the traditions of the people "to defeat individual rights claims as sacrificing the constitutional text to enhance majoritarianism and judicial restraint."[9] Gerhardt does not criticize the justices for the different results their textualisms produce. Rather, he blames the form of constitutional interpretation itself. The Constitution cannot be interpreted on its own terms, devoid of human influence. Unfortunately, Gerhardt's critical analysis stops short of offering a prescription for constitutional interpretation.

Critiques of textualism (Scalia's textualism in particular) draw attention to the need for a systematic approach to textual interpretation. In his speeches and extrajudicial writings, Scalia advocates textualism, but he does not provide a prescription for how to apply textual interpretation to a legal text. Such a prescription, beyond calling for a reasonable reading of the constitutional text, would offer three benefits: first, it would provide lower court judges with a guideline by which to interpret the Constitution; second, it would enhance the predictability of the law, because lower courts could interpret the law based upon clear textual guidelines; and third, it would provide a model of judicial decision-making by which to hold judges accountable.

What criteria would Scalia's systematic guideline for textual interpretation prioritize, if he were to have such a guideline? From his speeches and law review articles, we can glean:

(1) if the text of the Constitution directly mentions a right or a liberty, that right or liberty is constitutionally protected; and
(2) if the text of the Constitution does not mention a right or a liberty, no such right or liberty needs to be protected under the federal Constitution.

The distinction between constitutionally protected rights and rights not constitutionally protected is crude. Moreover, it does not account for competing values or govern the interpretation of those rights that the Constitution does guarantee. Therefore, the above construction of textualist criteria for constitutional interpretation would have to be elaborated. To continue this thought experiment, we might understand Scalia's speeches and writings to suggest the following:

(1) the Constitution protects a very limited set of rights and liberties;
(2) the Supreme Court should not accept but a very limited set of cases that are clearly constitutional questions;
(3) the court should protect fundamental rights and liberties, meaning those rights and liberties that are necessary to perpetuate a democratic system of government;
(4) rights and liberties outside the Constitution's purview are to be protected by the states (if the states choose to protect those rights and liberties);
(5) when reading the Constitution, justices are to give the language of the text the narrowest meaning possible; and
(6) articles of the Constitution and clauses in the amendments should not be linked together to create legal doctrine.

This more developed hierarchy of values includes provisions for judicial restraint, explicating the types of cases the Supreme Court should agree to hear, before clarifying how decisions should be interpreted.

The construction of a schema by which to interpret the Constitution highlights the contradictions in Scalia's advocacy of textualism. He claims that the text of the Constitution should have a plain meaning that can be reasonably interpreted, yet he stresses the need for experts in legal tradition to be the persons to interpret the law. The schema presented does not include other information that would aid in understanding the constitutional text, from letters written by the Founding Fathers to notes from state ratification debates. Rather, it works from the presumption that the text can be given a plain meaning and that a moderately educated person should be able to interpret the document, without legal training. This construction of textualism, however, neglects Scalia's argument that reasonable readings of the law must be grounded in the legal tradition.[10] Scalia gives primacy to the text of the Constitution, but he suggests that only those trained in the law may interpret that text. A reasonable person, however, might find these claims confusing.

This textualist schema might facilitate judicial interpretation that is as faithful to the constitutional text as possible. Yet just as scholars within the rhetoric and law movement disagree with Judge Posner's critique that the law is objective, I disagree with Justice Scalia's contention that textualism can be applied in an unbiased fashion that removes personal judgment from judicial decision-making. No form of judicial interpretation, textualism included, can impart meaning apart from extrinsic influences. Nevertheless, a more systematic schema for interpreting the Constitution is possible as well as desirable. Such a schema is desirable because it would clarify the role and the function of this form of judicial interpretation in a democratic society.

The Guardian of Democratic Principles

While Scalia's practice of textualism does not always conform to his judicial philosophy, or to his stated political and philosophical goals, his goals of limiting judicial activism and restoring deliberative democracy are worthy goals. Scalia advocates that democracy be enacted at the local and state levels and through the legislative branch of government rather than through the courts. The judicial and the political fulfill different purposes; the people should elect representatives to ensure their political rights and liberties through the political realm. If there were a guiding question to Scalia's judicial philosophy, it would seem to be the question posed in Juvenal's *Satires*: "*Quis custodiet ipsos custodes*?" "Who will guard the guards?" The Supreme Court is the guardian of the Constitution, the document that founded our nation and created our liberties, but who will guard the guardian?

Scalia's view that political control should be granted to the local and state governments, instead of to the courts, means that the responsibilities of the courts would decrease. A decrease in the role of the courts would equate to a decrease in opportunities for the misuse of judicial power. The courts would protect minority rights when fundamental liberties (such as the freedom of speech, the freedom to assemble, the freedom from self-incrimination, etc.) were challenged. The courts would not, however, invent new laws in an activist fashion, as some courts have done in the past.

I agree with Scalia's goals. Although discouraged by his lack of a systematic approach to constitutional interpretation, I nevertheless agree that judicial interpretation of the Constitution should be limited to allow for more democratic deliberation and decision-making. Although the public might not make the "right" decision all of the time, the purpose of a democracy is to empower the people to make their own decisions. Struggle and disagreement are inherent to a democratic system. We should not allow our deliberative system (imperfect though it may be) to be replaced by a system that looks to the courts to sort through our most difficult social issues.

Final Remarks

Constitutional interpretation remains one of the most important issues facing the United States today. The United States has come to rely upon the courts as the protectors and perpetuators of democracy. Yet as we can see from this analysis of Scalia's judicial rhetoric, the guardians of the Constitution can be inconsistent and opportunistic. Perceived as the most forceful advocate of conservative ideals on the court, the vitriol cast upon Scalia following his death shows that many critics did not trust him to rise above partisan politics and adjudicate cases in an impartial fashion. Paradoxically, what Scalia actually advocated in his public speeches and his law review articles was quite different from what can be inferred from his judicial opinions. Textualism, defined by Scalia as a reasonable interpretation of the Constitution that brings stability and predictability to the law, fails in practice to simplify and to clarify the law.

We need to discuss the problem of judicial interpretation—and textualism in particular—in more depth. This discussion needs to occur in classrooms, in scholarly journals, and in the public sphere. Justices have the power neither of the purse nor of the sword, but somehow their power of the pen has given them enormous control over communities and citizens. The United States has reached a point where democratic practice is supplanted by judicial activism. Conservatives and liberals alike race to the marble temple for answers to questions they are too scared, or too uncertain, to debate in public.

Scalia's biggest contribution to law was his call to return the power of democracy to the people. In case after case Scalia rejected the power of the judiciary to answer political questions, yet Scalia's message often became lost in his caustic rhetoric and dominant personality. Attention shifted from the issue to the man. When the Supreme Court agreed to hear *Cheney v. US District Court of Columbia* (2004), for example, newspapers focused on Scalia's allegedly questionable ethics in refusing to recuse himself from the case rather than on the legality of Vice President Cheney's business practices.[11] LexisNexis reported more than 125 articles in less than three weeks discussing Scalia's duck hunting trip with the vice president.[12] Scalia's call for strict interpretation of the Constitution was lost in the controversy over the person Scalia.

Scalia's legacy is that of an intellectual powerhouse who was a passionate and articulate advocate of textualism and originalism. For those individuals who agreed with him, he was a conservative hero who protected the rights and liberties the founders secured when they drafted the Constitution. For those individuals who disagreed with him, he was a misogynistic, homophobic racist who abused his powers as best he could to maintain white, male, heterosexual supremacy. Sound bites from his judicial opinions eloquently articulated the fears of conservatives and spewed institutional hatred according to liberals.

In his speeches and extrajudicial writings, Scalia crafted a textual tale in which the Constitution is a self-determining document that protects a limited number of rights. Within this narrative, judges play a minor role; they are to interpret the law in as narrow a fashion as possible. Legislators remain on the sidelines, ready to fulfill the will of the people when called upon. Scalia's jurisprudence, however, tells a different story. In Scalia's jurisprudence, judges use a variety of evidentiary support beyond the constitutional text, including British law, founding documents, dictionaries, case precedent, and doctrinal tests. Judges also have the ability to read the language of the law however they want. Herein lies the crux of the matter. Via Scalia's pen, language expands beyond the plain meaning of the text to include *alternative* legal meanings. Scalia's pen shifts the *focus* of language from questionable consequences to criminal actors. And Scalia's pen constructs groups and rights according to *different* linguistic frames. Language is malleable and supports a broad spectrum of linguistic possibilities within Scalia's jurisprudence.

More attention needs to be focused on Scalia's constitutional interpretation. Throughout his time on the bench, scholars and liberal-minded members of the public criticized Scalia, yet they did so largely for the wrong reasons. They criticized him for being hateful or for taking the wrong approach to constitutional interpretation. But what they needed to criticize him for was not doing what he says a judge should do. Scalia spun a textual tale he did not practice in his own jurisprudence. In the three areas of law examined here, Scalia rarely relied upon textualist reasoning and, when he did so, he did not apply textualism in a consistent manner. His textualism did not produce predictable, clear results, despite its supposed reliance upon the "plain meaning" of the Constitution.

Judges who employ textualism claim that their method of interpretation exists within the narrow confines of the constitutional document. Therefore, they argue that the material reality that results from their interpretation more closely corresponds to the system of governance that the Constitution created. Their approach is more democratic, in other words, because it separates the political from the legal and leaves the political to the people. Yet as this analysis shows, textualism is not beyond personal predilection and rhetorical choice. Textualism is just as rhetorical as other forms of constitutional interpretation.

More important than the myriad of results that textualism can produce is the political community that textualism creates. Judges who use textualism claim that theirs is an interpretation that exists within the narrow confines of the constitutional document. Therefore, the material reality that results from their interpretation more closely corresponds to the system of governance the Constitution was drafted to create. Theirs is, in other words, a truer democracy because it separates the political from the legal, leaving the political to the people.

As an informed and engaged citizenry, we need to have discussions about what constitutes political questions as opposed to legal questions. We also need to better understand how justices interpret the law. This book seeks to enhance the discussion of legal and political discourse by showing the conflict that occurs when a justice attempts to separate the judicial from the political. In the end I conclude that such a division is not possible. The judicial is the political, but the political does not have to be the judicial. One hopes that the sphere of the political is broader and more diverse than that of the judicial. Legal rhetoric scholar Per Fjelstad concludes, "The figure of legal judgment depends intrinsically on cultural judgments about the function of law."[13] He is correct. Many people conclude that democracy is hurt by judicial activism, while others argue that democracy is enhanced. Both can be true.

I examine the textual interpretation of Justice Antonin Scalia on its own terms. I use Scalia's speeches and extrajudicial writings in order to understand his adjudication in different areas of law. I find that Scalia makes strategic rhetorical choices in employing textualism as a function of the legal results he seeks. His choices result in an application of textualism that is opportunistic and not predictable. Therefore, although President Reagan sought to appoint a justice who would "interpret the law according to the intent of the Constitution," he nevertheless appointed a justice who also struck "down laws that displeased [him] politically or philosophically." I do not know that it is possible to appoint a justice who would adjudicate otherwise.

Notes

Introduction

1. Christopher E. Smith, *Justice Antonin Scalia and the Supreme Court's Conservative Moment* (Westport, CT: Praeger, 1993), 26.

2. Ronald Reagan. *Public Papers of the Presidents of the United States: Ronald Reagan.* 1986. Vol. 2. Washington, DC: GPO, 1067–69.

3. See, for example, David G. Savage, *Turning Right: The Making of the Rehnquist Supreme Court* (New York: John Wiley & Sons, 1992); Richard A. Brisbin Jr., *Justice Antonin Scalia and the Conservative Revival* (Baltimore: Johns Hopkins University Press, 1997); Smith, *Justice Antonin Scalia and the Supreme Court's Conservative Moment*; David A. Schultz and Christopher E. Smith, *The Jurisprudential Vision of Justice Antonin Scalia* (Lanham, MD: Rowman & Littlefield, 1996); Stanley H. Friedelbaum, *The Rehnquist Court: In Pursuit of Judicial Conservatism* (Westport, CT: Greenwood Press, 1994).

4. Ruben Bolling, "Tom the Dancing Bug," Salon.com (May 17, 2001), accessed June 14, 2001, http://archive.salon.com/comics/boll/2001/05/17/boll/.

5. Ruben Bolling, "Tom the Dancing Bug," Salon.com (March 13, 2013), accessed May 28, 2013, http://boingboing.net/2013/03/13/tom-the-dancing-bug-judge-sca-2.html.

6. See, for example, Noah Feldman, "Scalia's Classic 'Textualism' Will Be His Legacy," *Chicago Tribune*, February 19, 2016, Noah Feldman, "Scalia's Classic 'Textualism' Will Be His Legacy," *Chicago Tribune*, February 19, 2016; Janell Ross, "Antonin Scalia: A Brilliant Legal Mind Who Snubbed Civil Rights at Nearly Every Turn," *Washington Post*, February 14, 2016, https://www.washingtonpost.com/news/the-fix/wp/2016/02/14/antonin-scalia-a-brilliant-legal-mind-who-defied-civil-rights-at-nearly-every-turn/?hpid=hp_hp-top-table-main_fix-legalmind-1248pm%3Ahomepage%2Fstory&tid=a_inl; Robert Barnes, "Supreme Court Justice Antonin Scalia Dies at 79," *Washington Post*, February 13, 2016, https://www.washingtonpost.com/politics/supreme-court-justice-antonin-scalia-dies-at-79/2016/02/13/effe8184-a62f-11e3-a5fa-55f0c77bf39c_story.html.

7. See "Supreme Court Justices Weigh in on Antonin Scalia's Death," *USA Today*,

February 15, 2016, http://www.usatoday.com/story/news/politics/2016/02/14/statements-supreme-court-death-justice-scalia/80375976/.

8. "Supreme Court Justices Weigh In."

9. "Supreme Court Justices Weigh In."

10. "Supreme Court Justices Weigh In."

11. "Supreme Court Justices Weigh In."

12. "Supreme Court Justices Weigh In."

13. Ted Cruz, Twitter post, February 13, 2016, 4:27 p.m., http://twitter.com/tedcruz.

14. Marco Rubio, "Marco Rubio's Statement on Justice Antonin Scalia's Passing," February 13, 2016, http://blog.4president.org/2016/2016/02/marco-rubio-statement-on-justice-antonin-scalia.html.

15. Donald Trump, "Donald J. Trump Statement on Justice Scalia," February 13, 2016, https://www.donaldjtrump.com/press-releases/donald-j.-trump-statement-on-justice-scalia.

16. Liam Stack, "Jeb Bush Says Scalia Was 'My Favorite Justice,'" *New York Times*, February 13, 2016, http://www.nytimes.com/live/supreme-court-justice-antonin-scalia-dies-at-79/jeb-bush-says-scalia-was-my-favorite-justice/.

17. Patrick Howley, "Kasich: Scalia Was an 'Essential' Force for Conservative Thought," *Breitbart*, February 13, 2016, http://www.breitbart.com/big-government/2016/02/13/3028901/.

18. Barack Obama, "The President on the Passing of Supreme Court Justice Antonin Scalia," *The White House*, February 13, 2016, https://www.whitehouse.gov/photos-and-video/video/2016/02/13/president-passing-supreme-court-justice-antonin-scalia.

19. Hillary Clinton, "Hillary Clinton Statement on the Passing of Supreme Court Justice Antonin Scalia," HillaryClinton.com, February 13, 2016, https://www.hillaryclinton.com/briefing/statements/2016/02/13/justice-antonin-scalia-passing/.

20. Bernie Sanders, "Statement on Justice Scalia," *Bernie2016*, February 13, 2016, https://berniesanders.com/press-release/statement-on-justice-scalia/.

21. Cass R. Sunstein, "The Scalia I Knew Will Be Greatly Missed," *BloombergView*, February 13, 2016, https://www.bloomberg.com/view/articles/2016-02-14/the-scalia-i-knew-will-be-greatly-missed.

22. Richard Epstein, "Antonin Scalia, a Most Memorable Friend," *Hoover Institute*, February 15, 2016, http://www.hoover.org/research/antonin-scalia-most-memorable-friend.

23. See, for example, Paul T. Cappuccio, "Former Clerk Remembers Scalia's Personal Warmth," *New York Times*, February 13, 2016, http://www.nytimes.com/live/supreme-court-justice-antonin-scalia-dies-at-79/former-clerk-remembers-scalias-personal-warmth/; Matthew J. Franck, "Antonin Scalia, Persistent Champion of Constitutional Republicanism," *Witherspoon Institute*, May 2, 2016, http://www.thepublicdiscourse.com/2016/05/16871/; Soo Youn, "Antonin Scalia: Liberal Clerks Reflect on the Man They Knew and Admired," *Guardian*, February 15, 2016, https://www.theguardian.com/law/2016/feb/15/antonin-scalia-supreme-court-justice-liberal-clerks-reflect.

24. Hodgson, "Antonin Scalia Obituary."

25. Ilya Shapiro, "Scalia Will Be Impossible to Replace," CNN.com, February 15, 2016, http://www.cnn.com/2016/02/15/opinions/scalia-impossible-to-replace-shapiro/index.html.

26. Adam Liptak, "Antonin Scalia, Justice on the Supreme Court, Dies at 79," *New York Times*, February 13, 2016, http://www.nytimes.com/2016/02/14/us/antonin-scalia-death.html?rref=collection%2Ftimestopic%2FScalia%2C%20Antonin&action=click&

contentCollection=timestopics&region=stream&module=stream_unit&version=latest&contentPlacement=74&pgtype=collection.

27. George F. Will, "Why Antonin Scalia Was a Jurist of Colossal Consequence," *Washington Post*, February 14, 2016, https://www.washingtonpost.com/opinions/why-antonin-scalia-was-a-jurist-of-colossal-consequence/2016/02/14/6936b8fc-d359-11e5-9823-02b905009f99_story.html?utm_term=.a50c5fde02b4.

28. Andrew P. Napolitano, "Justice Scalia and Constitutional Fidelity," *Fox News*, February 18, 2016, http://www.foxnews.com/opinion/2016/02/18/justice-scalia-and-constitutional-fidelity.html.

29. Carolyn Shapiro, "How Scalia Played with Fire," CNN.com, February 16, 2016, http://www.cnn.com/2016/02/16/opinions/antonin-scalia-shapiro/index.html.

30. Carolyn Shapiro, "How Scalia Played with Fire," CNN.com, February 16, 2016, http://www.cnn.com/2016/02/16/opinions/antonin-scalia-shapiro/index.html.

31. Elena Kagan, The Nomination of Elena Kagan to be an Associate Justice of the Supreme Court of the United States Hearing Before the Committee on the Judiciary, United States Senate, One Hundred Eleventh Congress, Second Session, June 28–30 and July 1, 2010, 111th Congress 2 (2010), 62.

32. Lesley Stahl, "Justice Scalia on the Record: *60 Minutes*' Lesley Stahl Interviews Supreme Court Justice Antonin Scalia About His Public and Private Life," *60 Minutes*, April 24, 2008, http://www.cbsnews.com/news/justice-scalia-on-the-record/.

33. "Why People Hate Antonin Scalia," *Economist*, April 25, 2008, http://www.economist.com/blogs/democracyinamerica/2008/04/why_people_hate_antonin_scalia.

34. Steven Rosenfeld, "Is Scalia the Most Vile Person in Washington?" *Salon*, March 5, 2013, http://www.salon.com/2013/03/05/is_scalia_the_most_vile_person_in_washington/.

35. Tal Kopan, "Harry Reid, John Lewis Assail 'Racist' Scalia Comments," CNN.com, December 10, 2015, http://www.cnn.com/2015/12/10/politics/harry-reid-antonin-scalia-racist-comments/index.html.

36. Tom Gualtieri, "The Worst Person in America: Antonin Scalia," *Weeklings*, July 2, 2015, http://www.theweeklings.com/tgualtieri/2015/07/02/the-worst-person-in-america-antonin-scalia/.

37. Rachel Dicker, "The 8 Most Horrible Reactions to Justice Scalia's Death," *US News & World Report*, February 16, 2016, https://www.usnews.com/news/articles/2016-02-16/antonin-scalias-death-unleashes-a-twitter-hate-storm-against-the-late-justice.

38. Tomás Ríos, Twitter post, February 13, 2016, 4:35 p.m., https://twitter.com/TheTomasRios.

39. David Ehrlich, Twitter post, February 13, 2016, 1:59 p.m., https://twitter.com/davidehrlich.

40. Silvia Killingsworth, Twitter post, February 13, 2016, 4:22 p.m., https://twitter.com/silviakillings.

41. "Truly Evil Supreme Court Justice Antonin Scalia Is Dead, and I'm Not Sure How to Feel," *Daily News Bin*, February 13, 2016, http://www.dailynewsbin.com/opinion/evil-supreme-court-justice-antonin-scalia-is-dead-and-im-not-sure-how-to-feel/23822/.

42. Dahlia Lithwick, "Why Liberals Loved to Hate Antonin Scalia: He Presented Cruel, Demeaning Views in Thought-Provoking and Stirring Ways," *Slate*, February 14, 2016, http://www.slate.com/articles/news_and_politics/jurisprudence/2016/02/why_liberals_loved_to_hate_antonin_scalia.html.

43. Lithwick, "Why Liberals Loved to Hate Antonin Scalia."

44. Robert Gehl, "Here Comes the Evil: The Left Reacts to the Death of Antonin

Scalia," *Federalist Papers Project*, February 13, 2016, http://www.thefederalistpapers.org/us/here-comes-the-evil-the-left-reacts-to-the-death-of-antonin-scalia.

45. Rachel Anspach, "Scalia Was Not a Hero. He Was a Bigot," *Huffington Post*, February 17, 2016, http://www.huffingtonpost.com/rachel-anspach/scalia-was-not-a-hero-he-_b_9245850.html, and Eric Zuesse, "Face It: Antonin Scalia Is Just a Bigot in a Black Robe," *Washington's Blog*, March 27, 2013, http://www.washingtonsblog.com/2013/03/face-it-antonin-scalia-is-just-a-bigot-in-a-black-robe.html.

46. Michael Leff, "Textual Criticism: The Legacy of G.P. Mohrmann," *Quarterly Journal of Speech* 72 (1986): 378, doi: 10.1080/00335638609383783.

Chapter 1

1. Philip Bobbitt, *Constitutional Fate: Theory of the Constitution* (New York: Oxford University Press, 1982), 3

2. See Bobbitt, *Constitutional Fate.*

3. Mark Tushnet, "The Possibilities of Comparative Constitutional Law," *Yale Law Journal* 108 (1999): 1289, doi: 10.2307/797327

4. John F. Manning, "Textualism and the Equity of the Statute," *Columbia Law Review* 101, no. 1 (2001): 108–9, doi: 10.2307/1123509.

5. See Walter Wheeler Cook, "'Substance' and 'Procedure' in the Conflict of Laws," *Yale Law Journal* 42 (1933): 337, doi: 10.2307/791291.

6. Strauss, "Textualism and the Bill of Right," 1154.

7. A 1998 issue of *George Washington Law Review* was devoted to textualism. See Jed Rubenfeld, "Textualism and Democratic Legitimacy: The Moment and the Millennium," *George Washington Law Review* 66 (1998): 1085–1111; Lillian R. BeVier, "Textualism and Democratic Legitimacy: The Moment and the Millennium; A Question of Time, or Law?" *George Washington Law Review* 66 (1998): 1112–18; Frank H. Easterbrook, "Textualism and Democratic Legitimacy: Textualism and the Dead Hand," *George Washington Law Review* 66 (1998): 1119–26; Michael W. McConnell, "Textualism and Democratic Legitimacy: Textualism and the Dead Hand of the Past," *George Washington Law Review* 66 (1998): 1127–47; Suzanna Sherry, "Textualism and the Bill of Right: Textualism and Judgment," *George Washington Law Review* 66 (1998): 1148–52; David A. Strauss, "Textualism and the Bill of Right: The New Textualism in Constitutional Law," *George Washington Law Review* 66 (1998): 1153–60; Bradford R. Clark, "Textualism and Federalism: A Structural Approach," *George Washington Law Review* 66 (1998): 1161–97; Gregory E. Maggs, "Textualism and Federalism: Translating Federalism; A Textualist Reaction," *George Washington Law Review* 66 (1998): 1198–268; Michael Kent Curtis, "Textualism and the Civil War Amendment: Two Textual Adventures; Thoughts on Reading Jeffrey Rosen's Paper," *George Washington Law Review* 66 (1998): 1269–300; William N. Eskridge Jr., "Textualism and Original Understanding: Should the Supreme Court Read the Federalist but Not Statutory Legislative History?" *George Washington Law Review* 66 (1998): 1301–23; Ira C. Lupu, "Textualism and Original Understanding: Time, the Supreme Court, and The Federalist," *George Washington Law Review* 66 (1998): 1324–36; John F. Manning, "Textualism and Original Understanding: Textualism and the Role of the Federalist in Constitutional Adjudication," *George Washington Law Review* 66 (1998): 1337–72; Steven G. Calabresi, "Concluding Essay: Textualism and the Countermajoritarian Difficulty," *George Washington Law Review* 66 (1998): 1373–94.

8. William F. Harris II, *The Interpretable Constitution* (Baltimore: Johns Hopkins University Press, 1993), 30.

9. Woodrow Wilson, "What Is Progress?" in *The New Freedom: A Call for the Emancipation of the Generous Energies of a People* (New York: Doubleday, Page, and Company, 1913), 33–54. Available at Gutenberg.org, September 16, 2014, http://www.gutenberg.org/files/14811/14811-h/14811-h.htm.

10. Gompers v. United States, 233 U.S. 604 (1914) at 610.

11. Olmstead v. United States, 277 U.S. 438 (1928) at 473, citing Weems v. United States 217 U.S. 349 (1910) at 373.

12. Benjamin Nathan Cardozo, *The Nature of the Judicial Process* (New Haven: Yale University Press, 1921), 17.

13. Franklin Delano Roosevelt, "'Only Thing We Have to Fear Is Fear Itself': FDR's First Inaugural Address," *History Matters*, September 11, 2014, http://historymatters.gmu.edu/d/5057/.

14. Howard Lee McBain, *The Living Constitution: A Consideration of the Realities and Legends of Our Fundamental Law* (New York: Workers' Education Bureau Press, 1927).

15. James M. Beck, "The Changed Conception of the Constitution," *Proceedings of the American Philosophical Society* 69 (1930): 99–115.

16. James M. Beck, "The Changed Conception of the Constitution," *Proceedings of the American Philosophical Society* 69 (1930): 102.

17. Horace H. Hagan, "The Elasticity of the Federal Constitution," *Virginia Law Review* 20, no.4 (Feb. 1934): 391–401, doi: 10.2307/1066399.

18. Edward S. Corwin, "Moratorium over *Minnesota*," *University of Pennsylvania Law Review* 82, no. 4 (1934), 311–16, 314, doi: 10.2307/3308506.

19. James Hart, "A Unified Economy and States' Rights," *Annals of the American Academy of Political and Social Science* 185 (May 1936), 102–14.

20. Charles A. Beard, "The Living Constitution," *Annals of the American Academy of Political and Social Science* 185, no. 1 (May 1936), 29–34, 31.

21. West Coast Hotel Company v. Parrish, 300 U.S. 379 (1937).

22. See Cass Sunstein, "Justice Breyer's Democratic Pragmatism," *Yale Law Journal* 115, no. 7 (2006): 1719–43.

23. Lino A. Graglia, "Does Constitutional Law Exist?" *National Review* (June 26, 1995): 31–35.

24. William H. Rehnquist, "The Notion of a Living Constitution," *Texas Law Review* 54 (1976): 693–706.

25. William H. Rehnquist, "The Notion of a Living Constitution," *Harvard Journal of Law & Public Policy* 29, no. 2 (Spring 2006): 401–15.

26. Missouri v. Holland, 252 U.S. 416 (1920).

27. Rehnquist, "The Notion of a Living Constitution," 403.

28. Marbury v. Madison, 5 U.S. 137 (1803).

29. Attorney General Edwin Meese, "Address" House of Delegates, American Bar Association, Washington, DC, July 9, 1985.

30. Antonin Scalia, "Common-Law Courts in a Civil-Law System: The Role of United States Federal Courts in Interpreting the Constitution and Laws," in *A Matter of Interpretation: Federal Courts and the Law*, ed. Amy Gutmann (Princeton: Princeton University Press, 1997).

31. Robert Bork, *The Tempting of America: The Political Seduction of the Law* (New York: Touchstone, 1990).

32. See John Ely, "The Wages of Crying Wolf: A Comment on *Roe v. Wade*," *Yale Law Review* 82 (1973): 920–49.

33. Thomas C. Grey, "Do We Have an Unwritten Constitution?" *Stanford Law Review* 27, no. 3 (1975): 703–18, doi: 10.2307/1228335.

34. Associate Justice William J. Brennan Jr., "The Constitution of the United States: Contemporary Ratification," Address delivered at Text and Teaching Symposium, Georgetown University, Washington, DC, October 12, 1985.

35. Stephen Breyer, *Active Liberty: Interpreting Our Democratic Constitution* (New York: Knopf, 2005).

36. James Boyd White, *When Words Lose Their Meanings: Constitutions and Reconstitutions of Language, Character, and Community* (Chicago: University of Chicago Press, 1984).

37. Grey, "Do We Have an Unwritten Constitution?"

38. J. M. Balkin, "A Night in the Topics: The Reason of Legal Rhetoric and the Rhetoric of Legal Reason," in *Law's Stories: Narrative and Rhetoric in the Law*, ed. Peter Brooks and Paul Gewirth (New Haven, CT: Yale University Press, 1996), 211–24.

39. See, for example, Jack N. Rakove, "Mr. Meese, Meet Mr. Madison," *Atlantic Monthly* (December 1986), 77–86; Howard Kurtz, "Meese's View on Court Rulings Assailed, Defended," *Washington Post* (October 24, 1986): A12; Michael Kinsley, "Meese's Stink Bomb," *Washington Post* (October 29, 1986): A19; Anthony Lewis, "Law or Power?" *New York Times* (October 27, 1986): A23; "Mr. Meese's Contempt of Court," *New York Times* (November 2, 1986): § 4 at 23, col. 1; Pete Yost, "Meese's View of Supreme Court Would Lead to Chaos, Critics Say," *Associated Press* (October 24, 1986), accessed August 26, 2014, http://www.apnewsarchive.com/1986/Meese-s-Views-of-Supreme-Court-Would-Lead-to-Chaos-Critics-Say/id-3ff4063b92d5df2901ea2d339a563a92.

40. Edwin Meese, "The American Bar Association," The United States Department of Justice (July 9, 1985): 1–8, accessed March 10, 2017, https://www.justice.gov/sites/default/files/ag/legacy/2011/08/23/07-09-1985.pdf.

41. "The Great Debate: Interpreting Our Written Constitution," The Federalist Society for Law and Public Policy Studies (1986), accessed March 10, 2017, http://www.ruleoflawus.info/Constitutional%20Interpretation/Federalist%20Soc.-Great%20Debate-Interpreting%20Our%20Constitution.pdf.

42. Meese, "Address Before the D.C. Chapter of the Federalist Society Lawyers Division," 11.

43. Meese, "The American Bar Association," 7.

44. Brennan, "Speech Given at the Text and Teaching Symposium."

45. Brennan, "Speech Given at the Text and Teaching Symposium."

46. Brennan, "Speech Given at the Text and Teaching Symposium."

47. John Paul Stevens, "Before the Federal Bar Association," The Federalist Society for Law and Public Policy Studies (October 23, 1985), accessed March 20, 2017, http://www.ruleoflawus.info/Constitutional%20Interpretation/Federalist%20Soc.-Great%20Debate-Interpreting%20Our%20Constitution.pdf.

48. Meese, "Address Before the D.C. Chapter of the Federalist Society Lawyers Division," 1–15.

49. Robert Bork, "Before the University of San Diego Law School," The Federalist Society for Law and Public Policy Studies (November 18, 1985), accessed March 10, 2017, http://www.ruleoflawus.info/Constitutional%20Interpretation/Federalist%20Soc.-Great%20Debate-Interpreting%20Our%20Constitution.pdf.

50. Bork, "Before the University of San Diego Law School."

51. Bork, "Before the University of San Diego Law School."

52. Examples include Dred Scott v. Sandford, 60 U.S. 393 (1857); Roe v. Wade, 410 U.S. 113 (1973); and *Citizens United v. Federal Election Commission*, 558 U.S. 310 (2010).

53. See David Adamany, "Legitimacy, Realigning Elections, and the Supreme Court," *Wisconsin Law Review* 3 (1973): 790–846, doi: 10.1177/106591299404700306.

54. In James L. Gibson and Michael J. Nelson, "Is the U.S. Supreme Court's Legitimacy Grounded in Performance Satisfaction and Ideology," *American Journal of Political Science* 59, no. 1 (January 2015): 162–74, the authors argue that, generally speaking, the public is satisfied with what the court does even if individuals will disagree about a single decision of the court.

Chapter 2

1. See Jean Kirtley, "Scalia and His Speeches," *American Journal Review* 26, no. 3 (June/July 2004), accessed July 15, 2014, http://ajrarchive.org/article.asp?id=3686. In fact, the Supreme Court has a Web page where speeches the justices have delivered can be posted, and Scalia does not allow any of his to be posted. See "Speeches," Supreme Court of the United States, accessed July 15, 2014, http://www.supremecourt.gov/publicinfo/speeches/speeches.aspx.

2. Accessed July 26, 2016, https://www.supremecourt.gov/publicinfo/speeches/speeches.aspx.

3. David Savage, in the *Los Angeles Times*, reports, "Scalia is one of the most talkative, but least seen, of the nine Supreme Court justices." David G. Savage, "Some 'Mystified' by Award to Scalia for Free Speech," *Los Angeles Times* (March 20, 2003), A28.

4. One exception exists: Antonin Scalia, "Reflections on the Future of the Legal Academy," William and Mary Law School 2014 Commencement Exercises (May 11, 2014), accessed July 15, 2014, https://law.wm.edu/news/stories/2014/documents-2014/2014WMCommencementSpeech.pdf. This exception was noted by the *Washington Post*. See Will Baude, "Justice Scalia's Commencement Speech at William & Mary Law School," *Washington Post* (May 16, 2014), accessed July 15, 2014, http://www.washingtonpost.com/news/volokh-conspiracy/wp/2014/05/16/justice-scalias-commencement-speech-at-william-mary-law-school/.

5. One will find many such examples if one searches YouTube.com for "Antonin Scalia."

6. Savage, "Some 'Mystified' by Award to Scalia for Free Speech," A28.

7. See Marshall McLuhan, *Understanding Media: The Extensions of Man* (Boston, MA: MIT Press, 1964), 7–23.

8. See Robert A. Ferguson, "The Judicial Opinion as Literary Genre," *Yale Journal of Law & the Humanities* 2, no. 1 (1990): 201–19.

9. See Catherine L. Langford, "Toward a Genre of Judicial Dissent: *Lochner* and *Casey* as Exemplars," *Communication Law Review* 9 (2009): 1–12.

10. Not all of these speeches remain available online. The author has hard copies of all of them in her files. Antonin Scalia, "1989 Sibley Lecture: Reflections on the Constitution," *Sibley Lecture Series* (1989), accessed June 12, 2003, http://digitalcommons.law.uga.edu/lectures_pre_arch_lectures_sibley/63/; Antonin Scalia, "A Theory of Constitutional Interpretation," Catholic University of America (October 18, 1996), accessed March 10, 2017, http://www.proconservative.net/PCVol5Is225ScaliaTheoryConstlInterpretation

.shtml; Antonin Scalia, "On Interpreting the Constitution," *Manhattan Institute for Policy Research* (November 17, 1997), accessed March 10, 2017, https://www.manhattan-institute.org/html/1997-wriston-lecture-interpreting-constitution-8063.html; Antonin Scalia, "God's Justice and Ours," PewForum.org (January 2, 2002), accessed March 10, 2017, https://www.firstthings.com/article/2002/05/gods-justice-and-ours; Antonin Scalia, "Constitutional Interpretation the Old Fashioned Way," CFIF.org (March 14, 2005), accessed March 10, 2017, https://www.bc.edu/content/dam/files/centers/boisi/pdf/Symposia/Symposia%202010-2011/Constitutional_Interpretation_Scalia.pdf.

11. This is his thought regardless of what he states. For example, in his "Constitutional Interpretation the Old Fashioned Way," Scalia maintains, "My Constitution is a very flexible Constitution. You think the death penalty is a good idea—persuade your fellow citizens and adopt it. You think it's a bad idea—persuade them the other way and eliminate it." In his statement Scalia recognizes that the document is not flexible at all—it is static and must be altered through the process of constitutional amendment.

12. Scalia, Sibley Lecture.

13. Scalia, Sibley Lecture.

14. Stephen Breyer, *Active Liberty: Interpreting Our Democratic Constitution* (New York: Alfred A. Knopf, 2005). The liberty of the ancients, Breyer explains, is an "activity liberty," which asserts that the power to rule lies in the hands of the citizens themselves through "participatory self-government." The liberty of the moderns, on the other hand, enables the government to protect the minority from the tyranny of the majority. Breyer calls for judicial restraint but nevertheless locates the right to protect such liberty in judicial review and loose forms of constitutional interpretation.

15. Scalia's assertion that constitutional law is more enduring than statutory law is a bit ironic, since he just declared that the Constitution should be interpreted as a statute. Nevertheless, this is the argument he makes.

16. Scalia, "A Theory of Constitution Interpretation."

17. *Minor v. Happersett*, 88 U.S. 162 (1874).

18. Scalia, "A Theory of Constitution Interpretation."

19. Scalia, "On Interpreting the Constitution."

20. Scalia, "On Interpreting the Constitution."

21. Scalia, "On Interpreting the Constitution."

22. Scalia, "God's Justice and Ours."

23. See Scalia, "Constitutional Interpretation the Old Fashioned Way."

24. See Wayne A. Meeks, "Apocalyptic Discourse and Strategies of Goodness," *Journal of Religion* 80 (July 2000): 461–75.

25. See Edward W. Said, *Orientalism* (New York: Vintage, 1979); Jacques Derrida, "Violence and Metaphysics," in *Writing and Difference*, trans. Alan Bass (Chicago: University of Chicago Press, 1978); John Muckelbauer, "Rhetoric, Asignification, and the Other: A Response to Diane Davis," *Philosophy & Rhetoric* 40, no. 2 (2007): 238–47, doi:10.1353/para.2007.0023; Luke A. Winslow, "The Imaged Other: Style and Substance in the Rhetoric of Joel Osteen," *Southern Communication Journal* 79, no. 3 (July–August 2014): 250–71; Fernando Resende, "Inventing Muslims as the Other in Nineteenth-century Brazil," *Middle East Journal of Culture & Communication* 6, no. 2 (2013): 178–93; and Luke Winslow, "Promise Keepers and the Rhetoric of the Stylized Other," *Journal of Communication & Religion* 35, no. 1 (March 2012): 73–89.

26. Scalia, "Constitutional Interpretation the Old Fashioned Way."

27. Scalia, "Constitutional Interpretation the Old Fashioned Way."
28. Scalia, "Constitutional Interpretation the Old Fashioned Way."
29. Scalia, "Constitutional Interpretation the Old Fashioned Way."
30. Scalia, "Constitutional Interpretation the Old Fashioned Way."
31. Scalia, "Constitutional Interpretation the Old Fashioned Way."
32. Scalia, "Constitutional Interpretation the Old Fashioned Way."
33. Scalia, "Constitutional Interpretation the Old Fashioned Way."
34. Scalia, "Common-Law Courts in a Civil-Law System," 17.
35. Scalia, "The Rule of Law as a Law of Rules"; Scalia, "Originalism: The Lesser Evil"; Scalia, "Common-Law Courts in a Civil-Law System"; and Scalia and Garner, *Reading Law*.
36. Scalia, "The Rule of Law as a Law of Rules," 1176.
37. Scalia, "The Rule of Law as a Law of Rules," 1183.
38. Scalia, "The Rule of Law as a Law of Rules," 1183–84.
39. Scalia, "Originalism," 862.
40. Scalia, "Originalism," 857.
41. Scalia, "Common-Law Courts in a Civil-Law System," 3.
42. Scalia, "Common-Law Courts in a Civil-Law System," 17.
43. Scalia, "Common-Law Courts in a Civil-Law System," 16.
44. Scalia, "Common-Law Courts in a Civil-Law System," 23. In "Constitutional Interpretation the Old Fashioned Way," Scalia repeats this idea: "I do not think the Constitution, or any text should be interpreted either strictly or sloppily; it should be interpreted reasonably."
45. Scalia, "Common-Law Courts in a Civil-Law System," 24.
46. Scalia, "Common-Law Courts in a Civil-Law System," 37.
47. Scalia, "Common-Law Courts in a Civil-Law System," 37.
48. Scalia, "Common-Law Courts in a Civil-Law System," 38.
49. Scalia, "Common-Law Courts in a Civil-Law System," 41.
50. Richard A. Posner, "The Incoherence of Antonin Scalia," *New Republic* (August 24, 2012), accessed October 24, 2014, http://www.newrepublic.com/article/magazine/books-and-arts/106441/scalia-garner-reading-the-law-textual-originalism.
51. Scalia and Garner, *Reading Law*, 16.
52. Scalia and Garner, *Reading Law*, 15.
53. Scalia and Garner, *Reading Law*, 15.
54. For a discussion of secular time, see Michael Leff, "Dimensions of Temporality in Lincoln's Second Inaugural," *Communication Reports* 1 (1988): 27–31, doi: 10.1080/08934218809367458. For a discussion of public time, see Roger Stahl, "A Clockwork War: Rhetorics of Time in a Time of Terror," *Quarterly Journal of Speech* 94, no. 1 (2008): 73–99.
55. Robert Hariman, *Political Style: The Artistry of Power* (Chicago: University of Chicago Press, 1995), 95–140.
56. J. Michael Hogan and Glen Williams, "Republican Charisma and the American Revolution: The Textual Persona of Thomas Paine's *Common Sense*," *Quarterly Journal of Speech* 86, no. 1 (February 2000): 8, doi: 10.1080/00335630009384276.
57. Scalia and Garner, *Reading Law*, 16–17.
58. Scalia and Garner, *Reading Law*, 414.
59. Scalia, "On Interpreting the Constitution."
60. Scalia, "God's Justice and Ours."

Chapter 3

1. See Sir William Blackstone, *Commentaries on the Laws of England* (Oxford, England: Clarendon Press, 1765–1769), accessed January 23, 2014, http://www.lonang.com/exlibris/blackstone/index.html.

2. See Anthony F. Granucci, "Nor Cruel and Unusual Punishments Inflicted: The Original Meaning," *California Law Review* 57, no. 4 (1969): 839–65.

3. See Granucci, "Nor Cruel and Unusual Punishments Inflicted," 853.

4. Granucci, "Nor Cruel and Unusual Punishments Inflicted," 847.

5. Louisiana ex rel. Francis v. Resweber, 329 U.S. 459 (1947).

6. Robinson v. California, 370 U.S. 660 (1962).

7. In re Kemmler, 136 U.S. 436 at 447.

8. Wilkerson v. Utah, 99 U.S. 130 (1878); In re Kemmler, 136 U.S. 436 (1890); Rummel v. Estelle (1980); Harmelin v. Michigan, 501 U.S. 957 (1991); and Lockyer v. Andrade, 538 U.S. 63 (2003).

9. Weems v. United States, 217 U.S. 349 (1910); Trop v. Dulles, 356 U.S. 86 (1958); Robinson v. California, 370 U.S. 660 (1962); Coker v. Georgia, 433 U.S. 584 (1977); Enmund v. Florida, 458 U.S. 782 (1982); Solem v. Helm, 463 U.S. 277 (1983); and Kennedy v. Louisiana, 554 U.S. 407 (2008).

10. Furman v. Georgia, 408 U.S. 238 (1972).

11. Gregg v. Georgia, 428 U.S. 153 (1976); Proffitt v. Florida, 428 U.S. 242 (1976); Jurek v. Texas, 428 U.S. 262 (1976); and Woodson v. North Carolina, 428 U.S. 280 (1976).

12. Lockett v. Ohio, 438 U.S. 586 (1978); Bell v. Ohio, 438 U.S. 637 (1978); Eddings v. Oklahoma, 455 U.S. 104 (1982); and Enmund v. Florida, 458 U.S. 782 (1982).

13. See *Weems*.

14. *Coker*.

15. Hutto v. Finney, 437 U.S. at 685.

16. *Solem*, 463 U.S. at 288.

17. *Solem*, 463 U.S. at 290.

18. McCleskey v. Kemp, 481 U.S. 279 (1987).

19. See Atkins v. Virginia, 536 U.S. 304 (2002).

20. *Trop*, 356 U.S. at 101.

21. See Thompson v. Oklahoma, 487 U.S. 815 (1988).

22. Stanford v. Kentucky, 492 U.S. 361 (1989).

23. Roper v. Simmons, 543 U.S. at 554.

24. *Atkins*, 536 U.S. at 321.

25. *Atkins*, 536 U.S. at 314.

26. See *Wilkerson* (1879); *In re Kemmler* (1890); *Resweber* (1947); and Baze v. Rees, 553 U.S. 35 (2008).

27. In Gray v. Lucas, 463 U.S. 1237 (1983), Chief Justice John Marshall dissented from a stay of execution in a gas chamber execution. In Glass v. Louisiana, 471 U.S. 1080 (1985), Justice Brennan and Justice Blackmun both dissented in a denial of certiorari for a case involving the electric chair. In Gomez v. US District Court, 503 U.S. 654 (1992), Justice Stevens dissented from an order vacating a stay of execution in a gas chamber case. In each of their dissents the justices challenged the method of execution as inhumane or a violation of human dignity.

28. The opinions include Scalia's majority opinions: *Stanford*; Wilson v. Seiter, 501 U.S. 294 (1991); and *Harmelin*; Scalia's concurring opinions: West v. Atkins, 487 U.S. 42

(1988); Walton v. Arizona, 497 U.S. 639 (1990); Payne v. Tennessee, 501 U.S. 808 (1991); Austin v. United States, 509 U.S. 602 (1993); Herrera v. Collins, 506 U.S. 390 (1993); Johnson v. Texas, 509 U.S. 350 (1993); Tuilaepa v. California, 512 U.S. 967 (1994); Buchanan v. Angelone, 522 U.S. 269 (1998); Oregon v. Guzek, 546 U.S. 517 (2006); Ornaski v. Belmontes, 549 U.S. (2006); and Baze v. Rees, 553 U.S. 35 (2008); Scalia's dissenting opinions: *Thompson*; South Carolina v. Gathers, 490 U.S. 805 (1989); McKoy v. North Carolina, 494 U.S. 433 (1990); Espinosa v. Florida, 505 U.S. 1079 (1992); *Atkins*; Moore v. Texas, 535 U.S. 1044 (2002); Patterson v. Texas, 536 U.S. 984 (2002); *Roper*; Abdul-Kabir v. Quarterman, 550 U.S. 233 (2007); and Brown v. Plata, 563 U.S. 493 (2011); and Scalia's concurring in part and dissenting in part: Penry v. Lynaugh, 492 U.S. 302 (1989); and Sochor v. Florida, 504 U.S. 527 (1992).

29. See *Thompson*, 487 U.S. at 864.
30. *Atkins*, 536 U.S. at 349.
31. *Harmelin*, 501 U.S. at 995.
32. *Atkins*, 536 U.S. at 343.
33. *Stanford*, 492 U.S. at 373–74.
34. Stanford v. Kentucky, 492 U.S. at 378.
35. *Stanford*, 492 U.S. at 370.
36. *Penry*, 492 U.S. at 351.
37. *Walton*, 497 U.S. at 670.
38. *Harmelin*, 501 U.S. at 967.
39. *Thompson*, 487 U.S. at 870.
40. *Walton*, 497 U.S. at 670.
41. *Harmelin*, 501 U.S. at 974.
42. *Harmelin*, 501 U.S. at 974.
43. *Harmelin*, 501 U.S. at 975–76.
44. *Harmelin*, 501 U.S. at 976.
45. *Stanford*, 492 U.S. at 378.
46. Leviticus 17:10 NASB and Leviticus 26:17 NASB, respectively.
47. Ezekiel 15:7 NASB.
48. Luke 9:51.
49. *Wilson*, 501 U.S. at 300.
50. *Wilson*, 501 U.S. at 302.
51. *Atkins*, 536 U.S. at 307.
52. *Atkins*, 536 U.S. at 338.
53. *Atkins*, 536 U.S. at 338.
54. *Thompson*, 487 U.S. at 860.
55. *Thompson*, 487 U.S. at 862.
56. *Walton*, 497 U.S. at 674.
57. Simmons v. South Carolina, 512 U.S. at 181.
58. *Simmons*, 512 U.S. at 182.
59. *Simmons*, 512 U.S. at 181.
60. *Atkins*, 536 U.S. at 350.
61. *Atkins*, 536 U.S. at 350.
62. *Atkins*, 536 U.S. at 351.
63. *Atkins*, 536 U.S. at 351.
64. *Atkins*, 536 U.S. at 350.
65. *Moore*, 535 U.S. at 1045.

66. *Roper*, 543 U.S. at 619.

67. *Roper*, 543 U.S. at 619.

68. *Baze*, 553 U.S. at 91.

69. The Model Penal Code, § (3)h as quoted in footnote 44 of *Gregg*.

70. Idaho, for example, published ICJI 1713 HAC Instruction defining each of the terms. Available at http://www.isc.idaho.gov/jury/criminal/1700/ICJI_1713.doc.

71. *Atkins*, 536 U.S. at 339.

72. *Atkins*, 536 U.S. at 339.

73. *Moore*, 535 U.S. at 1045.

74. *Moore*, 535 U.S. at 1046.

75. *Roper*, 543 U.S. at 618.

76. *Roper*, 543 U.S. at 619.

77. *Roper*, 543 U.S. at 619.

78. See *Thompson*, 487 U.S. at 860–61.

79. *Simmons*, 512 U.S. at 181.

80. *Brown*, 563 U.S. at 1957.

81. *Walton*, 497 U.S. at 662–65.

82. *Atkins*, 536 U.S. at 344.

83. *Walton*, 497 U.S. at 669.

84. *Walton*, 497 U.S. at 658.

85. *Tuilaepa*, 512 U.S. 967 (1994).

86. *Herrera*, 506 U.S. at 429.

87. See *Harmelin*, 501 U.S. 957 (1991).

88. See *Baze*, 553 U.S. at 89.

89. *Brown*, 563 U.S. at 1956.

90. *Baze*, 553 U.S. at 90.

91. *Walton*, 497 U.S. at 657.

92. *Atkins*, 536 U.S. at 354.

93. See *Thompson* (1988).

94. *Roper*, 543 U.S. at 609.

95. *Thompson*, 487 U.S. at 867.

96. *Thompson*, 487 U.S. at 868.

97. *Thompson*, 487 U.S. at 870.

98. *Atkins*, 536 U.S. at 342.

99. *Baze*, 553 U.S. at 89, quoting *Gregg*, 96 S.Ct. at 175.

100. *Atkins*, 536 U.S. at 341.

101. *Walton*, 497 U.S. at 660.

Chapter 4

1. Noah Feldman, "The Intellectual Origins of the Establishment Clause," *New York University Law Review* 77, no. 2 (2002): 346–428.

2. 1 *Annals of Congress* 451 (Joseph Gales ed., 1789).

3. *Journal of the First Session of the Senate of the United States*, August 1789, reprinted in 1 *Documentary History of the First Federal Congress of the United States of America* 104, 136 (Linda Grant DePauw ed., 1972).

4. Thomas J. Curry, *The First Freedoms: Church and State in America to the Passage of the First Amendment* (1986), 207 (quoting 1 *Documentary History of the First Federal Congress of the United States of America* 151, 166 [Linda Grant DePauw ed., 1977]).

5. Isaiah Berlin, "Two Concepts of Liberty," in Berlin's *Four Essays on Liberty* (Oxford: Oxford University Press, 1969), 3–57.

6. Everson v. Board of Education, 330 U.S. 1 (1947) and Mueller v. Allen, 463 U.S. 388 (1983).

7. Tilton v. Richardson, 403 U.S. 672 (1971).

8. Santa Fe Independent School District v. Jane Doe, 530 U.S. 290 (2000) and Lee v. Weisman, 505 U.S. 577 (1992).

9. McCreary County v. American Civil Liberties Union, 545 U.S. 844 (2005); *Van Orden* (2005).

10. Agostini v. Felton, 521 U.S. 203 (1997).

11. County of Allegheny v. American Civil Liberties Union, 492 U.S. 573 (1989).

12. Lynch v. Donnelly, 465 U.S. 668 (1984).

13. See Reynolds v. United States, 98 U.S. 145 (1878).

14. See Sherbert v. Verner, 374 U.S. 398 (1963).

15. See Wisconsin v. Yoder, 406 U.S. 205 (1972).

16. United States v. Lee, 455 U.S. 252 (1982).

17. Bowen v. Roy, 476 U.S. 693 (1986).

18. Goldman v. Weinberger, 475 U.S. 503 (1986).

19. Lyng v. Northwest Indian Cemetery Protective Association, 485 U.S. 439 (1988).

20. In his analysis of the First Amendment, Feldman concludes that the intellectual origins of the religion clauses can be traced to John Locke's thoughts about the "freedom of conscience." See Feldman, "The Intellectual Origins of the Establishment Clause."

21. Arizona Christian School Tuition Organization v. Winn, 131 S.Ct. 1436 (2011).

22. *Good News Club*, 533 U.S. at 121.

23. *Capitol Square*, 515 U.S. at 767.

24. *Capitol Square*, 515 U.S. at 767.

25. *McCreary County*, 545 U.S. at 886.

26. Perry Education Association v. Perry Local Educators' Association, 460 U.S. 37 (1983).

27. *Capitol Square*, 515 U.S. at 770.

28. *Capitol Square*, 515 U.S. at 768.

29. *Pleasant Grove*, 555 U.S. at 483.

30. *Good News Club*, 533 U.S. at 124.

31. Edwards v. Aguillard, 482 U.S. at 615.

32. Lee v. Weisman, 505 U.S. at 646.

33. *Edwards*, 482 U.S. at 628.

34. *McCreary County*, 545 U.S. at 902–03.

35. *Weisman*, 505 U.S. at 640.

36. *Weisman*, 505 U.S. at 634.

37. *Edwards*, 482 U.S. at 613.

38. *Edwards*, 482 U.S. at 636.

39. Kiryas Joel v. Grumet, 512 U.S. 687 (1994) at 741.

40. *Kiryas Joel*, 512 U.S. at 751.

41. *Kiryas Joel*, 512 U.S. at 901.

42. *McCreary County*, 545 U.S. 844 at 902.

43. Employment Division v. Smith, 494 U.S. 872 (1990) at 877–78.

44. *Employment Division*, 494 U.S. at 877–78.

45. Locke v. Davey, 540 U.S. at 731.

46. See Oregon Revised Statues §161.605 (2001) and §161.625 (2001).

47. See *Employment Division*, 494 U.S. at 878.

48. *Locke*, 540 U.S. at 733.

49. "America's Changing Religious Landscape: Christians Decline Sharply as Share of Population; Unaffiliated and Other Faiths Continue to Grow," Pew Research Center, accessed February 6, 2016, http://www.pewforum.org/2015/05/12/americas-changing-religious-landscape/.

50. See Robert Bellah, "Civil Religion in America," *Daedalus* 96, no. 1 (1967):1–21.

51. *Employment Division*, 494 U.S. at 877.

52. *Employment Division*, 494 U.S. at 880.

53. *Employment Division*, 494 U.S. at 877.

54. *Employment Division*, 494 U.S. at 890.

55. Church of Lukumi Babalu Aye, Inc. v. City of Hialeah, 508 U.S. at 558.

56. Antonin Scalia, "Common-Law Courts in a Civil-Law System: The Role of the United States Federal Courts in Interpreting the Constitution and Laws," in *A Matter of Interpretation* (Princeton: Princeton University Press, 1997), 17.

Chapter 5

1. Olmstead v. United States, 277 U.S. at 478.

2. *Olmstead*, 277 U.S. at 478.

3. Meyer v. Nebraska, 262 U.S. 390 (1923).

4. Pierce v. Society of Sisters, 268 U.S. 510 (1925).

5. Griswold v. Connecticut, 381 U.S. at 484.

6. Roe v. Wade, 410 U.S. 113 (1973).

7. City of Akron v. Akron Center for Reproductive Health, 462 U.S. 416 (1983).

8. Whole Woman's Health v. Hellerstedt, 136 S.Ct. 2292 (2016).

9. Webster v. Reproductive Health Services, 492 U.S. 490 (1989) (concurring in part and concurring in judgment); Hodgson v. Minnesota, 497 U.S. 417 (1990) (concurring in the judgment in part and dissenting in part); Ohio v. Akron Center for Reproductive Health, 497 U.S. 502 (1990) (concurring); Planned Parenthood v. Casey, 505 U.S. 833 (1992) (concurring in judgment in part and dissenting in part); Bray v. Alexandria, 506 U.S. 263 (1993) (majority opinion); and Stenberg v. Carhart, 530 U.S. 490 (1989) (dissenting).

10. George Lakoff and Mark Johnson, *Metaphors We Live By* (Chicago: University of Chicago Press, 1962), 2.

11. Lakoff and Johnson, *Metaphors We Live By*, 2.

12. *Akron II*, 497 U.S. at 520.

13. *Hodgson*, 497 U.S. at 480.

14. *Webster*, 492 U.S. at 535.

15. *Casey*, 505 U.S. at 1000.

16. Other metaphors are used. See, for example, Michael Osborn, "Archetypal Metaphor in Rhetoric: The Light-Dark Family," *Quarterly Journal of Speech* 53, no. 2 (1967): 115–26; Kathleen Hall Jamieson, "The Metaphoric Cluster in the Rhetoric of Pope Paul VI and Edmund G. Brown Jr.," *Quarterly Journal of Speech* 66, no. 1 (1980): 51–72; J. Vernon Jenson, "British Voices on the Eve of the American Revolution: Trapped by the Family Metaphor," *Quarterly Journal of Speech* 63, no. 1 (1977): 43–50; William Gribbin, "The Juggernaut Metaphor in American Rhetoric," *Quarterly Journal of Speech* 59, no. 3 (1973): 297–303; Ronald H. Carpenter, "America's Tragic Metaphor: Our Twentieth-

Century Combatants as Frontiersmen," *Quarterly Journal of Speech* 76, no. 1 (1990): 1–22; Roger C. Aden, "Entrapment and Escape: Inventional Metaphors in Ronald Reagan's Economic Rhetoric," *Southern Communication Journal* 54, no. 4 (1988): 384–400; Suzanne M. Daughton, "Metaphorical Transcendence: Images of the Holy War in Franklin Roosevelt's First Inaugural," *Quarterly Journal of Speech* 79, no. 4 (1993): 427–46; Thomas B. Ferrell and G. Thomas Goodnight, "Accidental Rhetoric: The Root Metaphors of Three Mile Island," *Communication Monographs* 48, no. 4 (1981): 271–300; Robert L. Ivie, "Fire, Flood, and Red Fever: Motivating Truman Doctrine Speech," *Presidential Studies Quarterly* 29 (1999): 570–91; Robert L. Ivie, "The Ideology of Freedom's 'Fragility' in American Foreign Policy Argument," *Journal of the American Forensic Association* 24 (1987): 27–36; Ben Voth, "The Wall Separating Church and State: A Longitudinal Analysis of Metaphor as Argument," *Argumentation & Advocacy* 34 (1998): 127–39.

17. *Casey*, 505 U.S. at 979 (emphasis added).
18. *Carhart*, 530 U.S. at 953 (emphasis added).
19. *Casey*, 505 U.S. at 980 (emphasis added).
20. *Bray*, 530 U.S. at 278.
21. *Casey*, 505 U.S. at 980 (emphasis added).
22. *Carhart*, 530 U.S. at 955 (emphasis added).
23. *Hodgson*, 497 U.S. at 480.
24. *Webster*, 492 U.S. at 532.
25. *Akron*, 497 U.S. at 520.
26. *Hodgson*, 497 U.S. at 480.
27. *Casey*, 505 U.S. at 989–90.
28. *Casey*, 505 U.S. at 1002.
29. *Bray*, 530 U.S. at 956.
30. *Carhart*, 530 U.S. at 955.
31. *Hodgson*, 497 U.S. at 479.
32. *Casey*, 505 U.S. at 983.
33. *Casey*, 505 U.S. at 993.
34. *Casey*, 505 U.S. at 993.
35. *Casey*, 505 U.S. at 995.
36. Catherine L. Langford, "Race and Racism in the Collective Memory of the Law: A Rhetorical Analysis of Roger B. Taney and *Dred Scott v. Sandford*," *Communication Law Review* 11 (2011): 1–21. Available at http://commlawreview.org/Archives/CLVv11i2/Race_and_Racism_in_the_Collective_Memory_of_the_Law.pdf.
37. *Bray*, 530 U.S. at 269.
38. *Bray*, 530 U.S. at 273.
39. *Bray*, 530 U.S. at 278 (emphasis added).
40. *Bray*, 530 U.S. at 278.
41. *Bray*, 530 U.S. at 270.
42. *Carhart*, 530 U.S. at 953.

Conclusion

1. Feldman, "The Intellectual Origins of the Establishment Clause," 404.
2. Robert G. Natelson, "The Original Meaning of the Establishment Clause," *William & Mary Bill of Rights Journal* 14, no. 1 (2005): 73–140.
3. Natelson, "The Original Meaning of the Establishment Clause."

4. Vincent Phillip Muñoz, "The Original Meaning of the Free Exercise Clause: The Evidence from the First Congress," *Harvard Journal of Law & Public Policy* 31, no. 3 (2008): 1083–120.

5. See David J. Garrow, *Liberty and Sexuality: The Right to Privacy and the Making of Roe v. Wade* (Berkeley: University of California Press, 1998).

6. See Symposium, "The Model Penal Code," *Columbia Law Review* 63, no. 4 (1963): 589–93.

7. Paul H. Robinson and Markus D. Dubber, "The American Model Penal Code: A Brief Overview," *New Criminal Law Review* 10, no. 3 (2007): 319–41. doi: 10.1525/nclr.2007.10.3.319.

8. Carolyn Shapiro, "How Scalia Played with Fire," CNN.com, February 16, 2016, http://www.cnn.com/2016/02/16/opinions/antonin-scalia-shapiro/index.html.

9. Michael J. Gerhardt, "A Tale of Two Textualists: A Critical Comparison of Justices Black and Scalia," *Boston University Law Review* 74 (1994): 27.

10. See Scalia, "Common-Law Courts in a Civil-Law System," 3–47.

11. Cheney v. US District Court of Columbia, 542 U.S. 367 (2004).

12. As of February 22, 2004.

13. Per Fjelstad, "Legal Judgment and Cultural Motivation: Enthymematic Form in *Marbury v. Madison*," *Southern Communication Journal* 60, no. 1 (1994), 22, doi: 10.1080/10417949409372959.

Bibliography

Abdul-Kabir v. Quarternman, 550 U.S. 233 (2007).

Adamany, David. "Legitimacy, Realigning Elections, and the Supreme Court." *Wisconsin Law Review* 3 (1973): 790–846. doi: 10.1177/106591299404700306.

Aden, Roger C. "Entrapment and Escape: Inventional Metaphors in Ronald Reagan's Economic Rhetoric." *Southern Communication Journal* 54, no. 4 (1988): 384–400.

Akron v. Akron Center for Reproductive Health, 462 U.S. 416 (1983).

"America's Changing Religious Landscape: Christians Decline Sharply as Share of Population; Unaffiliated and Other Faiths Continue to Grow." Pew Research Center. Accessed February 6, 2016. http://www.pewforum.org/2015/05/12/americas-changing-religious-landscape/.

Anspach, Rachel. "Scalia Was Not a Hero. He Was a Bigot." *The Huffington Post*, February 17, 2016. http://www.huffingtonpost.com/rachel-anspach/scalia-was-not-a-hero-he-_b_9245850.html.

Atkins v. Virginia, 536 U.S. 304 (2002).

Austin v. United States, 509 U.S. 602 (1993).

Balkin, J. M. "A Night in the Topics: The Reason of Legal Rhetoric and the Rhetoric of Legal Reason." In *Law's Stories: Narrative and Rhetoric in the Law*, edited by Peter Brooks and Paul Gewirth, 211–24. New Haven, CT: Yale University Press, 1996.

Barnes, Robert. "Supreme Court Justice Antonin Scalia Dies at 79." *Washington Post* (Washington, DC), February 13, 2016. https://www.washingtonpost.com/politics/supreme-court-justice-antonin-scalia-dies-at-79/2016/02/13/effe8184-a62f-11e3-a5fa-55f0c77bf39c_story.html.

Baude, Will. "Justice Scalia's Commencement Speech at William & Mary Law School." *Washington Post* (Washington, DC), May 16, 2014. Accessed July 15, 2014. http://www.washingtonpost.com/news/volokh-conspiracy/wp/2014/05/16/justice-scalias-commencement-speech-at-william-mary-law-school/.

Baze v. Rees, 553 U.S. 35 (2008).

Beard, Charles A. "The Living Constitution." *Annals of the American Academy of Political and Social Science* 185, no. 1 (May 1936): 29–34.

Beck, James M. "The Changed Conception of the Constitution." *Proceedings of the American Philosophical Society* 69 (1930): 99–115.

Bell v. Ohio, 438 U.S. 637 (1978).

Bellah, Robert. "Civil Religion in America." *Daedalus* 96, no. 1 (1967): 1–21.

BeVier, Lillian R. "Textualism and Democratic Legitimacy: The Moment and the Millennium: A Question of Time, or Law?" *George Washington Law Review* 66 (1998): 1112–18.

Blackstone, Sir William. *Commentaries on the Laws of England* (Oxford, England: Clarendon Press, 1765–1769). Accessed January 23, 2014. http://www.lonang.com/exlibris/blackstone/index.html.

Bobbitt, Philip. *Constitutional Fate: Theory of the Constitution*. New York: Oxford University Press, 1982.

Bolling, Ruben. "Tom the Dancing Bug." Salon.com (May 17, 2001). Accessed June 14, 2001. http://archive.salon.com/comics/boll/2001/05/17/boll/.

———. "Tom the Dancing Bug." Salon.com (Mar. 13, 2013). Accessed May 28, 2013. http://boingboing.net/2013/03/13/tom-the-dancing-bug-judge-sca-2.html.

Bork, Robert. "Before the University of San Diego Law School." The Federalist Society for Law and Public Policy Studies (November 18, 1985). Accessed May 23, 2013. http://www.ruleoflawus.info/Constitutional%20Interpretation/Federalist%20Soc.-Great%20Debate-Interpreting%20Our%20Constitution.pdf.

———. *The Tempting of America: The Political Seduction of the Law*. New York: Touchstone, 1990.

Bray v. Alexandria, 506 U.S. 263 (1993).

Brennan Jr., William J. "The Constitution of the United States: Contemporary Ratification." Address delivered at Text and Teaching Symposium, Georgetown University, Washington, DC, October 12, 1985.

Breyer, Stephen. *Active Liberty: Interpreting Our Democratic Constitution*. New York: Knopf, 2005.

Brisbin Jr., Richard A. *Justice Antonin Scalia and the Conservative Revival*. Baltimore: Johns Hopkins University Press, 1997.

Brown v. Plata, 563 U.S. 493 (2011).

Buchanan v. Angelone, 522 U.S. 269 (1998).

Calabresi, Steven G. "Concluding Essay: Textualism and the Countermajoritarian Difficulty." *George Washington Law Review* 66 (1998): 1373–94.

Cappuccio, Paul T. "Former Clerk Remembers Scalia's Personal Warmth." *New York Times*, February 13, 2016. http://www.nytimes.com/live/supreme-court-justice-antonin-scalia-dies-at-79/former-clerk-remembers-scalias-personal-warmth/.

Cardozo, Benjamin Nathan. *The Nature of the Judicial Process*. New Haven, CT: Yale University Press, 1921.

Carpenter, Ronald H. "America's Tragic Metaphor: Our Twentieth-Century Combatants as Frontiersmen." *Quarterly Journal of Speech* 76 (1990): 1–22.

Cheney v. US District Court of Columbia, 542 U.S. 367 (2004).

Church of Lukumi Babalu Aye, Inc. v. City of Hialeah, 508 U.S. 520 (1993).

Citizens United v. Federal Election Commission, 558 U.S. 310 (2010).

Clark, Bradford R. "Textualism and Federalism: A Structural Approach." *George Washington Law Review* 66 (1998): 1161–97.

Clinton, Hillary. "Hillary Clinton Statement on the Passing of Supreme Court Justice Antonin Scalia." HillaryClinton.com. February 13, 2016. https://www.hillaryclinton.com/briefing/statements/2016/02/13/justice-antonin-scalia-passing/.

Coker v. Georgia, 433 U.S. 584 (1977).

Cook, Walter Wheeler. "'Substance' and 'Procedure' in the Conflict of Laws." *Yale Law Journal* 42 (1933): 333–58. doi: 10.2307/791291.

Corwin, Edward S. "Moratorium over *Minnesota*." *University of Pennsylvania Law Review* 82, no. 4 (1934), 311–16. doi: 10.2307/3308506.

Cruz, Ted. Twitter post. February 13, 2016, 4:27 p.m. http://twitter.com/tedcruz.

Curtis, Michael Kent. "Textualism and the Civil War Amendment: Two Textual Adventures: Thoughts on Reading Jeffrey Rosen's Paper." *George Washington Law Review* 66 (1998): 1269–1300.

Daughton, Suzanne M. "Metaphorical Transcendence: Images of the Holy War in Franklin Roosevelt's First Inaugural." *Quarterly Journal of Speech* 79, no. 4 (1993): 427–46.

Derrida, Jacques. "Violence and Metaphysics." In *Writing and Difference*, translated by Alan Bass. Chicago: University of Chicago Press, 1978.

Dicker, Rachel. "The 8 Most Horrible Reactions to Justice Scalia's Death." *US News & World Report*, February 16, 2016. https://www.usnews.com/news/articles/2016-02-16/antonin-scalias-death-unleashes-a-twitter-hate-storm-against-the-late-justice.

Dred Scott v. Sandford, 60 U.S. 393 (1857).

Easterbrook, Frank H. "Textualism and Democratic Legitimacy: Textualism and the Dead Hand." *George Washington Law Review* 66 (1998): 1119–26.

Eddings v. Oklahoma, 455 U.S. 104 (1982).

Ehrlich, David. Twitter post. February 13, 2016. 1:59 p.m. https://twitter.com/davidehrlich.

Ely, John. "The Wages of Crying Wolf: A Comment on *Roe v. Wade*." *Yale Law Review* 82 (1973): 920–49.

Employment Division v. Smith, 494 U.S. 872 (1990).

Enmund v. Florida, 458 U.S. 782 (1982).

Epstein, Richard. "Antonin Scalia, A Most Memorable Friend." *Hoover Institute*. February 15, 2016. http://www.hoover.org/research/antonin-scalia-most-memorable-friend.

Eskridge Jr., William N. "Textualism and Original Understanding: Should the Supreme Court Read the Federalist but Not Statutory Legislative History?" *George Washington Law Review* 66 (1998): 1301–23.

Espinosa v. Florida, 505 U.S. 1079 (1992).

Feldman, Noah. "Scalia's Classic 'Textualism' Will Be His Legacy." *Chicago Tribune* (Chicago, IL), February 19, 2016.

Ferguson, Robert A. "The Judicial Opinion as Literary Genre." *Yale Journal of Law & the Humanities* 2, no. 1 (1990): 201–19.

Fjelstad, Per. "Legal Judgment and Cultural Motivation: Enthymematic Form in *Marbury v. Madison*." *The Southern Communication Journal* 60, no. 1 (1994), 22–32. doi: 10.1080/10417949409372959.

Franck, Matthew J. "Antonin Scalia, Persistent Champion of Constitutional Republicanism." *Witherspoon Institute*. May 2, 2016. http://www.thepublicdiscourse.com/2016/05/16871/.

Friedelbaum, Stanley H. *The Rehnquist Court: In Pursuit of Judicial Conservatism*. Westport, CT: Greenwood Press, 1994.

Furman v. Georgia, 408 U.S. 238 (1972).

Garrow, David J. *Liberty and Sexuality: The Right to Privacy and the Making of Roe v. Wade*. Berkeley: University of California Press, 1998.

Gehl, Robert. "Here Comes the Evil: The Left Reacts to the Death of Antonin Scalia." *Federalist Papers Project*. February 13, 2016. http://www.thefederalistpapers.org/us/here-comes-the-evil-the-left-reacts-to-the-death-of-antonin-scalia.

Gerhardt, Michael J. "A Tale of Two Textualists: A Critical Comparison of Justices Black and Scalia." *Boston University Law Review* 74 (1994): 25–66.

Gibson, James L., and Michael J. Nelson. "Is the US Supreme Court's Legitimacy Grounded in Performance Satisfaction and Ideology." *American Journal of Political Science* 59, no. 1 (January 2015): 162–74.

Glass v. Louisiana, 471 U.S. 1080 (1985).

Gomez v. US District Court, 503 U.S. 654 (1992).

Gompers v. United States, 233 U.S. 604 (1914).

Graglia, Lino A. "Does Constitutional Law Exist?" *National Review* (June 26, 1995): 31–35.

Granucci, Anthony F. "Nor Cruel and Unusual Punishments Inflicted: The Original Meaning." *California Law Review* 57, no. 4 (1969): 839–65.

Gray v. Lucas, 463 U.S. 1237 (1983).

"The Great Debate: Interpreting Our Written Constitution." The Federalist Society for Law and Public Policy Studies (1986). Accessed March 10, 2017. http://www.fed-soc.org/publications/detail/the-great-debate-interpreting-our-written-constitution.

Gregg v. Georgia, 428 U.S. 153 (1976).

Grey, Thomas C. "Do We Have an Unwritten Constitution?" *Stanford Law Review* 27, no. 3 (1975): 703–18. doi: 10.2307/1228335.

Gribbin, William. "The Juggernaut Metaphor in American Rhetoric." *Quarterly Journal of Speech* 59, no. 3 (1973): 297–303.

Griswold v. Connecticut, 381 U.S. 479 (1965) at 484.

Gualtieri, Tom. "The Worst Person in America: Antonin Scalia." *The Weeklings*, July 2, 2015. http://www.theweeklings.com/tgualtieri/2015/07/02/the-worst-person-in-america-antonin-scalia/.

Hagan, Horace H. "The Elasticity of the Federal Constitution." *Virginia Law Review* 20, no. 4 (Feb. 1934): 391–401. doi: 10.2307/1066399.

Hariman, Robert. *Political Style: The Artistry of Power*. Chicago: University of Chicago Press, 1995.

Harmelin v. Michigan, 501 U.S. 957 (1991).

Harris II, William F. *The Interpretable Constitution*. Baltimore: Johns Hopkins University Press, 1993.

Hart, James. "A Unified Economy and States' Rights." *Annals of the American Academy of Political and Social Science* 185 (May 1936): 102–14.

Herrera v. Collins, 506 U.S. 390 (1993).

Hodgson v. Minnesota, 497 U.S. 417 (1990).

Hogan, J. Michael, and Glen Williams. "Republican Charisma and the American Revolution: The Textual Persona of Thomas Paine's *Common Sense*." *Quarterly Journal of Speech* 86, no. 1 (February 2000): 1–18. doi: 10.1080/00335630009384276.

Howley, Patrick. "Kasich: Scalia Was an 'Essential' Force for Conservative Thought." *Breitbart*. February 13, 2016. http://www.breitbart.com/big-government/2016/02/13/3028901/.

Hutto v. Finney, 437 U.S. 678 (1978).

In re Kemmler, 136 U.S. 436 (1890).
Ivie, Robert L. "The Ideology of Freedom's 'Fragility' in American Foreign Policy Argument." *Journal of the American Forensic Association* 24 (1987): 27–36.
———. "Fire, Flood, and Red Fever: Motivating Truman Doctrine Speech." *Presidential Studies Quarterly* 29 (1999): 570–91.
Jamieson, Kathleen Hall. "The Metaphoric Cluster in the Rhetoric of Pope Paul VI and Edmund G. Brown, Jr." *Quarterly Journal of Speech* 66, no. 1 (1980): 51–72.
Jenson, J. Vernon. "British Voices on the Eve of the American Revolution: Trapped by the Family Metaphor." *Quarterly Journal of Speech* 63, no. 1 (1977): 43–50.
Johnson v. Texas, 509 U.S. 350 (1993).
Jurek v. Texas, 428 U.S. 262 (1976).
Kagan, Elena. The Nomination of Elena Kagan to be an Associate Justice of the Supreme Court of the United States Hearing Before the Committee on the Judiciary. United States Senate. One Hundred Eleventh Congress, Second Session. June 28–30 and July 1, 2010. 111th Congress 2 (2010).
Kennedy v. Louisiana, 554 U.S. 407 (2008).
Killingsworth, Silvia. Twitter post. February 13, 2016. 4:22 p.m. https://twitter.com/silviakillings.
Kinsley, Michael. "Meese's Stink Bomb." *Washington Post* (October 29, 1986): A19.
Kirtley, Jean. "Scalia and His Speeches." *American Journal Review* (June/July 2004). Accessed July 15, 2014. http://ajrarchive.org/article.asp?id=3686.
Kopan, Tal. "Harry Reid, John Lewis Assail 'Racist' Scalia Comments." CNN.com, December 10, 2015. http://www.cnn.com/2015/12/10/politics/harry-reid-antonin-scalia-racist-comments/index.html.
Kurtz, Howard. "Meese's View on Court Rulings Assailed, Defended." *Washington Post* (October 24, 1986): A12.
Lakoff, George, and Mark Johnson. *Metaphors We Live By*. Chicago: University of Chicago Press, 1962.
Langford, Catherine L. "Race and Racism in the Collective Memory of the Law: A Rhetorical Analysis of Roger B. Taney and *Dred Scott v. Sandford*." *Communication Law Review* 11 (2011): 1–21. http://commlawreview.org/Archives/CLVv11i2/Race_and_Racism_in_the_Collective_Memory_of_the_Law.pdf.
———. "Toward a Genre of Judicial Dissent: *Lochner* and *Casey* as Exemplars." *Communication Law Review* 9 (2009): 1–12.
Leff, Michael. "Dimensions of Temporality in Lincoln's Second Inaugural." *Communication Reports* 1 (1988): 27–31. doi: 10.1080/08934218809367458.
———. "Textual Criticism: The Legacy of G.P. Mohrmann." *Quarterly Journal of Speech* 72 (1986): 377–89. doi: 10.1080/00335638609383783.
Lewis, Anthony. "Law or Power?" *New York Times* (October 27, 1986): A23.
Liptak, Adam. "Antonin Scalia, Justice on the Supreme Court, Dies at 79." *New York Times*, February 13, 2016. http://www.nytimes.com/2016/02/14/us/antonin-scalia-death.html?rref=collection%2Ftimestopic%2FScalia%2C%20Antonin&action=click&contentCollection=timestopics&region=stream&module=stream_unit&version=latest&contentPlacement=74&pgtype=collection.
Lithwick, Dahlia. "Why Liberals Loved to Hate Antonin Scalia: He Presented Cruel, Demeaning Views in Thought-Provoking and Stirring Ways." *Slate*, February 14, 2016. http://www.slate.com/articles/news_and_politics/jurisprudence/2016/02/why_liberals_loved_to_hate_antonin_scalia.html.
Locke v. Davey, 540 U.S. 712 (2004).

Lockett v. Ohio, 438 U.S. 586 (1978).

Lockyer v. Andrade, 538 U.S. 63 (2003).

Louisiana ex rel. Francis v. Resweber, 329 U.S. 459 (1947).

Lupu, Ira C. "Textualism and Original Understanding: Time, the Supreme Court, and The Federalist." *George Washington Law Review* 66 (1998): 1324–36.

Maggs, Gregory E. "Textualism and Federalism: Translating Federalism; A Textualist Reaction." *George Washington Law Review* 66 (1998): 1198–268.

Manning, John F. "Textualism and the Equity of the Statute." *Columbia Law Review* 101, no. 1 (2001): 1–127. doi: 10.2307/1123509.

Marbury v. Madison, 5 U.S. 137 (1803).

McBain, Howard Lee. *The Living Constitution: A Consideration of the Realities and Legends of Our Fundamental Law*. New York: Workers' Education Bureau Press, 1927.

McCleskey v. Kemp, 481 U.S. 279 (1987).

McConnell, Michael W. "Textualism and Democratic Legitimacy: Textualism and the Dead Hand of the Past." *George Washington Law Review* 66 (1998): 1127–47.

McCreary County, 545 U.S. 844 (2005).

McKoy v. North Carolina, 494 U.S. 433 (1990).

McLuhan, Marshall. *Understanding Media: The Extensions of Man*. Boston, MA: MIT Press, 1964.

Meeks, Wayne A. "Apocalyptic Discourse and Strategies of Goodness." *Journal of Religion* 80 (July 2000): 461–75.

Meese, Edwin. "Address Before the DC Chapter of the Federalist Society Lawyers Division." The United States Department of Justice (November 15, 1985). Accessed March 10, 2017. https://www.justice.gov/sites/default/files/ag/legacy/2011/08/23/11-15-1985.pdf.

———. "The American Bar Association." The United States Department of Justice (July 9, 1985): 1–8. Accessed March 10, 2017. https://www.justice.gov/sites/default/files/ag/legacy/2011/08/23/07-09-1985.pdf.

Meyer v. Nebraska, 262 U.S. 390 (1923).

Minor v. Happersett, 88 U.S. 162 (1874).

Missouri v. Holland, 252 U.S. 416 (1920).

Moore v. Texas, 535 U.S. 1044 (2002).

"Mr. Meese's Contempt of Court." *New York Times* (November 2, 1986): § 4 at 23, col. 1.

Muckelbauer, John. "Rhetoric, Asignification, and the Other: A Response to Diane Davis." *Philosophy & Rhetoric* 40, no. 2 (2007): 238–47. doi: 10.1353/para.2007.0023.

Muñoz, Vincent Phillip. "The Original Meaning of the Free Exercise Clause: The Evidence from the First Congress." *Harvard Journal of Law & Public Policy* 31, no. 3 (2008): 1083–120.

Napolitano, Andrew P. "Justice Scalia and Constitutional Fidelity." *Fox News*, February 18, 2016. http://www.foxnews.com/opinion/2016/02/18/justice-scalia-and-constitutional-fidelity.html.

Natelson, Robert G. "The Original Meaning of the Establishment Clause." *William & Mary Bill of Rights Journal* 14, no. 1 (2005): 73–140.

Obama, Barack. "The President on the Passing of Supreme Court Justice Antonin Scalia." *The White House*. March 10, 2017. https://obamawhitehouse.archives.gov/photos-and-video/video/2016/02/13/president-passing-supreme-court-justice-antonin-scalia.

Ohio v. Akron Center for Reproductive Health, 497 U.S. 502 (1990) at 520.

Olmstead v. United States, 277 U.S. 438 (1928).

Oregon Revised Statues § 161.605 (2001) and § 161.625 (2001).
Oregon v. Guzek, 546 U.S. 517 (2006).
Ornaski v. Belmontes, 549 U.S. (2006).
Osborn, Michael. "Archetypal Metaphor in Rhetoric: The Light-Dark Family." *Quarterly Journal of Speech* 53, no. 2 (1967): 115–26.
Patterson v. Texas, 536 U.S. 984 (2002).
Payne v. Tennessee, 501 U.S. 808 (1991).
Penry v. Lynaugh, 492 U.S. 302 (1989).
Pierce v. Society of Sisters, 268 U.S. 510 (1925).
Planned Parenthood v. Casey, 505 U.S. 833 (1992).
Posner, Richard A. "The Incoherence of Antonin Scalia." *New Republic*, August 24, 2012. Accessed October 24, 2014. http://www.newrepublic.com/article/magazine/books-and-arts/106441/scalia-garner-reading-the-law-textual-originalism.
Proffitt v. Florida, 428 U.S. 242 (1976).
Rakove, Jack N. "Mr. Meese, Meet Mr. Madison." *Atlantic Monthly* (December 1986): 77–86.
Reagan, Ronald. *Public Papers of the Presidents of the United States: Ronald Reagan*. 1986. Vol. 2. Washington, DC: Government Printing Office, 1067–69.
Rehnquist, William H. "The Notion of a Living Constitution." *Texas Law Review* 54 (1976): 693–706.
———. "The Notion of a Living Constitution." *Harvard Journal of Law & Public Policy* 29, no. 2 (Spring 2006): 401–15.
Resende, Fernando. "Inventing Muslims as the Other in Nineteenth-century Brazil." *Middle East Journal of Culture & Communication* 6, no. 2 (2013): 178–93.
Ríos, Tomás. Twitter post. February 13, 2016. 4:35 p.m. https://twitter.com/TheTomasRios.
Robinson, Paul H., and Markus D. Dubber. "The American Model Penal Code: A Brief Overview." *New Criminal Law Review* 10, no. 3 (2007): 319–41. doi: 10.1525/nclr.2007.10.3.319.
Robinson v. California, 370 U.S. 660 (1962).
Roe v. Wade, 410 U.S. 113 (1973).
Roosevelt, Franklin Delano. "'Only Thing We Have to Fear Is Fear Itself': FDR's First Inaugural Address." *History Matters*, September 11, 2014. http://historymatters.gmu.edu/d/5057/.
Roper v. Simmons, 543 U.S. 551 (2005).
Rosenfeld, Steven. "Is Scalia the Most Vile Person in Washington?" *Salon*, March 5, 2013. http://www.salon.com/2013/03/05/is_scalia_the_most_vile_person_in_washington/.
Ross, Janell. "Antonin Scalia: A Brilliant Legal Mind Who Snubbed Civil Rights at Nearly Every Turn." *Washington Post* (Washington, DC), February 14, 2016. https://www.washingtonpost.com/news/the-fix/wp/2016/02/14/antonin-scalia-a-brilliant-legal-mind-who-defied-civil-rights-at-nearly-every-turn/?hpid=hp_hp-top-table-main_fix-legalmind-1248pm%3Ahomepage%2Fstory&tid=a_inl.
Rubenfeld, Jed. "Textualism and Democratic Legitimacy: The Moment and the Millennium." *George Washington Law Review* 66 (1998): 1085–111.
Rubio, Marco. "Marco Rubio's Statement on Justice Antonin Scalia's Passing." February 13, 2016. http://blog.4president.org/2016/2016/02/marco-rubio-statement-on-justice-antonin-scalia.html.
Rummel v. Estelle, 445 U.S. 263 (1980).
Said, Edward W. *Orientalism*. New York: Vintage, 1979.

Sanders, Bernie. "Statement on Justice Scalia." *Bernie2016*. February 13, 2016. https://berniesanders.com/press-release/statement-on-justice-scalia/.

Savage, David G. "Some 'Mystified' by Award to Scalia for Free Speech." *Los Angeles Times* (March 20, 2003): A28.

———. *Turning Right: The Making of the Rehnquist Supreme Court*. New York: John Wiley & Sons, 1992.

Scalia, Antonin. "1989 Sibley Lecture: Reflections on the Constitution." *Sibley Lecture Series*, 1989. Accessed June 12, 2003. http://digitalcommons.law.uga.edu/lectures_pre_arch_lectures_sibley/63/.

———. "A Theory of Constitutional Interpretation." Catholic University of America, October 18, 1996. Accessed June 12, 2003. http://www.proconservative.net/PCVol5Is225ScaliaTheoryConstlInterpretation.shtml.

———. "Common-Law Courts in a Civil-Law System: The Role of United States Federal Courts in Interpreting the Constitution and Laws." In *A Matter of Interpretation: Federal Courts and the Law*, edited by Amy Gutmann, 3–47. Princeton: Princeton University Press, 1997.

———. "God's Justice and Ours." PewForum.org, January 2, 2002. Accessed June 12, 2003. https://www.firstthings.com/article/2002/05/gods-justice-and-ours.

———. "Constitutional Interpretation the Old Fashioned Way." CFIF.org, March 14, 2005. Accessed July 15, 2014. https://www.bc.edu/content/dam/files/centers/boisi/pdf/Symposia/Symposia%202010-2011/Constitutional_Interpretation_Scalia.pdf.

———. "On Interpreting the Constitution," *Manhattan Institute for Policy Research*, November 17, 1997. Accessed June 12, 2003. https://www.manhattan-institute.org/html/1997-wriston-lecture-interpreting-constitution-8063.html.

———. "Reflections on the Future of the Legal Academy." William and Mary Law School 2014 Commencement Exercises, May 11, 2014. Accessed July 15, 2014. https://law.wm.edu/news/stories/2014/documents-2014/2014WMCommencementSpeech.pdf.

Schultz, David A., and Christopher E. Smith. *The Jurisprudential Vision of Justice Antonin Scalia*. Lanham, MD: Rowman & Littlefield, 1996.

Shapiro, Carolyn. "How Scalia Played with Fire." CNN.com, February 16, 2016. http://www.cnn.com/2016/02/16/opinions/antonin-scalia-shapiro/index.html.

Shapiro, Ilya. "Scalia Will Be Impossible to Replace." CNN.com, February 15, 2016. http://www.cnn.com/2016/02/15/opinions/scalia-impossible-to-replace-shapiro/index.html.

Sherry, Suzanna. "Textualism and the Bill of Right: Textualism and Judgment." *George Washington Law Review* 66 (1998): 1148–52.

Smith, Christopher E. *Justice Antonin Scalia and the Supreme Court's Conservative Moment*. Westport, CT: Praeger, 1993.

Sochor v. Florida, 504 U.S. 527 (1992).

Solem v. Helm, 463 U.S. 277 (1983).

South Carolina v. Gathers, 490 U.S. 805 (1989).

Stack, Liam. "Jeb Bush Says Scalia Was 'My Favorite Justice.'" *New York Times*, February 13, 2016. http://www.nytimes.com/live/supreme-court-justice-antonin-scalia-dies-at-79/jeb-bush-says-scalia-was-my-favorite-justice/.

Stahl, Lesley. "Justice Scalia on the Record: *60 Minutes'* Lesley Stahl Interviews Supreme Court Justice Antonin Scalia about His Public and Private Life." *60 Minutes*. April 24, 2008. http://www.cbsnews.com/news/justice-scalia-on-the-record/.

Stahl, Roger. "A Clockwork War: Rhetorics of Time in a Time of Terror." *Quarterly Journal of Speech* 94, no. 1 (2008): 73–99.

Stanford v. Kentucky, 492 U.S. 361 (1989).

Stenberg v. Carhart, 530 U.S. 490 (1989).

Stevens, John Paul. "Before the Federal Bar Association." The Federalist Society for Law and Public Policy Studies (October 23, 1985). Accessed May 23, 2013. http://www.fed-soc.org/publications/detail/the-great-debate-justice-john-paul-stevens-october-23-1985.

Strauss, David A. "Textualism and the Bill of Right: The New Textualism in Constitutional Law." *George Washington Law Review* 66 (1998): 1153–60.

Sunstein, Cass. "Justice Breyer's Democratic Pragmatism." *Yale Law Journal* 115, no. 7 (2006): 1719–43.

Sunstein, Cass R. "The Scalia I Knew Will Be Greatly Missed." *BloombergView*, February 13, 2016. https://www.bloomberg.com/view/articles/2016-02-14/the-scalia-i-knew-will-be-greatly-missed.

"Supreme Court Justices Weigh in on Antonin Scalia's Death." *USA Today*, February 15, 2016. http://www.usatoday.com/story/news/politics/2016/02/14/statements-supreme-court-death-justice-scalia/80375976/.

Symposium. "The Model Penal Code." 63 *Columbia Law Review* 589 (1963).

Thompson v. Oklahoma, 487 U.S. 815 (1988).

Trop v. Dulles, 356 U.S. 86 (1958).

"Truly Evil Supreme Court Justice Antonin Scalia is Dead, and I'm Not Sure How to Feel." *Daily News Bin*. February 13, 2016. http://www.dailynewsbin.com/opinion/evil-supreme-court-justice-antonin-scalia-is-dead-and-im-not-sure-how-to-feel/23822/.

Trump, Donald. "Donald J. Trump Statement on Justice Scalia." February 13, 2016. https://www.donaldjtrump.com/press-releases/donald-j.-trump-statement-on-justice-scalia.

Tuilaepa v. California, 512 U.S. 967 (1994).

Tushnet, Mark. "The Possibilities of Comparative Constitutional Law." *Yale Law Journal* 108 (1999): 1225–309. doi: 10.2307/797327.

Voth, Ben. "The Wall Separating Church and State: A Longitudinal Analysis of Metaphor as Argument." *Argumentation & Advocacy* 34 (1998): 127–39.

Walton v. Arizona, 497 U.S. 639 (1990).

Webster v. Reproductive Health Services, 492 U.S. 490 (1989).

Weems v. United States, 217 U.S. 349 (1910).

West Coast Hotel Company v. Parrish, 300 U.S. 379 (1937).

West v. Atkins, 487 U.S. 42 (1988).

White, James Boyd. *When Words Lose Their Meanings: Constitutions and Reconstitutions of Language, Character, and Community*. Chicago: University of Chicago Press, 1984.

Whole Woman's Health v. Hellerstedt, 136 S.Ct. 2292 (2016).

"Why People Hate Antonin Scalia." *Economist*, April 25, 2008. http://www.economist.com/blogs/democracyinamerica/2008/04/why_people_hate_antonin_scalia.

Wilkerson v. Utah, 99 U.S. 130 (1878).

Will, George F. "Why Antonin Scalia Was a Jurist of Colossal Consequence." *Washington Post*, February 14, 2016. https://www.washingtonpost.com/opinions/why-antonin-scalia-was-a-jurist-of-colossal-consequence/2016/02/14/6936b8fc-d359-11e5-9823-02b905009f99_story.html?utm_term=.a50c5fde02b4.

Wilson v. Seiter, 501 U.S. 294 (1991).

Wilson, Woodrow. "What Is Progress?" *The New Freedom: A Call for the Emancipation of the Generous Energies of a People*, 33–54. New York: Doubleday, Page, and Company, 1913. Accessed September 16, 2014. http://www.gutenberg.org/files/14811/14811-h/14811-h.htm.

Winslow, Luke A. "The Imaged Other: Style and Substance in the Rhetoric of Joel Osteen." *Southern Communication Journal* 49, no. 3 (July-August 2014): 250–71.

———. "Promise Keepers and the Rhetoric of the Stylized Other." *Journal of Communication & Religion* 35, no. 1 (March 2012): 73–89.

Woodson v. North Carolina, 428 U.S. 280 (1976).

Yost, Pete. "Meese's View of Supreme Court Would Lead to Chaos, Critics Say." *Associated Press* (October 24, 1986). Accessed August 26, 2014. http://www.apnewsarchive.com/1986/Meese-s-Views-of-Supreme-Court-Would-Lead-to-Chaos-Critics-Say/id-3ff4063b92d5df2901ea2d339a563a92.

Youn, Soo. "Antonin Scalia: Liberal Clerks Reflect on the Man They Knew and Admired." *Guardian*, February 15, 2016. https://www.theguardian.com/law/2016/feb/15/antonin-scalia-supreme-court-justice-liberal-clerks-reflect.

Zuesse, Eric. "Face It: Antonin Scalia Is Just a Bigot in a Black Robe." *Washington's Blog*, March 27, 2013. http://www.washingtonsblog.com/2013/03/face-it-antonin-scalia-is-just-a-bigot-in-a-black-robe.html.

Index

Abdul-Kabir v. Quarternman, 67
abortion, Scalia on, 100–114; on abortion as a political rather than a legal issue, 106–9, 114–15, 119; in *Akron*, 105, 107; argument that Constitution does not protect a woman's right to an elective abortion, 100, 104, 115; argument that courts lack power to adjudicate the issue, 100–102, 105–7, 114–15, 119; argument that states have the power to decide the issue, 114–15; *Bray* majority opinion, 101, 105, 107, 111–15; brevity of responses to abortion cases, 105–6, 114; in *Carhart*, 105, 107, 113; *Casey* dissent, 101–2, 104–5, 109–11, 114–15; comparison of Court's decision-making in abortion to *Dred Scott* opinion, 111; disagreement with Court's use of stare decisis to support abortion, 105; on division between the political and the judicial, 107–8; example of Scalia's justification of textual interpretation when the Constitution is silent on the issue, 100; in *Hodgson*, 105–8; personification of Constitution as authority figure, protector, and educator, 103; reasons why judges should not legislate, 108–9; *Roe* caused increased societal hostilities and division, 111; Socratic dialogue between Scalia and plurality opinion in *Casey*, 109–11, 114; *Stenberg* dissent, 101; support of pro-life efforts to discourage women from obtaining abortions, 113–14; textualism and historicism, 104, 114; use of container metaphor and organic metaphor to argue that the Constitution does not cover the right to abortion, 101–4; in *Webster*, 105–7
abortion law and decisions: decisions considering constraints on right to abortion, 99–100; and Operation Rescue, 111–12; *Roe v. Wade*, 98–100; silence of Constitution on right to an abortion, 97, 118; state laws proscribing abortion and permitting it under certain circumstances, 119
accommodationist approach, to Establishment Clause, 73
Adamany, David, 22
Adams, John, 83
Alito, Justice Samuel, 4
Allegheny County v. American Civil Liberties Union, 73
American Law Institute (ALI), Model Penal Code, 64, 119
Amish, 75, 89
Anspach, Rachel, 7
Anthony, Susan B., appeal of denial of voting rights in *Minor v. Happersett*, 30
argumentum ad antiquitatum, and fixed nature of Constitution, 27–28

Arizona Christian School Tuition Organization v. Winn, 76
Atkins, Daryl Renard, 62–63
Atkins v. Virginia, 53, 54, 62–63, 67–68

Balkin, Jack M., 18
Baze v. Rees, 63, 66, 68
Beard, Charles A., "The Living Constitution," 17
Beck, James M., "The Changed Conception of the Constitution," 15–16
Berlin, Isaiah, "Two Concepts of Liberty," 72–73
Bill of Rights, and "cruel and unusual punishments" clause, 51
Black, Justice Hugo, 21, 117; textualism, 121–22
Blackmun, Justice Harry, extension of right of privacy to woman's ability to abort a fetus, 98–100, 114
Bobbitt, Philip, *Constitutional Fate: Theory of the Constitution*, 9–10, 44
Bolling, Ruben, "Tom the Dancing Bug" cartoon, 3
Booth v. Maryland, 67
Bork, Robert, 1; on constitutional interpretation, 20–21; and judicial interpretation, 18; support for strict reading of law, 19
Brandeis, Justice Louis, *Olmstead* judicial dissent, and right of individuals to be "let alone," 14, 97–98
Bray v. Alexandria Women's Health Clinic, 101, 105, 107, 111–14
Brennan, Justice William: and Constitution as aspirational document altered by changing conditions, 20; and judicial interpretation, 18–19
Breyer, Justice Stephen: *Active Liberty: Interpreting Our Democratic Constitution*, 136n14; advocate of pragmatic judicial interpretation, 18, 28; speeches posted on Web page, 25
Brisbin, Richard A., Jr., 2
Brown v. Plata, 66
Burke, Kenneth, *A Grammar of Motives*, 17
Bush, George H. W., 84
Bush, Jeb, 4

Calhoun, John C., nullification doctrine, 15
capital punishment, consistently viewed by Supreme Court as constitutional, 54–55
Capitol Square Review and Advisory Board v. Pinette, 76–79, 81, 84
Cardozo, Benjamin, *The Nature of the Judicial Process*, 14
Cheney, Richard, 125
Cheney v. US District Court of Columbia, 125
Church of the Lukumi Babulu Aye v. City of Hialeah, 88–89, 93–94, 96
City of Akron v. Akron Center for Reproductive Health, 99, 107, 112
City of Boerne v. Flores, 75
Clinton, Hillary, 4–5
coercion test, and Establishment Clause, 74
Coker v. Georgia, 52, 53
consensus legitimacy, 21–22
constitutional interpretation: debate about, and myth that law can be interpreted in unbiased manner, 9; debate about, and role of judge, 12; debate about as part of public discourse, 22; doctrinal (precedent), 10; ethical (telic ends), 10; and expansion of meaning of Constitution using unwritten law, 17; "Great Debate," 19–21; guidelines for, Scalia and Garner, 46; historical (original intent/meaning), 10; Justice Brennan on, 18–19; Justice Breyer on, 18, 28; Justice Scalia on, 1–2; Justice Stevens on, 19; "loose" interpretation, 9, 10, 12; and material effects on social reality, 21; necessitated by competing constitutional values, 120; prudential (cost/benefit analysis), 10; in response to contemporary social needs, 17–18; and split courts, 9; "strict" interpretation, 9; structural (macro interpretation), 10; textual (plain meaning), 10. *See also* living constitution
constitutional interpretation, Scalia on: "anti-argument," 35–36; citation of speech by Benjamin Franklin to support claim for fixed nature of Constitution, 28, 36; claim that Constitution guarantees legal process but not legal result, 31, 35; claim that idea of Constitution as living document debases text and harms democratic process, 31, 33–35; Constitutional text at center of interpretation, 1–2; and Due Process Clause, 35; on fixed nature of Constitution altered only through political process, 26, 29–30, 136n11; on fixed nature of Constitution based on *argumentum ad antiquitatum*, 27–28; guidelines for interpretation, 46; and legislative history and intent, 40–42, 93; on loose interpre-

tations as threat to individual liberty and democratic processes, 37, 43; on Nineteenth Amendment as example for Constitutional amendment, 24, 29–31; and plain meaning of text, 31, 48, 123; "reasonable" readings of law, 41–42, 48–49; role of Supreme Court justices in maintenance of constitutional covenants, 29; strict interpretation, 37, 86. *See also* textualism, Scalia on
constitutional law, written and unwritten, 16
constitutional law textbooks, inclusion of Constitution after Scalia's seat on Court, 6
content legitimacy, 22
Corwin, Edward, 16–17
creation science, 76, 82
Cruz, Ted, 4

decisional liberty, 100
Douglas, Justice William O. Douglas, 98
Dred Scott decision, Scalia on, 111
Dworkin, Ronald, commentary on Scalia's "Common-Law Courts" essay, 50

Edwards v. Aguillard, 76, 77, 80, 87
Ehrlich, David, 7
Eighth Amendment, "cruel and unusual punishments" clause: as clear constitutional clause, 55, 116; Court agreement that clause forbids "inhuman and barbarous" forms of punishment, 52; Court's consistent view of capital punishment as constitutional, 54–55; Court's wavering on what it deems cruel and unusual punishment, 53; and doctrine of evolving standards of decency, 52, 54; history of jurisprudence, 51–55, 138n27; language of, and English Bill of Rights of 1689, 51; and proportional punishment, 53–54
Eighth Amendment, "cruel and unusual punishments" clause, Scalia on, 55–70; assertion that certain types of crime are worthy of death, 63–65, 70; in *Atkins*, 56, 62–64; in *Baze*, 63; claim that justices who disagree with him are inconsistent, 68–69; construction of meaning of cruel and unusual punishments, 55–61, 70; criticism of court for violation of separation of powers, 66–67; difference in Scalia's reading of clause and plain meaning supported by text, 61, 116; on execution of minors and mentally handicapped, 56, 67–70; in *Hamelin*, 56, 58–60; and irrelevance of cruelty if punishment is not unusual, 57–58; and irrelevance of proportionality, 58, 60; in *Lee*, 63, 65; measure of "unusual" punishment, 57–60, 70; in *Moore*, 63–64; notion that crime is innate in certain criminals, 65; and original meaning of text, 56–57; in *Penry*, 57, 60; rejection of cruelty of excessive punishment, 56; rejection of evolving standards of decency in understanding of, 60–61; rejection of incidental suffering as cruel and unusual punishment, 61; reliance on British law for evidentiary support, 56, 59; religious framing for interpretation of clause, 60–61, 70–71; rhetorical strategies emphasizing guilt of accused, 61; in *Roper v. Simmons*, 54, 63–65; shift of interpretation from cruelty of punishment to cruelty of crime, 61–65, 71, 116; in *Simmons*, 63–65; specific examples of what constitutes capital crime, 64–65; in *Stanford*, 57, 60; and state as arbiter of capital punishment, 65–71; statement of facts in *Atkins*, 62–63; in *Thompson*, 58, 63, 65; variation in citing precedents to support claim that states have the power to punish, 68–69; in *Walton*, 57–59, 63
Ely, John, 18
Employment Division v. Smith, 75–76, 88–93
Enmund v. Florida, 52, 53
Epstein, Richard, 5
Equal Protection Clause, 29
Espinosa v. Florida, 67
Establishment Clause, 72; accommodationist approach, 73; application to national government at adoption of Constitution, 95; and coercion test, 74; components of unconstitutional advancement of religion, 74; contested meaning of establishment at time of founding, 117; Court's difficulty in determining what constitutes an establishment of religion, 94; doctrinal tests to determine existence of, 74; endorsement test, 74; *Lemon* test, 74, 76; as negative liberty right (requiring government not to institute a religion), 73, 117; nonpreferentialism approach, 73; plain reading of, 117; and questions concerning school funding, 73; and questions outside of education, 73–74; strict separation approach to, 73. *See also* Free Exercise Clause

Establishment Clause, Scalia on: argument that government should allow religious expression in public sphere, 77, 80, 96; consideration of original intent of clause in *Edwards* dissent, 82–84; consideration of original meaning of clause in *Weisman* opinion, 82, 84, 88; definition of unconstitutional establishments of religion in *Weisman*, 83; dissents arguing that legislators can use religious convictions when passing laws, 77; doctrinal arguments, 82, 86–88, 95–96; establishment of religion as free speech, 77–81, 94–95; failure to provide evidence that historic practices of people support public religious activity, 84–88; failure to use strict forms of interpretation advocated in extrajudicial writings and speeches, 94; and *Lemon* test, 82, 86–87, 95–96; list of religious practices of early political leaders in *McCreary*, 83; modification of meaning of establishment from legal status to geographic space, 79; opinions consistently furthering interests of religion, 76–77; preference for accommodation and nonpreferential approaches to establishment, 84; understanding of academic freedom as freedom from indoctrination, 82; use of original intent of founders and original meaning of text to deny strict separation of church and state, 77, 81–84, 95

Everson v. Board of Education, 73

Federalist Society, 19

Feldman, Noah, 117, 141n20

First Amendment, 72. *See also* Establishment Clause; Free Exercise Clause

Fjelstad, Per, 127

Foot Resolution, 15

Fourteenth Amendment, 56, 71, 98

Free Exercise Clause: belief/action division, 74–76; case law centering on excusal of person from compliance with law based on religious beliefs, 74–75; plain reading of, 117–18; positive liberty right (allowing citizens to practice whatever religion they wish), 73; three-prong *Sherbert* test, 75–76; variations in accommodation for religious differences, 75. *See also* Establishment Clause

Free Exercise Clause, Scalia on: in *Church of the Lukumi Babulu Aye v. City of Hialeah*, 88–89, 93–94, 96; claim that minority practices can be proscribed if deemed illegal by community, 89–90; differing definitions of religious minority, 91–93, 118; inconsistency between *Employment Division* and *Locke* decisions, 90–93; reliance on doctrinal arguments with no textual grounding in Constitution, 89, 91, 94, 96; and separation of belief and action, 89–91, 96; textual analysis of in *Employment Division v. Smith*, 88–90, 96; textual analysis of in *Locke v. Davey*, 88–91; transformation of plain meaning from "without restraint" to "without financial cost," 90, 95

Free Speech Clause, and distinction between types of public spaces, 78

Fuller, Chief Justice, 52

Furman v. Georgia, 53, 71

Garner, Bryan, 37

Gerhardt, Michael, "A Tale of Two Textualisms," 121–22

Ginsburg, Justice Ruth Bader, 4, 25

Glendon, Mary Ann, commentary on Scalia's "Common-Law Courts" essay, 50

Goldman v. Weinberger, 75

Gompers v. United States, 14, 18

Good News Club v. Milford Central School, 77, 78

Granucci, Anthony F., 51

"Great Debate," and Constitutional interpretation, 19–22

Great Depression, 15

Gregg v. Georgia, 53, 54, 68

Grey, Thomas, 18

Griswold v. Connecticut, 98

Gualtieri, Tom, 6

Hagan, Horace H., "The Elasticity of the Federal Constitution," 16–17

Hamelin v. Michigan, 52, 56, 59–60

Hariman, Robert, "republican style," 45

Harris, William F., II, 13

Hart, James, 17

Hayne, Robert Y., 15–16

Hein v. Freedom From Religion Foundation, 77

Henry, Patrick, 118

Hodgson, Godfrey, 5

Hodgson v. Minnesota, 99, 105–6, 112

Hogan, J. Michael, 45

Holmes, Justice Oliver Wendell: opinion in

Gompers v. United States, 14; opinion in *Missouri v. Holland*, 18
Hutto v. Finney, 53

In re Kemmler, 52
involuntary servitude, 112

Jefferson, Thomas, 83, 84, 118
Johnson, Mark, 101–2
judicial decision-making, Scalia on: claim that courts cannot adjudicate matters not mentioned in Constitution, 31, 47, 49; claim that judges should follow originalism when deciding cases, 28, 34–35; claim that judicial decision-making should be formulaic, 37–38; distinction between judicial action and personal belief, 25–26, 32, 36–37, 47–48; on influence of text on judge's reading, 38; on nature of legitimate legal decisions regarding constitutional questions, 43, 49; on problems with judicial legislating, 32
Jurek v. Texas, 53
Juvenal, *Satires*, 124

Kagan, Justice Elena, 4, 6
Kasich, John, 4
Katz v. United States, 95
Kennedy, Justice Anthony, 4
Kennedy v. Louisiana, 52
Killingsworth, Silvia, 7
Kiryas Joel, 77, 81, 87–88
Ku Klux Klan, 76

Lakoff, George, 101–2
Lamb's Chapel, 81
law and justice, Scalia on: characterization of common law as art within which judges can create legal rules, 40, 49; characterization of statutory and constitutional law as science, 39–40; distinction between political and judicial, 48; and impact of legal canons and presumptions on judicial decision-making, 41–42; lack of differentiation between statutory and constitutional construction, 42; limited vision of role of judiciary in governance, 37; role of public in changing law, 31, 48; on state as "minister of God" in administration of justice, 32–33
Lee v. Weisman, 63, 65, 73, 76–77, 81–85
Liptak, Adam, 5
Lithwick, Dahlia, 7
living Constitution, 13–19; and Constitutional changes in response to contemporary social needs, 16–17; contemporary rhetorical constructions of, 17–19; and nonoriginalist readings, 16–17; pushback against, 19; Scalia on, 31, 33–35, 46–47, 101; two versions of identified by William Rehnquist, 18
Locke, John, "freedom of conscience," 76, 141n20
Locke v. Davey, 88–93, 96
Louisiana ex rel. Francis v. Resweber, 52
Lynch v. Donnelly, 73, 74
Lyng v. Northwest Indian Cemetery Protective Association, 75

Madison, James, 51, 72, 83, 85, 118
Marbury v. Madison, 18
Marshall, Justice Thurgood, 68; defense of judicial review in *Marbury v. Madison*, 18
Mason, George, 51
McBain, Howard Lee, *The Living Constitution*, 15, 17
McCleskey v. Kemp, 54
McCreary County, 77–78, 83–85, 87
McKoy v. North Carolina, 67, 68
McLuhan, Marshall, 25
McReynolds, Justice James Clark, 98–99
Meese, Edwin: and debate over constitutional interpretation, 9, 18; and ethic of original intent, 19–20; remarks to DC chapter of Federalist Society, 20
menorahs, and Establishment Clause cases, 73
Merian, Anna, 7
Metaphors We Live By (Lakoff and Johnson), 101–2
Meyer v. Nebraska, 98
Minor v. Happersett, 30
Missouri v. Holland, 18
Moore v. Texas, 63–64, 67
Mormon polygamy, and free exercise clause, 74
Mueller v. Allen, 73

Napolitano, Andrew P., 5
Natelson, Robert G., 118
Native American Church, 90–93
nativity scenes, and Establishment Clause cases, 73
Nesbitt, Eric, 62–63
new textualism, 10–11
New York Times v. Sullivan, 35

nondenominational prayer, and Establishment Clause cases, 73
nonpreferentialist approach, and Establishment Clause, 73
Northwest Ordinance, and "cruel and unusual punishments," 51

Obama, Barack, 4
O'Connor, Justice Sandra Day, 74, 105
Olmstead v. United States, 14, 95, 97–98
Operation Rescue, 111–12
opportunistic textualism, and Scalia, 8, 116–24; altering of Free Exercise Clause to justify decision in church and state questions, 118; altering of linguistic meaning of Cruel and Unusual Punishments clause, 116–17, 120; application of textualism only in area of abortion, 119–20; failure to apply textualism in consistent manner, 126; failure to describe how to apply textual interpretation to a legal text, 122; justification of decisions using interpretive forms criticized in his speeches and articles, 119–21, 127; twisting of terms beyond plain meaning, 121
originalism, 5, 19–20; textual originalism, 22, 44
originalism, Scalia on: acknowledgment that originalism is difficult to apply correctly, 38–39; original meaning as textualism, 44; shift in language from textualism to originalism, 35–36; view that judges should follow originalism when deciding cases, 28, 34–35

Payne, Thomas, *Common Sense*, 37
Payne v. Tennessee, 68
Penry v. Lynaugh, 57, 60
Perry Educational Association v. Perry Local Educator's Association, 79
Pierce v. Society of Sisters, 98
"plain meaning" of Constitution: Establishment Clause, 117; Free Exercise Clause, 117–18; Scalia on, 31, 48, 123; Scalia's deviation from, 61, 90, 95, 116, 121; and textualism, 3, 10
Planned Parenthood v. Casey: grounded in Fourteenth Amendment's Due Process Clause, 99–100, 114–15; Scalia's dissent, 101–2, 104–5, 109–11
Plato, *Gorgias*, 39
Pleasant Grove City v. Summum, 77, 80
Posner, Richard, 44, 123
Powell, Justice Lewis F., Jr., and *Gregg* opinion, 68
prayer, at public school graduation ceremonies, 77, 85
privacy, doctrine of, 97–98
procedural due process, 98
Proffitt v. Florida, 53
proportionality, doctrine of, 53–54, 58, 60

Reagan, Ronald: desire to appoint strict constructionists to bench, 2, 127; remarks following appointments of Rehnquist as chief justice and Scalia as associate justice, 2, 19, 21
Rehnquist, Chief Justice William, 111; appointment to chief justice, 2; on two meanings of a living Constitution, 18
Reid, Harry, 6
religious displays, on public property, 77
Religious Freedom Restoration Act (RFRA), 75–76
religious publications, tax-exempt status, 77
Reynolds v. United States, 74–75, 90–91
Richmond v. Lewis, 67
rigorous textualism, 10–11
Ríos, Tomás, 7
Robert, Justice Owen, vote in *West Coast Hotel Company v. Parrish*, 17
Robinson v. California, 52
Roe v. Wade: 1973 decision based on right to privacy, 97–99, 104, 112; Scalia on, 105–6, 109–11. *See also* abortion, Scalia on; abortion law and decisions
Roosevelt, Franklin Delano, and idea that Constitution has ability to respond to contemporary social needs, 15
Roper v. Simmons, 54, 63–65, 67–68
Rubenfeld, Jed, 12
Rubio, Marco, 4
Rummel v. Estelle, 52

Salazar v. Buono, 77
Sanders, Bernie, 4–5
Santa Fe Independent School District v. Jane Doe, 73
Savage, David, 25
Scalia, Antonin: death on February 13, 2016, 3; effect on Supreme Court, 3; elevator anecdote, 1; as judicial revivalist, 5; liberal response to, 6–7, 125; pre-Court advocacy of deregulation and increased power for executive branch, 2; reaction of peers

and politicians to death of, 3–5; self-description as skilled minority member of legal intellectuals, 34
Scalia, Antonin, extrajudicial writings, 36–46; "Common-Law Courts in a Civil-Law System," 39–44, 95; *Matter of Interpretation, A: Federal Courts and the Law*, 37; "Originalism: The Lesser Evil," 38–39; *Reading Law: The Interpretation of Legal Texts* (with Bryan Garner), 37, 44–46; "Rule of Law as a Law of Rules," 37–38. *See also specific topics*
Scalia, Antonin, opinions: and overturning of New Deal decisions, 2–3. *See also* abortion, Scalia on; Eighth Amendment, "cruel and unusual punishments" clause, Scalia on; Establishment Clause, Scalia on; Free Exercise Clause, Scalia on
Scalia, Antonin, speeches, 24–36; "Constitutional Interpretation, A": 1996 remarks to Catholic University of America, 29–30; "Constitutional Interpretation the Old-Fashioned Way": 2005 Address to the Woodrow Wilson International Center for Scholars, 26, 33–36, 136n11; "God's Justice and Ours": 2002 Pew Forum on Religion and Public Life Remarks, 32–33, 47–48; "On Interpreting the Constitution": 1997 Wriston Lecture to the Manhattan Institution for Policy Research, 30–32; "Reflections on the Constitution": 1989 Sibley Lecture to the University of George School of Law, 27–29; refusal to allow recording or posting of, 25, 135n1; repetition of themes in, 25–26; "Theory of Constitutional Interpretation, A": 1996 remarks to Catholic University of America, 29–30. *See also specific topics*
Shapiro, Carolyn, 121
Shapiro, Ilya, 5, 6
Sherbert v. Verner, 75, 93, 96
Smith, Christopher E., 2
Socrates, 39
Solem v. Helm, 52, 53
Souter, Justice David, 6
South Carolina v. Gathers, 67
Stahl, Lesley, 6
Stanford v. Kentucky, 54, 57, 60
Stenberg v. Carhart, 100, 105, 112
Stern, Mark Joseph, 6
Stevens, Justice John Paul: disagreement with Meese on strict judicial interpretation, 19; permission for speeches to be posted on Web page, 25; Scalia on *Gregg* opinion of, 68; statement of facts in *Atkins*, 62; view of original intent as unachievable goal, 20
Stewart, Justice Potter, *Gregg* opinion, 54, 68
Strauss, David, 12
strict textualism, 10–11
substantive due process, 98
Sunstein, Cass, 5
Supreme Court: conservative turn of modern, 2; Web page with speeches delivered by justices, 25
Supreme Court justices: alteration of interpretations of Constitution toward consistency with FDR's political ideology, 17; speeches posted on Web page, 25. *See also specific justices*
symbolic legitimacy, 22

Taney, Justice Roger B., 111
Ten Commandments displays, and Establishment Clause cases, 74, 77
Tennard v. Dretke, 67
Texas Monthly, 77, 84–85
textualism, as method of Constitutional interpretation, 5; critical challenges to, 11–12; inherent problems with, 120, 125–26; and judicial restraint, 11; new textualism, 10–11; reliance on "plain meaning" of Constitution, 3, 10; rigorous textualism, 10–11; strict textualism, 10–11
textualism, Scalia on: and claim that courts should defer to legislature in matters of social policy unless a right is expressly protected in Constitution, 24; and conservative agendas that overturn New Deal decisions, 21; and limited range of meaning of Constitution, 24; Scalia's self-reference as "textualist" or "originalist," 21; textualism as "commonsensical," 44–45; textualism as effort to understand original meaning rather than original intent of Constitution, 29; textualism as only acceptable form of constitutional interpretation, 7; textualism as set of general rules, 38; textualism focusing on original meaning of text for members of founding generation, 42–43; theory of textualism, 44–45. *See also* opportunistic textualism, and Scalia
textual originalism, 22, 44

Thomas, Clarence, on Scalia, 3
Thompson v. Oklahoma, 54, 58, 63, 65, 67, 68
Tilton v. Richardson, 73
Tribe, Lawrence H., commentary on Scalia's "Common-Law Courts" essay, 50
Trop v. Dulles, 52, 54
Trump, Donald, 4

United States v. Lee, 75
US New & World Report, eight worst tweets about Scalia, 6–7

Van Orden v. Perry, 74, 77
Virginia Declaration of Rights, and "cruel and unusual punishments," 51

Walton v. Arizona, 57–58, 58–59, 63, 66, 68
Warren, Chief Justice Earl, 54
Warren Court, reading of the Constitution, 17
Washington, George, 83, 85
Webster, Daniel, 15–16, 21
Webster v. Reproductive Health Services, 99, 105–7, 112
Weems v. United States, 14, 52, 53
West Coast Hotel Company v. Parrish, 17
White, James Boyd, and judicial interpretation, 18
Whole Woman's Health, 100
"Why People Hate Antonin Scalia" *(Economist)*, 6
Wilkerson v. Utah, 52
Will, George, 5
Williams, Glen, 45
Wilson, Woodrow: and role of judge in interpretation of Constitution, 13; view of constitutional text as organic, 13; "What is Progress?", 13–14
Wisconsin v. Yoder, 75
Wood, Gordon S., commentary on Scalia's "Common-Law Courts" essay, 50
Woodson v. North Carolina, 53

Zuesse, Eric, 7